IF
CLASSROOMS
MATTER

IF CLASSROOMS MATTER

PROGRESSIVE VISIONS OF EDUCATIONAL ENVIRONMENTS

Edited by
Jeffrey R. Di Leo and Walter R. Jacobs

Routledge
New York • London

Published in 2004 by
Routledge
270 Madison Avenue
New York, NY 10016
www.routledge-ny.com

Published in Great Britain by
Routledge
2 Park Square
Milton Park, Abingdon
Oxon, OX14 4RN
www.routledge.co.uk

Library of Congress Cataloging in Publication Data
If classrooms matter : progressive visions of educational environments / edited by
    Jeffrey R. Di Leo and Walter R. Jacobs.
        p. cm.
    Includes bibliographical references.
    ISBN 0-415-97157-8 (hb : alk. paper) — ISBN 0-415-97158-6 (pb : alk. paper)
    1. Classroom environment—Social aspects—United States. 2. Classrooms—United
States—Planning. 3. Critical pedagogy—United States. 4. Educational technology—
Social aspects—United States.   I. Di Leo, Jeffrey R. II. Jacobs, Walter R., 1968–
    LB3013.I4 2004
    370.11'5—dc22

                                                            2004014167

Teachers who have a vision of democratic education
assume that learning is never confined solely
to an institutionalized classroom.
—bell hooks, *Teaching Community: A Pedagogy of Hope*

An analysis of the interaction of teachers and students on the
level of place, pedagogy, and politics has the potential to
radically reconfigure the values that we associate with
pedagogical sites. If pedagogy and education matter, then we
are compelled to reevaluate some of the fundamental biases
that we hold regarding where we teach and learn.
—from the Editors' Introduction

Permissions and Acknowledgments

Essays by Michael W. Apple, Andrew Hoberek, and Elizabeth Ellsworth were first published in symplokē *10.1/2 (2002). Copyright © symplokē 2002. Published by the University of Nebraska Press. Reprinted with permission.*

Sharon O'Dair's "Class Work: Site of Egalitarian Activism or Site of Embourgeoisement?" originally appeared in College English *65 (July 2003): 593–606. Copyright 2003 by the National Council of Teachers of English. Reprinted with permission.*

Carol Becker's essay was first published by the College Art Association in the Winter 2003 issue of Art Journal. *Copyright © Carol Becker. Reprinted by permission.*

Critical scholarship on the classroom is among the most important work being conducted today in the academy. The scholars working in this field are to be commended for their investigation of a subject vital to American education and society. We would especially like to thank our contributors for sharing their essays and insights with us.

We would also like to thank Candice Chovanec Melzow for her assistance in the preparation of the index, and our significant others, Nina and Valerie, for their support and encouragement.

Contents

Section III: The Actualities of Media Interventions

Place, Pedagogy, Politics
Reflections on Contemporary Classroom Reconfigurations

JEFFREY R. DI LEO
WALTER R. JACOBS

The American classroom is currently undergoing an unprecedented process of radical reconfiguration. With more and more Americans juggling work and school, there is now a growing population of students who seldom set foot in a traditional classroom. Their pedagogical sites center on computer screens, televisions, and printed study guides. In addition to these market- and technology-driven changes, innovative teachers are taking their teaching outside the traditional classroom. Whether it is trips to locations of interest or job training in the field, learning outside the classroom is becoming more popular. The increase in the number of sites of learning poses a challenge for teachers, students, and administrators. We must learn how to adjust our pedagogy to account for the changing nature of the classroom.

The contemporary reconfiguration of the classroom can be broken down into three interrelated modes or dimensions. The first mode concerns physical transformations of the classroom, that is to say, reconfigurations of the place or space of teaching and learning. The second mode concerns pedagogical transformations, or reconfigurations of the relations between the place of learning and the human participants engaged in learning and teaching. The third mode concerns institutional or political transformations at work regarding the classroom, that is to say, the cultural and political aspects. These dimensions of classroom reconfiguration, which are at play in

1

each of the essays in this volume, might be more simply termed *place*, *pedagogy*, and *politics*.[1]

Places and Possibilities

At its most fundamental or basic level, the classroom is simply a *place* or *space*. Consideration of classrooms on this level must refrain from ascriptions of value, and regard each and every teaching space as a site of pure potential and possibility. Actualization of a classroom's potential is only realizable in the interaction of the classroom space with a set of human participants. The reconfiguration of the American classroom is most readily apparent in these changes to the physical space for learning and teaching.

Traditionally, the American classroom was dominated by a specific set of physical features: rows of desks facing a blackboard. The variations of this defined classroom space were minimal. In recent years, classrooms have undergone considerable alterations, ranging from the arrangement of desks in circles or groups and the replacement of blackboards with dry erase boards to the installation of sophisticated film and computer equipment. Yet even these significant physical changes are minor when compared to the changes currently underway.

Whereas the traditional classroom was a space designed to be inhabited by all of the students in the class and the teacher at the same time, and was part of a larger complex of classrooms, the radically reconfigured American classroom offers this classroom as one option among many. Demand for more accessible sites of pedagogy, technological innovations, and progressive pedagogical methods have resulted in an array of new types of sites of pedagogy.

Some sites of pedagogy, including off-campus locations such as shopping malls and foreign locales such as Carol Becker's class "pilgrimage" to Vietnam (see chapter 6), afford teachers and students the opportunity to be in the same space, albeit one that differs radically phenomenologically from the "traditional" classroom space. Others, such as integrated televised class meetings at multiple locations, and online classes that utilize chatrooms, allow teachers and students simultaneously *to effectively be* in the same pedagogical space. Still others, such as online classes that do not utilize simultaneous communications where the students can see the instructor but not vice versa, reconfigure the classroom space by multiplying it by the number of students in the course: one's classroom is wherever one chooses to "tune in" or "log on" that day.

We must regard all classroom spaces—from the traditional rows of desks to the emerging use of computer screens—as *possibility* or *potential*. In themselves, each of these sites of pedagogy are no better or worse than any other potential space. Such an evaluation is important in an educational culture often quick to assume the superiority of traditional sites of pedagogy and to dismiss others as necessarily inferior. No conclusions as to teaching and learning effectiveness can be deduced merely from the basis of a change in pedagogical site. One must always be open to the value of reconfigurations in sites of pedagogy.

Pedagogy: Interaction and Struggle

In themselves, the sites of pedagogy are simply the locations of pedagogical address. They are the spaces or places in which interactions between teacher and student can occur. Without a pedagogical site, pedagogical address is unrealizable; without a pedagogical address, pedagogical sites are empty. The meeting point of pedagogical address and pedagogical site is the absolute horizon of learning.

The next level for considering contemporary reconfigurations of the classroom focuses attention on the *classroom as a site of interaction between a place* (non-ego—some type of classroom) *and individuals* (ego—some set of students and teachers). Viewed from this perspective, the classroom becomes a site of *struggle* or *hereness and nowness* (hic et nunc) whose very essence is its *thisness*. The *thisness* of the classroom is always already uniquely defined through the interrelation of its place with a particular set of individuals. The factual character of the classroom considered at this level consists of pure individuality, excluding both possibility and generality. As in the case of the classroom regarded in itself, the classroom as site of interaction or struggle is not generalizable. It is a specific interaction between a place and individuals: the key features here are its *individuality* and *existential status.* All sites wherein individuals are interacting with each other as well as with (and within) a space should be regarded as local and contingent (non-generalizable and non-universalizable).

If pedagogy at its core involves contingent and local interactions of place and individuals, then the pedagogical theory and analysis that regards classrooms and/or the individuals that enter into relations with classrooms as *constants* is no longer acceptable. Pedagogical theory and analysis must be prepared to open up the space of the pedagogical to multifarious relations between class space and individuals. The experiences resultant upon the interaction—or struggle—between place and individuals are singular, and should be regarded as such at the level of the pedagogical. A view of pedagogy that encourages us to see classrooms as sites of interaction rightly encourages us to look at each interaction between a classroom space and individuals as unique. Considered as a site of *struggle*, pedagogy is not a rule-bound enterprise or generalizable activity, but an individualized and particular one. Classrooms viewed in this way reveal interaction and struggle as inherent in the phenomenological structure of the sites of pedagogy.

The Politics of Pedagogical Space

The political is the third and final mode of understanding the classroom. It goes beyond and incorporates both the potentialities of classroom space and the specific struggles between the place of learning and the individuals interacting with the learning space. The political brings the potentialities of classrooms, and the pedagogical interactions of specific sites into relation with each other, encouraging us to find them meaningful and make generalizations about them. Places of learning in themselves, and the struggles of individuals with them are brought into wider relief at this level: into what contemporary cultural theorists have called "the circuit of culture."[2]

This dimension encourages abstraction of universal meanings from the potentialities of classroom space and the actualities of classroom struggles. The classroom as viewed from this perspective not only becomes the subject of universalization, but is also drawn into a dialogue with general aspects of culture and society. The politicalization of the classroom is achieved by drawing it out of the context of its particular existences or instantiations—its existential context—and putting it into play with other aspects of culture and society.

As the political necessarily involves generalities about the classroom, it draws us into looking at "the big picture." The classroom becomes not just a *potential* site of pedagogy or a *particular* interaction between a place and a set of participants—both local and non-totalizing aspects—but rather a meaningful and generalizable entity. Through the political, we are encouraged to make generalizations about classroom struggles, to formulate laws regarding classrooms, and to bring the classroom into relation with the wider realm of culture and society.

It is also important to note that any "politics of the classroom" necessarily involves considerations of the classroom in itself, and the classroom in relation to specific teachers and students: the political always already involves them. In other words, while a politics of the classroom can involve grand narratives and totalizing statements, these statements cannot be made *without assuming some set of local conditions*: namely, both sites of pedagogy in themselves and specific interactions between pedagogical sites and pedagogical addresses. All politics and generalizations are thus reducible to local conditions, whereas the inverse is not true.[3] Following Marx, we derive our politics and generalities from specific sets of possibilities and actualities.[4]

Each of the essays in this collection shares this sense of the political by closely connecting political vision to the potentialities and actualities of varying sites of pedagogy. Analyses of the politics of pedagogical space can sometimes become caught up in sweeping theoretical visions. In the process, the analysis neglects to attend to the much harder work of testing, critiquing, and revising those visions. The initial section of essays in the volume interrogate such grand declarations, arguing that they should serve as mere starting points for pedagogical analysis.

Henry A. Giroux's "The Politics of Public Pedagogy" commences the collection with an investigation of how the ascendancy of neoliberal corporate culture into all aspects of American life has impoverished public discourse, in which "there is no vocabulary for political or social transformation, democratically inspired visions, or critical notions of social agency to expand the meaning and purpose of democratic public life." Drawing on the works of Raymond Williams and Cornelius Castoriadis, Giroux shows cultural studies advocates how to problematize and pluralize the political, and engage new sites of pedagogy in an ongoing project that contests a variety of forms of domination deployed by contemporary neoliberalism.

The next essay, "Education, Social Class, and the Sites of Pedagogy" by Stanley Aronowitz, presents a history of popular culture, labor, and neighborhood movements as educational sites. He argues that the demise of these movements created conservative practices and positions that are obstacles to "the requisite changes that would transform schools from credential mills and institutions of control to a site of education that prepares young people to see themselves as active participants in the world." Aronowitz details steps to reform—not abandon—public education, in which "the best chance for education resides in the communities, in social movements, and in the kids themselves."

Michael W. Apple's "Interrupting the Right," the third essay in this section, analyzes a rightist resurgence—what Apple calls "conservative modernization"—in education and finds spaces for interrupting it. Apple explains how the positions of this new hegemonic bloc strongly resonate with aspects of the realities that people experience. He contends, therefore, that the Left must engage in an ongoing set of crucial debates about the means and ends of educational institutions and about their connections to larger institutions and power relations. Keeping such debates alive and vibrant is one of the best ways of challenging "the curriculum of the dead."

The final essay, Peter McLaren and Nathalia E. Jaramillo's "Critical Pedagogy in a Time of Permanent War," deploys lessons learned in recent anti-Capitalist struggles around the globe to extend two of the themes of previous essays. Focusing on the *asambleas* street protest movement of Argentina and the Bolivarian Circle mobilizations of Venezuela, McLaren and Jaramillo offer "both a commentary on the domestication of critical pedagogy, and a challenge for revivifying its political roots and role in the civil societarian left." Further, McLaren and Jaramillo—indeed, all of the authors of this opening section—conclude that "there is a need for teacher educators to bring more radical discourse into the educational literature."

Re-Ruling the Classroom: The Possibilities of Places

If the preceding group of essays can be said to call for more radical *discourse* in the educational *literature*, then the next group of essays might be said to call for a more radical *vision* of educational *environments*. These essays remind us that just as we must think carefully about the materials we bring into the classroom, so too must we consider what the site of instruction in itself, and in interaction with individuals, brings to the subject matter of our classes. Critical theory has shown us how the medium in which messages are addressed affects the contents of those messages. These media form receiver expectations—we might even go so far as to say *construct* them.

As an educational community, we need to place a premium on scholarship that works to articulate the relationship between pedagogical site and pedagogical address. It is not enough to simply say that the context or medium in which pedagogical addresses occur affects the content of those messages. We must understand *how* it does this and privilege scholarship that works towards an understanding of this issue. The middle set of essays works towards such an understanding by examining the consequences of the transposition of traditional rules of pedagogical practice. These essays detail actualized sites where places, teachers, and students questioned received wisdom and co-created new possibilities to critically examine their social and cultural worlds.

The first essay in this section, Elizabeth Ellsworth's "The U.S. Holocaust Memorial Museum as a Scene of Pedagogical Address," views the permanent exhibit of the U.S. Holocaust Memorial Museum as a concrete materialization of a particular pedagogical approach. It provides a rich context for studying key challenges and opportunities involved in teaching the Holocaust in particular, and in teaching about and across social and cultural difference in general. Ellsworth focuses on how the museum's narrative form, visual design, and point of view construct its pedagogical address. She argues that the power of the address of this museum's pedagogy lies in its indeterminacy. This museum, with its primary objective of education, paradoxically embraces the ways that histories of the Holocaust throw the pedagogical relation between teacher and student into crisis. Far from leading to paralysis or despair, an analysis of this museum's pedagogical address offers specific examples of how the paradoxes of teaching and learning can be productive, and can assist teachers and students in accessing moral imperatives without absolutes.

The next contribution, Carol Becker's "Pilgrimage to My Lai: Social Memory and the Making of Art," continues Ellsworth's analysis of the effects of the sites of pedagogy on students' moral faculties. Becker investigates the nature of pilgrimages, where "the intention of this type of journey is not to change the world, but to change oneself: to achieve a consciousness and spiritual transformation while connecting with the history of others who have 'troden' the same path." Focusing specifically on a 2002 pilgrimage to Vietnam with two other faculty members and ten students, Becker demonstrates how students "will find a way to alchemize their internalization of the event into yet another event or manifestation, filtered through the particularity of individual consciousness," such as a performance in which a Vietnamese student teaches an American student to speak, in correct Vietnamese, each name on the list of 504 civilians killed in the My Lai massacre.

Whereas the first two essays in this section introduce us to the use of innovative teaching spaces, the next two show us how to refashion any teaching space into a politically and professionally progressive one. In "Professionalism: What Graduate Students Need," Andrew Hoberek argues that we need to think more seriously about graduate education as professional training: that is, as training geared towards preparing students to perform the work of professional academics. Specifically, graduate students need more training in the administrative service component of the research/ teaching/service triad of academic life. "Professionalism" constructs a plan of action that might accomplish this goal.

If Hoberek's essay recreates graduate teaching space as a site of professionalization, then the next essay might be said to recreate undergraduate teaching space as a site of politicalization. Sharon O'Dair's "Class Work: Site of Egalitarian Activism or Site of Embourgeoisement?" charges that "The Standard Model" of the composition classroom—pedagogy should be counter-hegemonic, the literacy students achieve should be critical, and all participants should seek positive change in our communities—frequently oppresses working class students. The composition classroom, O'Dair believes, ought to be a site that does not privilege the middle class world of the university. It should include frank talk that enables working-class students to get out of the university classroom if they do not want and/or need to be there, and to investigate opportunities for political participation and viable alternatives for training and work, including efforts to decouple occupational opportunity and higher education. O'Dair argues that such frank talk would enable such students to accept help in teaching them how to become middle class.

The Actualities of Media Interventions

If it is the case that pedagogical site deeply affects pedagogical address, then one should also expect that pedagogical site affects student expectations. Consequently, students need to become more finely aware of how the context of their educational experiences temper their learning expectations. If they expect that learning can only occur against the backdrop of a blackboard, then every time that their class leaves this setting or the instructor brings in media such as film, they will *turn off* their learning expectations, and *turn on* other anticipations, such as those for entertainment. Students must be taught how to be learners outside of the traditional classroom setting, and realize the learning potential of alternative sites of pedagogy. This is, in part, the subject of the concluding set of essays. Particular attention is paid to "new media," media embedded in electronic computer technologies.

The first essay in this section, Jacqueline Bobo's "Media, Activism, and the Classroom: Teaching Black Feminist Cultural Criticism," investigates classroom reception of three films by Black women that can be instrumental in erasing destructive racial ideologies. Bobo demonstrates how the use of media products can be particularly effective in critically engaging students in such sensitive subject matter. She concludes, "through meticulous concentration on Black women's history, faithfully representing their lives, Black women's films magnify female viewers' perception of their material circumstances, potentially motivating them toward activism, thereby strengthening their viability as a potent social force."

In "Back to Cyberschool: Some of the Learning, None of the Fun," David Trend highlights a destructive side of media: the ways digital media are facilitating the growing privatization of schools and universities, in which schools become sites for commerce, university research shifts to product development, and students in both sites are turned into commodities. Trend argues that "the challenge is to engage the possibilities that these new technologies offer, while being cautious of how they may silently undermine the institution."

TyAnna K. Herrington's "Where in the World is the Global Classroom Project?" discusses the *Global Classroom Project,* a shared online course in cross-cultural, digital communication joining students and professors from St. Petersburg, Russia, Karlskrona, Sweden, and Atlanta, USA, through the Internet. Since students' classes occur in shared spaces that are independent of time and place, the *Global Classroom Project* both creates new questions and forces new insights in how to adapt pedagogy to this alternative learning space. The *Global Classroom Project*—ongoing since spring 2000—provides a means to reconsider how space, or lack thereof, impacts our concepts of culture, pedagogy, and communication, and leads us not only to recreate notions of "the classroom," but also to reconceptualize our definitions of learning.

Mark Poster's "History in the Digital Domain" closes this section by asking: what is at stake in the alteration of the material structure of cultural objects from the paper forms of manuscript and print to the digital form of computer files? In particular, how is the change affecting academic disciplines that rely upon stable forms of symbolic records? More specifically still, how is the discipline of History affected by the digitization of writing? Is digitization simply a more efficient means of reproduction, storage and transmission of documents, whose availability in space and time is enhanced for the application by historians of research techniques and methods? Or does digitization cause an alteration for historians in the constitution of truth? Poster investigates how rapid change of media implies a rapid change of analytic categories, leading to the recognition of the tentative nature of questions such as these. He concludes that we are thus well outside the binary structure of certainty/relativism, and in a new age of conditional truth regimes.

The essays by Trend, Herrington and Poster suggest that the mandate for change in our beliefs about the role of sites of pedagogy must not only come from students and educators, but also from institutions. Institutional culture in America is largely premised on the belief that a classroom has four walls, desks, and a blackboard. What goes on in this space is regarded as teaching whereas what goes on outside of it is regarded, at best, as peripheral education. If we are to take seriously the belief that new media hold opportunities for improving learning in America, then a change in attitude by institutions is paramount. Without the support of institutions, these attempts will fail to affect a systemic change in view, despite classroom reconfigurations and the efforts of students and teachers.

Moreover, the work in this section facilitates a reconsideration of the bias in education today to value pedagogy that goes on through correspondence and other non-traditional classroom spaces as being inferior to work that is done in the classroom. This bias is in part premised upon a particular belief as to what a "true" classroom is as opposed to its "false" instantiations (e.g., computer-screens, televisions, and shopping malls). Evaluative judgments as to the value of classrooms should be suspended until one has a more complete account of the interactions of these spaces with particular individuals and pedagogical addresses. Again, we must regard all sites of pedagogy in themselves as pure possibility and potential. Their value and meaning is to be gleaned, as the contributions indicate, only after these sites have been made particular through an interaction with individuals and forms of address.

The essays in this section compel us to consider how site of address affects differences in the styles of both teachers and learners. As pedagogical theory becomes increasingly aware of differences in student learning styles, we must be sensitive to how students will react to new sites of pedagogy. For example, how does an entirely text-based form of address affect the performance of a student who reads slowly and relies on spoken word to reinforce learning? Similarly, we must consider how successful teachers will adapt their proven teaching practices to new sites of pedagogy. How will teachers who are accustomed to addressing students in person in a classroom adapt their style to sites outside of the university campus or on-line?

When Classrooms Matter

Education in America today demands a comprehensive rethinking of the classroom spaces where we teach and learn. While it may be obvious that pedagogical processes are affected by the setting in which they occur, we understand far too little about this relationship to be able to maximize its learning and social potential. The essays in this collection maintain that gaining a better understanding of the dynamics of the places in which we teach and learn is critical to improving education and society.

Pedagogical theory premised upon the classroom as a fixed entity is no longer acceptable. We must learn how to adjust our pedagogy to account for the changing nature of the classroom. A student watching a teacher present a lecture on a computer screen has a qualitatively different experience than a student who is face to face with a teacher. Pedagogical theorists must account for how these and related experiences affect learning.

Treating all the places where we teach and learn as potential classrooms entails a deconstruction of our value system as to legitimate sites of pedagogy. While the site of pedagogy is an important variable in the quality of education, it is never an absolute indicator of value. Only after evaluation of the particularities or local conditions at play in any particular site should judgment be rendered as to their value. This attitude toward the value of classrooms requires a suspension of our commonly held beliefs about classrooms: the traditional classroom loses its position of privilege over other sites of pedagogy.

The implications of this reconfiguration of the value hierarchy of places of learning has ramifications that go far beyond the particularities of classroom performance. As academic culture begins to support a wider sense of the sites of pedagogy, so too will academic identities shift. In particular, the dislocation of our value hierarchy regarding classrooms has the potential of reconfiguring the identities and values associated with students, teachers, institutions, and education in general.

Students who learn in non-traditional sites of pedagogy need not feel that their educational experience is compromised because of its non-traditional setting. Academic culture must reserve value judgment of the performance of these students until the particularities of classroom experience have been examined. There are no, by definition, second-class students in an academic culture open to local determinations of classroom value. The widespread effect of this is an undermining of our beliefs about student identities based solely on assumptions about the value of particular sites of pedagogy.

A similar value scenario holds among teachers as well. The adjunct who teaches in a shopping mall and the professor who grades lessons submitted online need no longer feel that they are second-class teachers simply on the basis of site of pedagogy. If they have worked to establish a pedagogical address that maximizes the potential of their site of pedagogy, and the performance of their students is on par with student performance in "traditional" classroom settings, then the basis for regarding their contributions to the academy as secondary become ill-founded.

While judgments of educational value grounded simply in site of pedagogy are easier to make, those determined through an evaluation of the particularities of educational experience are more telling. Again, determinations of the value of interactions and struggles between sites of pedagogy and individuals are made locally. The effect of this on the identities of instructors is a suspension of value determination *until* the local conditions of pedagogical experience have been analyzed.

If it is the case that the value of students and instructors are not to be determined simply on the basis of their place of instruction, then a similar scenario holds for institutions as well. The value of colleges and universities that employ non-traditional sites of pedagogy is not determinable simply on the basis of value biases regarding these sites. Academic performance at these institutions needs to be more carefully assessed based on the local educational conditions that they are creating. On-line institutions of higher education cannot be considered inferior to traditional institutions merely on the basis of site of pedagogy.

As new sites of pedagogy are introduced into our schools, we must develop new methods and standards of evaluation and additional teacher training. To leave teachers unprepared for changes in pedagogical sites resulting from technological, economic, and political developments in American society is to risk educational failure. As new sites of pedagogy are developed, we must not allow our teachers to venture into these areas without training and without understanding how these changes in site affect teacher and student performance. This situation puts our students' education at risk and exposes our teachers to pedagogical disappointment and failure.

Moreover, as education is an integral part of the future well-being of American society, ignoring the changes occurring in the classroom puts our society at risk.

Moving forward, we must take time to reflect on the recent and future changes in pedagogical sites. The essays in this volume provide a basis for further inquiry. An analysis of the interaction of teachers and students on the level of place, pedagogy, and politics has the potential to radically reconfigure the values that we associate with pedagogical sites. If pedagogy and education matter, then we are compelled to reevaluate some of the fundamental biases that we hold regarding where we teach and learn.

Notes

1. Reduction of classroom reconfiguration to these three levels is based loosely on the phenomenlogy of Charles S. Peirce. In particular, his notion that all phenomena possess three modes of being or aspects: firstness, secondness and thirdness. See Charles S. Peirce, *Collected Papers of Charles Sanders Peirce*, Volume 1, ed. Charles Hartshorne and Paul Weiss (Cambridge, MA: Harvard University Press, 1931).
2. See, for example, Richard Johnson, "The Story So Far," in *Introduction to Contemporary Cultural Studies*, ed. D. Punter (London: Longman, 1986), 277–313; Richard Johnson, "What is Cultural Studies Anyway?" *Social Text* 6.1 (1987): 38–80; and Paul Du Gay, et al., *Doing Cultural Studies: The Story of the Sony Walkman* (London: Sage, 1997).
3. We maintain that sites of pedagogy are derivable from politics, but not vice versa. This insight on the relationship between politics and sites of pedagogy is arguably at odds with cultural studies accounts of the classroom that posit equal generative notions among particular pedagogical sites and the political.
4. In 1846, Karl Marx and Frederick Engels famously stated, "Life is not determined by consciousness, but consciousness by life." See Karl Marx and Frederick Engels, *The German Ideology, Part One*, ed. C. J. Arthur (New York: International Publishers, 1972), 47.

SECTION I

The Politics
of Pedagogical Space

CHAPTER 1

The Politics of Public Pedagogy

HENRY A. GIROUX

Neoliberalism as Public Pedagogy

> Our age is the time of "individual utopias," of utopias privatized, and
> so it comes naturally (as well as being a fashionable thing to do) to
> deride and ridicule such projects which imply a revision of the options
> which are collectively put at the disposal of individuals.[1]

The ascendancy of neoliberal corporate culture into every aspect of
American life both consolidates economic power in the hands of the few
and aggressively attempts to break the power of unions, decouple income
from productivity, subordinate the needs of society to the market, and deem
public services and goods an unconscionable luxury. And it does more. It
thrives on a culture of cynicism, insecurity, and despair. Conscripts in a
relentless campaign for personal responsibility, Americans are now convinced that they have little to hope for or gain from the government, non-
profit public spheres, democratic associations, public and higher education,
or other non-governmental social forces. With few exceptions, the project
of democratizing public goods has fallen into disrepute in the popular imagination as the logic of the market undermines the most basic social solidari-
ties. The consequences include not only a weakened state, but a growing
sense of insecurity, cynicism, and political retreat on the part of the general
public. The incessant calls for self-reliance that now dominate public discourse betray a hollowed out and refigured state that neither provides adequate safety nets for its populace, especially those who are young, poor, or
marginalized, nor gives any indication that it will serve the interests of its

citizens in spite of constitutional guarantees. In short, private interests trump social needs, and economic growth becomes more important than social justice. The brutal shredding of the social contract is mediated through the force of corporate power and commercial values that dominate those competing public spheres and value systems that are critical to a just society. The liberal democratic vocabulary of rights, entitlements, social provisions, community, social responsibility, living wage, job security, equality, and justice seem oddly out of place in a country in which the promise of democracy has been replaced by casino capitalism, a winner-take-all philosophy, suited to lotto players and day-traders alike. As corporate culture extends even deeper into the basic institutions of civil and political society, it is reinforced by a pervasive fear and insecurity about the present, and a deep-seated skepticism in the public mind that the future holds nothing beyond a watered down version of the present, buttressed daily by a culture industry largely in the hands of concentrated capital. As the prevailing discourse of neoliberalism seizes the public imagination, there is no vocabulary for political or social transformation, democratically inspired visions, or critical notions of social agency to expand the meaning and purpose of democratic public life. Against the reality of low wage jobs, the erosion of social provisions for a growing number of people and the expanding war against young people of color, the market-driven juggernaut of public pedagogy continues to mobilize desires in the interest of producing market identities and market relationships that ultimately sever the link between education and social change while reducing agency to the obligations of consumerism.

There is a simultaneous diminishing of non-commodified public spheres—those institutions such as public schools, churches, noncommercial public broadcasting, libraries, trade unions and various voluntary institutions engaged in dialogue, education, and learning—that address the relationship of the individual to public life, social responsibility, and provide a robust vehicle for public participation and democratic citizenship. As media theorists, Edward Herman and Robert McChesney observe, non-commodified public spheres have played an invaluable role historically "as places and forums where issues of importance to a political community are discussed and debated, and where information is presented that is essential to citizen participation in community life."[2] Without these critical public spheres, corporate power often goes unchecked and politics becomes dull, cynical, and oppressive.[3]

What becomes troubling under the rule of neoliberalism is not simply that ideas associated with freedom and agency are defined through the prevailing ideology and principles of the market, or that neoliberal ideology wraps itself in what appears to be an unassailable appeal to common sense, or finally that it prohibits or censors critics. What is troubling is that in the face of all sorts of political chicanery, the public at large seems to resist all non-market alternatives and remains convinced of its own helplessness.

Defined as the paragon of modern social relations by Friedrich A. von Hayek, Milton Friedman, Robert Nozick, Francis Fukuyama and other market fundamentalists, neoliberalism attempts to eliminate an engaged critique about its most basic principles and social consequences by embracing the "market as the arbiter of social destiny."[4] Not only does neoliberalism empty the public treasury, hollow out public services, limit the vocabulary and imagery available to recognize anti-democratic forms of power, and narrow models of individual agency, it also undermines the critical functions of any viable democracy by undercutting the ability of individuals to engage in the continuous translation between public considerations and private interests by collapsing the public into the realm of the private. As Bauman observes, "It is no longer true that the 'public' is set on colonizing the 'private.' The opposite is the case: it is the private that colonizes the public space, squeezing out and chasing away everything which cannot be fully, without residue, translated into the vocabulary of private interests and pursuits."[5] Divested of its political possibilities and social underpinnings, freedom offers few opportunities for people to translate private worries into public concerns and collective struggle.[6]

Within neoliberalism's market-driven discourse, corporate power marks the space of a new kind of public pedagogy, one in which the production, dissemination, and circulation of ideas emerges from the educational force of the larger culture. Public pedagogy in this sense refers to a powerful ensemble of ideological and institutional forces whose aim is to produce competitive, self-interested individuals vying for their own material and ideological gain. Corporate public pedagogy culture largely cancels out or devalues gender, class-specific, and racial injustices of the existing social order by absorbing the democratic impulses and practices of civil society within narrow economic relations. Corporate public pedagogy has become an all-encompassing cultural horizon for producing market identities, values, and practices. The good life, in this discourse, "is construed in terms of our identities as consumers—we are what we buy."[7]

For example, some neoliberal advocates argue that the answer to solving the health care and education crises faced by many states can be solved by selling off public assets to private interests. The Pentagon even considered, if only for a short time, turning the war on terror and security concerns over to futures markets, subject to on-line trading. Thus, non-commodified public spheres are replaced by commercial spheres as the substance of critical democracy is emptied out and replaced by a democracy of goods available to those with purchasing power and the increasing expansion of the cultural and political power of corporations throughout the world.

As a result of the corporate attack on public life, the maintenance of democratic public spheres from which to launch a moral vision or to engage in a viable struggle over politics loses all credibility—not to mention monetary support. As the alleged objectivity of public and political discourse remains unchallenged, individual critique and collective political struggles become more difficult. Under neoliberalism, dominant public pedagogy with its narrow and imposed schemes of classification and limited modes of identification use the educational force of the culture to negate the basic conditions for critical agency.

As the late Pierre Bourdieu has pointed out, political action is only "possible because agents, who are part of the social world, have knowledge of this world and because one can act on the social world by acting on their knowledge of this world."[8] Politics often begins when it becomes possible to make power visible, to challenge the ideological circuitry of hegemonic knowledge, and to recognize that "political subversion presupposes cognitive subversion, a conversion of the vision of the world."[9] But another element of politics focuses on where politics happens, how proliferating sites of pedagogy bring into being new forms of resistance, raise new questions, and necessitate alternative visions regarding autonomy and the possibility of democracy itself. As public space is increasingly commodified and the state is aligned more closely with capital, politics is defined largely by its policing functions. Its ideological counterpart is a public pedagogy that mobilizes power in the interest of a Darwinian world marked by the progressive removal of autonomous spheres of cultural production such as journalism, publishing, and film; the destruction of collective structures capable of counteracting the widespread imposition of commercial values and effects of the pure market; the creation of a reserve army of the unemployed globally; and the subordination of nation-states to the real masters of the economy. Bourdieu emphasizes the dystopian effects of neoliberalism on this world:

> First is the destruction of all the collective institutions capable of counteracting the effects of the infernal machine, primarily those of the state, repository of all of the universal values associated with the idea of the public realm. Second is the imposition everywhere, in the upper spheres of the economy and the state as at the heart of corporations, of that sort of moral Darwinism that, with the cult of the winner, schooled in higher mathematics and bungee jumping, institutes the struggle of all against all and cynicism as the norm of all action and behaviour.[10]

What is crucial to recognize in the work of theorists such as Raymond Williams, Stuart Hall, Pierre Bourdieu, Noam Chomsky, Robert McChesney, and others is that neoliberalism is more than an economic theory; it also constitutes the conditions for a radically refigured cultural politics. That is, it provides, to use Raymond Williams' term, a new mode of "permanent education" in which dominant sites of pedagogy engage in diverse forms of pedagogical address to put into play a limited range of identities, ideologies, and subject positions that both reinforce neoliberal social relations and undermine the possibility for democratic politics.[11] The economist William Greider goes so far as to argue that the diverse advocates of neoliberalism currently in control of the American government want to "roll back the twentieth century literally"[12] by establishing the priority of private institutions and market identities, values, and relationships as the organizing principles of public life. This is a discourse that wants to squeeze out ambiguity from public space, dismantle the social provisions and guarantees provided by the welfare state, and eliminate democratic politics by making the notion of the social impossible to imagine beyond the isolated consumer and the logic of the market.[13] The ideological essence of this new public pedagogy is well expressed by Grover Norquist, the president of Americans for Tax Reform and arguably Washington's leading right-wing strategist, who argues that "My goal is to cut government in half in twenty-five years, to get it down to the size where we can drown it in the bathtub."[14]

These new sites of public pedagogy which have become the organizing force of neoliberal ideology are not restricted to schools, blackboards, and test taking. Nor do they incorporate the limited forms of address found in schools. Such sites operate within a wide variety of social institutions and formats including sports and entertainment media, cable television networks, churches, and channels of elite and popular culture such as advertising. Profound transformations have taken place in the public space, producing new sites of pedagogy marked by a distinctive confluence of new digital and media technologies, growing concentrations of corporate power, and unparalleled meaning producing capacities. Unlike traditional forms of pedagogy, knowledge and desire are inextricably connected to modes of pedagogical address mediated through unprecedented electronic technologies that include high-speed computers, new types of digitized film and CD-ROMs. The result is a public pedagogy that plays a decisive role in producing a diverse cultural sphere that gives new meaning to education as a political force. What is surprising about the cultural politics of neoliberalism is that cultural studies theorists have either ignored or largely underestimated the symbolic and pedagogical dimensions of the struggle that neoliberal corporate power has put into place for the last thirty years, particularly under the ruthless administration of President George W. Bush.

Making the Pedagogical More Political

> The need for permanent education, in our changing society, will be met in one way or another. It is now on the whole being met, though with many valuable exceptions and efforts against the tide, by an integration of this teaching with the priorities and interests of a capitalist society, and of a capitalist society, moreover, which necessarily retains as its central principle the idea of a few governing, communicating with and teaching the many.[15]

At this point in American history, neoliberal capitalism is not simply too overpowering; on the contrary, "democracy is too weak."[16] Hence, the increasing influence of money over politics, corporate interests overriding public concerns, and the growing tyranny of unchecked corporate power and avarice. Culture combines with politics to turn struggles over power into entertainment, as is the case in the California recall of Governor Gray Davis and election of Arnold Schwarzenegger. But more importantly, under neoliberalism, pedagogy has become thoroughly politicized in reactionary terms as it constructs knowledge, values, and identities through a dominant media that has become a handmaiden of corporate power. For instance, soon after the invasion of Iraq, the *New York Times* released a survey indicating that 42 percent of the American public believed that Saddam Hussein was directly responsible for the September 11 attacks on the World Trade Center and the Pentagon. CBS also released a news poll indicating that 55 percent of the public believed that Saddam Hussein directly supported the terrorist organization Al Qaeda. A majority of Americans also believed that Saddam Hussein had weapons of mass destruction, was about to build a nuclear bomb, and that he would unleash it eventually on an unsuspecting American public. None of these claims had any basis in fact since no evidence existed to even remotely confirm that any of these assertions were true. Of course, these opinions held by a substantial number of Americans did not simply fall from the sky; they were ardently legitimated by President Bush, Vice President Dick Cheney, Secretary of State Colin Powell, and National Security Advisor Condolezza Rice, while daily reproduced uncritically in all of the dominant media. These misrepresentations and strategic distortions circulated in the dominant press either with uncritical, jingoistic enthusiasm, as in the case of the Fox News Channel, or through the dominant media's refusal to challenge such claims—both positions, of course, in opposition to foreign news sources such as the BBC which repeatedly challenged such assertions. Such deceptions are never innocent and in this case appear to have been shamelessly used by the Bush administration to both muster support for the Iraqi invasion and an ideologically driven agenda "that overwhelmingly favors the president's wealthy supporters and is driving the federal government toward a long-term fiscal catastrophe."[17]

While not downplaying the seriousness of government deception, I believe there is another serious issue that underlines these events in which the most important casualty is not simply the integrity of the Bush administration, but democracy itself. One of the central legacies of modern democracy, with its roots in the Enlightenment classical liberal tradition, and most evident in the twentieth century in work as diverse as W. E. B. Du Bois, Raymond Williams, Cornelius Castoriadis, John Dewey, and Paulo Freire, among others, is the important recognition that a substantive democracy cannot exist without educated citizens. For some, the fear of democracy itself translated into an attack on a truly public and accessible education for all citizens. For others such as the progressive Walter Lippman, who wrote extensively on democracy in the 1920s, it meant creating two modes of education. One mode for the elite who would rule the country and be the true participants in the democratic process, and the other branch of education for the masses, whose education would train them to be spectators rather than participants in shaping democratic public life. Du Bois recognized that such a bifurcation of educational opportunity was increasingly becoming a matter of common sense, but rejected it outright.[18] Similarly, in opposition to the enemies of democracy and the elitists, radical social critics such as Cornelius Castoriadis, Paulo Freire, Stuart Hall and others believed that education for a democratic citizenry was an essential condition of equality and social justice and had to be provided through public, higher, popular, and adult education.

While Castoriadis and others were right about linking education and democracy, they had no way in their time of recognizing that the larger culture would extend, if not supercede, institutionalized education as the most important educational force in the developed societies. In fact, education and pedagogy have been synonymous with schooling in the public mind. Challenging such a recognition does not invalidate the importance of formal education to democracy, but it does require a critical understanding of how the work of education takes place in a range of other spheres such as advertising, television, film, the Internet, video games, and the popular press.

Rather than invalidate the importance of schooling, public pedagogy extends the sites of pedagogy and, in so doing, broadens and deepens the meaning of cultural pedagogy. The concept of public pedagogy also underscores the central importance of formal spheres of learning that unlike their popular counter parts—driven largely by commercial interests that more often mis-educate the public—must provide citizens with those critical capacities, modes of literacies, knowledge, and skills that enable them to both read the world critically and participate in shaping and governing it.

Pedagogy at the popular level must now be a central concern of formal schooling itself. I am not claiming that public or higher education are free from corporate influence and dominant ideologies, but that such models of education, at best, provide the spaces and conditions for prioritizing civic values over commercial interests (i.e., it self-consciously educates future citizens capable of participating in and reproducing a democratic society). In spite of their present embattled status and contradictory roles, institutional schooling remains uniquely placed to prepare students to both understand and influence the larger educational forces that shape their lives. Such institutions along with their cultural studies advocates by virtue of their privileged position and dedication to freedom and democracy also have an obligation to draw upon those traditions and resources capable of providing a critical and humanistic education to all students in order to prepare them for a world in which information and power have taken on a new and powerful dimension. One entry into this challenge is to address the contributions that cultural studies and critical pedagogy have made in the last few decades to such issues, particularly with respect to how the relationship between culture and power constitute a new site of both politics and pedagogy.

Cultural Studies and the Question of Pedagogy

> City walls, books, spectacles, events educate—yet now they mostly *miseducate* their residents. Compare the lessons, taken by the citizens of Athens (women and slaves included), during the performances of Greek tragedies with the kind of knowledge which is today consumed by the spectator of *Dynasty* or *Perdue de vue*.[19]

My interest in cultural studies emerges out of an ongoing project to theorize the regulatory and emancipatory relationship among culture, power, and politics as expressed through the dynamics of what can be called public pedagogy. This project concerns, in part, the diverse ways in which culture functions as a contested sphere over the production, distribution, and regulation of power and how and where it operates both symbolically and institutionally as an educational, political, and economic force. Drawing upon a long tradition in cultural studies work, culture is viewed as constitutive and political, not only reflecting larger forces but also constructing them; in this instance, culture not only mediates history, it shapes it. In this formulation, power is a central element of culture just as culture is a crucial element of power.[20]

As Bauman observes, "Culture is a permanent revolution of sorts. To say 'culture' is to make another attempt to account for the fact that the human world (the world moulded by the humans and the world which moulds humans) is perpetually, unavoidably—and unremediably *noch nicht geworden* (not-yet-accomplished), as Ernst Bloch beautifully put it."[21]

I am suggesting that culture is a crucial terrain for theorizing and realizing the political as an articulation and intervention into the social, a space in which politics is pluralized, recognized as contingent, and open to many formations.[22] But culture is also a crucial sphere for articulating the dialectical and mutually constitutive dynamics between the global political circuits that now frame material relations of power and a cultural politics in which matters of representation and meaning shape and offer concrete examples of how politics is expressed, lived, and experienced through the modalities of daily existence. Culture, in this instance, is the ground of both contestation and accommodation. It is increasingly characterized by the rise of mega corporations and new technologies which are transforming radically the traditional spheres of the economy, industry, society, and everyday life. I am referring not only to the development of new information technologies but also the enormous concentration of ownership and power among a limited number of corporations that now control a diverse number of media technologies and markets.[23] Culture now plays a central role in producing narratives, metaphors, images, and desiring maps that exercise a powerful pedagogical force over how people think about themselves and their relationship to others. From this perspective, culture is the primary sphere in which individuals, groups, and institutions engage in the art of translating the diverse and multiple relations that mediate between private life and public concerns. It is also the sphere in which the translating and pedagogical possibilities of culture are under assault, particularly as the forces of neoliberalism dissolves public issues into utterly privatized and individualistic concerns.[24]

Central to any viable notion of cultural studies is the primacy of culture and power, organized through an understanding of how the political becomes pedagogical, particularly in terms of how private issues are connected to larger social conditions and collective forces; that is, how the very processes of learning constitute the political mechanisms through which identities are shaped, desires mobilized, and experiences take on form and meaning within those collective conditions and larger forces that constitute the realm of the social. In this context, pedagogy is no longer restricted to what goes on in schools, but becomes a defining principle of a wide ranging set of cultural apparatuses engaged in what Raymond Williams has called "permanent education." Williams rightfully believed that education in the broadest sense plays a central role in any viable form of cultural politics. He writes:

> What [permanent education] valuably stresses is the educational force of our whole social and cultural experience. It is therefore concerned, not only with continuing education, of a formal or informal kind, but with what the whole environment, its institutions and relationships,

actively and profoundly teaches. . . . [Permanent education also refers to] the field in which our ideas of the world, of ourselves and of
our possibilities, are most widely and often most powerfully formed
and disseminated. To work for the recovery of control in this field is
then, under any pressures, *a priority.* [25]

Williams argued that any viable notion of critical politics would have to
pay closer "attention to the complex ways in which individuals are formed
by the institutions to which they belong, and in which, by reaction, the
institutions took on the color of individuals thus formed."[26]

Williams also foregrounded the crucial political question of how agency
unfolds within a variety of cultural spaces structured within unequal relations of power.[27] He was particularly concerned about the connections between pedagogy and political agency, especially in light of the emergence of
a range of new technologies that greatly proliferated the amount of information available to people while at the same time constricting the substance and ways in which such meanings entered the public domain. The
realm of culture for Williams took on a new role in the latter part of the
twentieth century because the actuality of economic power and its atten-
dant networks of pedagogical control now exercised more influence than
ever before in shaping identities, desires, and everyday life, acquired largely
through the force of common sense.[28] Williams clearly understood that making the political more pedagogical meant recognizing that where and how
the psyche locates itself in public discourse, visions, and passions provides
the groundwork for agents to enunciate, act, and reflect on themselves
and their relations to others and the wider social order.

Unfortunately, Williams' emphasis on making the pedagogical more
political has not occupied a central place in the work of most cultural studies theorists. Pedagogy in most cultural studies accounts is either limited to
the realm of schooling, dismissed as a discipline with very little academic
cultural capital, or is rendered reactionary through the claim that it simply
accommodates the paralyzing grip of governmental institutions that normalize all pedagogical practices. Within this discourse, pedagogy largely
functions to both normalize relations of power and overemphasize agency
at the expense of institutional pressures, embracing what Tony Bennett calls
"all agency and no structure."[29] This criticism, however, does little to explore or highlight the complicated, contradictory, and determining ways in
which the institutional pressures of schools [and other pedagogical sites]
and the social capacities of educators are mediated within unequal relations
of power. Instead, Bennett simply reverses the formula and buttresses his
own notion of governmentality as a theory of structures without agents. Of
course, this position also ignores the role of various sites of pedagogy and

the operational work they perform in producing knowledge, values, identities, and subject positions. More importantly, it reflects the more general refusal on the part of many cultural studies theorists to take up the relationship between pedagogy and agency, on the one hand, and the relationship between the crisis of culture, education, and democracy on the other. Given such a myopic vision, left leaning intellectuals who are dismissive of formal education sites have no doubt made it easier for the more corporate and entrepreneurial interests to dominate colleges and universities.

Unfortunately, many cultural studies theorists have failed to take seriously Antonio Gramsci's insight that "[e]very relationship of 'hegemony' is necessarily an educational relationship"—with its implication that education as a cultural pedagogical practice takes place across multiple sites as it signals how, within diverse contexts, education makes us both subjects of and subject to relations of power.[30]

I want to build on Gramsci's insight by exploring in greater detail the connection among democracy, political agency, and pedagogy by analyzing some of the work of the late French philosopher, Cornelius Castoriadis. Castoriadis has made seminal, and often overlooked, contributions to the role of pedagogy and its centrality to political democracy. I focus on this radical tradition in order to reclaim a legacy of critical thinking that refuses to decouple education from democracy, politics from pedagogy, and understanding from public intervention.

This tradition of critical thought signals for educators and cultural studies advocates the importance of investing in the political as part of a broader effort to revitalize notions of democratic citizenship, social justice, and the public good. But it also signals the importance of cultural politics as a pedagogical force for understanding how people buy into neoliberal ideology, how certain forms of agency are both suppressed and produced, how neoliberals work pedagogically to convince the public that consumer rights are more important than the rights people have as citizens and workers, and how pedagogy as a force for democratic change enables understanding, action, and resistance.

Education and Radical Democracy

Let us suppose that a democracy, as complete, perfect, etc. as one might wish, might fall upon us from the heavens: this sort of democracy will not be able to endure for more than a few years if it does not engender individuals that correspond to it, ones that, first and foremost, are capable of making it function and reproducing it. There can be no democratic society without democratic *paideia*.[31]

Castoriadis was deeply concerned about what it meant to think about politics and agency in light of the new conditions of capitalism that threatened to undermine the promise of democracy at the end of the twentieth century. Moreover, he argues, like Raymond Williams, that education in the broadest sense, is a principle feature of politics because it provides the capacities, knowledge, skills, and social relations through which individuals recognize themselves as social and political agents. Linking such a broad-based definition of education to issues of power and agency also raises fundamental questions that go to the heart of any substantive notion of democracy: how do issues of history, language, culture, and identity work to articulate and legitimate particular exclusions?

If culture in this sense becomes the constituting terrain for producing identities and constituting social subjects, education becomes the strategic and positional mechanism through which such subjects are addressed, positioned within social spaces, located within particular histories and experiences, and always arbitrarily displaced and decentered as part of a pedagogical process that is increasingly multiple, fractured, and never homogenous.

Castoriadis has provided an enormous theoretical service over the last thirty years in analyzing the space of education as a constitutive site for democratic struggle. Castoriadis pursues the primacy of education as a political force by focusing on democracy as both the realized power of the people and as a mode of autonomy. In the first instance, he insists that "democracy means power of the people . . . a regime aspiring to social and personal" freedom.[32] Democracy in this view suggests more than a simply negative notion of freedom in which the individual is defended against power.

On the contrary, Castoriadis argues that any viable notion of democracy must reject this passive attitude toward freedom with its view of power as a necessary evil. In its place, he calls for a productive notion of power, one that is central to embracing a notion of political agency and freedom that affirms the equal opportunity of all to exercise political power in order to participate in shaping the most important decisions affecting their lives.[33] He ardently rejects the increasing "abandonment of the public sphere to specialists, to professional politicians."[34] Castoriadis rejects any conception of democracy that did not create the means for "unlimited interrogation in all domains" that closed off in "advance not only every political question as well as every philosophical one, but equally every ethical or aesthetic question."[35] He also refuses a notion of democracy restricted to the formalistic processes of voting while at the same time arguing that the notion of participatory democracy cannot remain narrowly confined to the political sphere.

Democracy, for Castoriadis, must also concern itself with the issue of cultural politics. He rightly argues that progressives are required to address the ways in which every society creates what he calls its "social imaginary significations," which provide the structures of representations that offer individuals selected modes of identification, provide the standards for both the ends of action and the criteria for what is considered acceptable or unacceptable behavior, while establishing the affective measures for mobilizing desire and human action.[36]

The fate of democracy for Castoriadis was inextricably linked to the profound crisis of contemporary knowledge, characterized by its increasing commodification, fragmentation, privatization, and the turn toward racial and patriotic conceits. As knowledge becomes abstracted from the demands of civic culture and is reduced to questions of style, ritual, and image, it undermines the political, ethical, and governing conditions for individuals and social groups to either participate in politics or construct those viable public spheres necessary for debate, collective action, and solving urgent social problems. As Castoriadis suggests, the crisis of contemporary knowledge provides one of the central challenges to any viable notion of politics. He writes:

> Also in question is the relation of . . . knowledge to the society that produces it, nourishes it, is nourished by it, and risks dying of it, as well as the issues concerning for whom and for what this knowledge exists. Already at present these problems demand a radical transformation of society, and of the human being, at the same time that they contain its premises. If this monstrous tree of knowledge that modern humanity is cultivating more and more feverishly every day is not to collapse under its own weight and crush its gardener as it falls, the necessary transformations of man and society must go infinitely further than the wildest utopias have ever dared to imagine.[37]

Castoriadis was particularly concerned about how progressives might address the crisis of democracy in light of how social and political agents were being produced through dominant public pedagogies in a society driven by the glut of specialized knowledge, consumerism, and a privatized notion of citizenship that no longer supported non-commercial values and increasingly dismissed as a constraint any view of society that emphasized public goods and social responsibility. What is crucial to acknowledge in Castoriadis's view of democracy is that the crisis of democracy cannot be separated from the dual crisis of representation and political agency.

In a social order in which the production of knowledge, meaning, and debate are highly restricted not only are the conditions for producing critical social agents limited, but also lost is the democratic imperative of affirming the primacy of ethics as a way of recognizing a social order's obligation to future generations. Ethics in this sense recognizes that the extension of power assumes a comparable extension in the field of ethical responsibility, a willingness to acknowledge that ethics means being able to answer in the present for actions that will be borne by generations in the future.[38]

Central to Castoriadis's work is the crucial acknowledgment that society creates itself through a multiplicity of organized pedagogical forms that provide the "instituting social imaginary" or field of cultural and ideological representations through which social practices and institutional forms are endowed with meaning, generating certain ways of seeing the self and its possibilities in the world. Not only is the social individual constituted, in part, by internalizing such meanings, but he or she acts upon such meanings in order to also participate and, where possible, to change society.

According to Castoriadis, politics within this framework becomes "the collective activity whose object" is to put into question the explicit institutions of society while simultaneously creating the conditions for individual and social autonomy.[39] Castoriadis's unique contribution to democratic political theory lies in his keen understanding that autonomy is inextricably linked to forms of civic education which provide the conditions for bringing to light how explicit and implicit power can be used to open up or close down those public spaces that are essential for individuals to meet, address public interests, engage pressing social issues, and participate collectively in shaping public policy. In this view, civic education brings to light "society's instituting power by rendering it explicit . . . it reabsorbs the political into politics as the lucid and deliberate activity whose object is the explicit [production] of society."[40]

Castoriadis asserts that political agency involves learning how to deliberate, make judgments, and exercise choices, particularly as the latter are brought to bear as critical activities that offer the possibility of change. Civic education as it is experienced and produced throughout a vast array of institutions provides individuals with the opportunity to see themselves as more than they simply are within the existing configurations of power of any given society. Every society has an obligation to provide citizens with the capacities, knowledge and skills necessary for them to be, as Aristotle claimed, "capable of governing and being governed."[41] A democracy cannot work if citizens are not autonomous, self-judging, and independent, qualities that are indispensable for them to make vital judgments and choices about participating in and shaping decisions that effect everyday life, institutional reform, and governmental policy. Hence, civic education becomes the cornerstone of democracy in that the very foundation of self-government is based on people not just having the "typical right to participate; they should also be educated [in the fullest possible way] in order to be *able* to participate."[42]

From a Pedagogy of Understanding to a Pedagogy of Intervention

> It is not the knowledge of good and evil that we are missing; it is the skill and zeal to act on that knowledge which is conspicuously absent in this world of ours, in which dependencies, political responsibility and cultural values part ways and no longer hold each other in check.[43]

Williams and Castoriadis were clear that pedagogy and the active process of learning was central to any viable notion of citizenship and inclusive democracy. Pedagogy looms large for both of these theorists not as a technique or *a priori* set of methods but as a political and moral practice. As a political practice, pedagogy illuminates the relationship among power, knowledge, and ideology, while self-consciously, if not self-critically, recognizing the role it plays as a deliberate attempt to influence how and what knowledge and identities are produced within particular sets of social relations. As a moral practice, pedagogy recognizes that what cultural workers, artists, activists, media workers and others teach cannot be abstracted from what it means to invest in public life, presuppose some notion of the future, or locate oneself in a public discourse.

The moral implications of pedagogy also suggest that our responsibility as public intellectuals cannot be separated from the consequences of the knowledge we produce, the social relations we legitimate, and the ideologies and identities we offer up to students. Refusing to decouple politics from pedagogy means, in part, that teaching in classrooms or in any other public sphere should not simply honor the experiences students bring to such sites, including the classroom, but should also connect their experiences to specific problems that emanate from the material contexts of their everyday life. Pedagogy in this sense becomes performative in that it is not merely about deconstructing texts but about situating politics itself within a broader set of relations that addresses what it might mean to create modes of individual and social agency that enables rather than shuts down democratic values, practices, and social relations. Such a project recognizes not only the political nature of pedagogy, but also situates it within a call for intellectuals to assume responsibility for their actions, to link their teaching to those moral principles that allow us to do something about human suffering, as Susan Sontag has recently suggested.[44]

Part of this task necessitates that cultural studies theorists and educators anchor their own work, however diverse, in a radical project that seriously engages the promise of an unrealized democracy against its really existing and radically incomplete forms. Of crucial importance to such a project is rejecting the assumption that theory can understand social problems without contesting their appearance in public life. Yet, any viable cultural politics needs a socially committed notion of injustice if we are to take seriously what it means to fight for the idea of the good society. I think Zygmunt Bauman is right in arguing that "If there is no room for the idea of *wrong* society, there is hardly much chance for the idea of a good society to be born, let alone make waves."[45]

Cultural studies theorists need to be more forceful, if not committed, to linking their overall politics to modes of critique and collective action that address the presupposition that democratic societies are never too just or just enough, and such a recognition means that a society must constantly nurture the possibilities for self-critique, collective agency, and forms of citizenship in which people play a fundamental role in critically discussing, administrating and shaping the material relations of power and ideological forces that bear down on their everyday lives.

At stake here is the task, as Jacques Derrida insists, of viewing the project of democracy as a promise, a possibility rooted in an ongoing struggle for economic, cultural, and social justice.[46] Democracy in this instance is not a sutured or formalistic regime, it is the site of struggle itself.

The struggle over creating an inclusive and just democracy can take many forms, offers no political guarantees, and provides an important normative dimension to politics as an ongoing process of democratization that never ends. Such a project is based on the realization that a democracy that is open to exchange, question, and self-criticism never reaches the limits of justice. As Bauman observes:

> Democracy is not an institution, but essentially an anti-institutional force, a 'rupture' in the otherwise relentless trend of the powers-that-be to arrest change, to silence and to eliminate from the political process all those who have not been 'born' into power. . . . Democracy expresses itself in a continuous and relentless critique of institutions; democracy is an anarchic, disruptive element inside the political system; essentially, a force for *dissent* and change. One can best recognize a democratic society by its constant complaints that it is *not* democratic enough.[47]

By linking education to the project of an unrealized democracy, cultural studies theorists who work in higher education can move beyond those approaches to pedagogy that reduce it to a methodology such as "teaching the conflicts" or relatedly opening up a culture of questioning. In the most immediate sense, these positions fail to make clear the larger political, normative, and ideological considerations that inform such views of education, teaching, and visions of the future, assuming that education is predicated upon a particular view of the future that students should inhabit. Furthermore, both positions collapse the purpose and meaning of higher education, the role of educators as engaged scholars, and the possibility of pedagogy itself into a rather short-sighted and sometimes insular notion of method, particularly one that emphasizes argumentation and dialogue. There is a disquieting refusal in such discourses to raise broader questions about the social, economic, and political forces shaping the very terrain of higher education—particularly unbridled market forces, or racist and sexist forces that unequally value diverse groups of students within relations of academic power, or what it might mean to engage pedagogy as a basis not merely for understanding but also for participating in the larger world.

There is also a general misunderstanding of how teacher authority can be used to create the conditions for an education in democracy without necessarily falling into the trap of simply indoctrinating students.[48] For instance, liberal educator Gerald Graff believes that any notion of critical pedagogy that is self conscious about its politics and engages students in ways that offer them the possibility for becoming critical—or what Lani Guinier calls the need to educate students "to participate in civic life, and to encourage graduates to give back to the community, which through taxes, made their education possible"[49]—either leaves students out of the conversation or presupposes too much and simply represents a form of pedagogical tyranny.

While Graff advocates strongly that educators create the educational practices that open up the possibility of questioning among students, he refuses to connect pedagogical conditions that challenge how they think at the moment to the next step of prompting them to think about changing the world around them so as to expand and deepen its democratic possibilities. George Lipsitz criticizes academics such as Graff who believe that connecting academic work to social change is at best a burden and, at worst, a collapse into a crude form of propagandizing suggesting that they are subconsciously educated to accept cynicism about the ability of ordinary people to change the conditions under which they live.[50] Teaching students how to argue, draw on their own experiences, or engage in rigorous dialogue says nothing about why they should engage in these actions in the first place. How the culture of argumentation and questioning relates to giving students the tools they need to fight oppressive forms of power, make the world a more meaningful and just place, and develop a sense of social responsibility is missing in work like Graff's because this is part of the discourse of political education, which Graff simply equates to indoctrination or speaking to the converted.[51] Here propaganda and critical pedagogy collapse into each other.

Propaganda is used to generally misrepresent knowledge, promote biased knowledge, or produce a view of politics that appears beyond question and critical engagement. While no pedagogical intervention should fall to the level of propaganda, a pedagogy which attempts to empower critical citizens cannot and should not avoid politics.

Pedagogy must address the relationship between politics and agency, knowledge and power, subject positions and values, and learning and social change while always being open to debate, resistance, and a culture of questioning. Liberal educators committed to simply raising questions have no language for linking learning to forms of public scholarship that would enable students to consider the important relationship between democratic public life and education, politics and learning. Disabled by a depoliticizing, if not slavish allegiance to a teaching methodology, they have little idea of how to encourage students pedagogically to enter the sphere of the political, enabling them to think about how they might participate in a democracy by taking what they learn "into new locations—a third grade classroom, a public library, a legislator's office, a park,"[52] or for that matter taking on collaborative projects that address the myriad of problems citizens face in a diminishing democracy.

In spite of the professional pretense to neutrality, academics need to do more pedagogically than simply teach students how to be adept at forms of argumentation. Students need to argue and question, but they need much more from their educational experience. The pedagogy of argumentation in and of itself guarantees nothing but it is an essential step towards opening up the space of resistance towards authority, teaching students to think critically about the world around them, and recognizing interpretation and dialogue as a condition for social intervention and transformation in the service an unrealized democratic order.

As Amy Gutmann brilliantly argues, education is always political because it is connected to the acquisition of agency, the ability to struggle with ongoing relations of power, and is a precondition for creating informed and critical citizens. For Gutmann, educators need to link education to democracy and recognize pedagogy as an ethical and political practice tied to modes of authority in which the "democratic state recognizes the value of political education in predisposing [students] to accept those ways of life that are consistent with sharing the rights and responsibilities of citizenship in a democratic society."[53] This is not a notion of education tied to the alleged neutrality of teaching methods, but to a vision of pedagogy that is directive and interventionist on the side of reproducing a democratic society. Democratic societies need educated citizens who are steeped in more than the skills of argumentation. It is precisely this democratic project that affirms the critical function of education and refuses to narrow its goals and aspirations to methodological considerations. This is what makes critical pedagogy different from training. It is the failure to connect learning to its democratic functions and goals that provides rationales for pedagogical approaches that strip the understanding of what it means to be educated from its critical and democratic possibilities.

Williams and Castoriadis recognized that the crisis of democracy was not only about the crisis of culture, but also about the crisis of pedagogy and education. Cultural studies theorists would do well to take account of the profound transformations taking place in the public sphere and reclaim pedagogy as a central category of cultural politics. The time has come for cultural studies theorists to distinguish professional caution from political cowardice and recognize that their obligations extend beyond deconstructing texts or promoting a culture of questioning. These are important pedagogical interventions, but they do not go far enough.

We need to link knowing with action and learning with social engagement. This requires addressing the responsibilities that come with teaching students and others to fight for an inclusive and radical democracy by recognizing that education, in the broadest sense, is not just about understanding, however critical, but must also provide the conditions for assuming the responsibilities we have as citizens to expose human misery and to eliminate the conditions that produce it.

I think Bauman is quite right in suggesting that as engaged cultural workers, we need to take up our work as part of a broader democratic project in which the good society

> is a society which thinks it is not just enough, which questions the sufficiency of any achieved level of justice and considers justice always to be a step or more ahead. Above all, it is a society which reacts angrily to any case of injustice and promptly sets about correcting it.[54]

Matters of responsibility, social action, and political intervention do not simply develop out of social critique but also forms of self-critique. The relationship between knowledge and power, on the one hand, and scholarship and politics, on the other, should always be self-reflexive about its effects, how it relates to the larger world, whether or not it is open to new understandings, and what it might mean pedagogically to take seriously matters of individual and social responsibility. In short, this project points to the need for educators to articulate cultural studies as not only a resource for theoretical competency and critical understanding, but also as a pedagogical practice that addresses the possibility of interpretation as an intervention in the world.

Neoliberalism not only places capital and market relations in a no-man's land beyond the reach of compassion, ethics, and decency, it also undermines those basic elements of the social contract and the political and pedagogical relations it presupposes in which self-reliance, confidence in others, and a trust in the longevity of democratic institutions provide the basis for modes of individual autonomy, social agency, and critical citizenship.

One of the most serious challenges faced by cultural studies is the need to develop a new language and set of theoretical tools for contesting a variety of forms of domination put into play by neoliberalism in the new millennium. Part of this challenge demands recognizing that the struggles over cultural politics cannot be divorced from the contestations and struggles put into play through the forces of dominant economic and cultural institutions and their respective modes of education. Cultural studies advocates must address the challenge of how to problematize and pluralize the political, engage new sites of pedagogy as crucial, strategic public spheres, and situate cultural studies within an ongoing project that recognizes that the crisis of democracy is about the interrelated crises of politics, culture, and education.

Notes

1. Zygmunt Bauman, *Work, Consumerism, and the New Poor* (Philadelphia: Open University Press, 1998), 97–98.
2. Edward S. Herman and Robert W. McChesney, *The Global Media: The New Missionaries of Global Capitalism* (Washington and London: Cassell, 1997), 3.
3. I address this issue in Henry A. Giroux, *Public Spaces, Private Lives: Democracy Beyond 9/11* (Lanham, MD: Rowman and Littlefield, 2003).
4. James Rule, "Markets, in Their Place," *Dissent* (winter 1998), 31.
5. Zygmunt Bauman, *The Individualized Society* (London: Polity Press, 2001), 107.
6. See Bauman, *The Individualized Society.*
7. Alan Bryman, *Disney and His Worlds* (New York: Routledge, 1995), 154.
8. Pierre Bourdieu, *Language and Symbolic Power* (Cambridge: Harvard University Press, 2001), 127.
9. Bourdieu, *Language and Symbolic Power*, 128.
10. Pierre Bourdieu, "The Essence of Neoliberalism," *Le Monde Diplomatique* (December 1998), 4. Online at http://www.en.mode-diplomatique.fr/1998/12/08bourdieu
11. For some general theoretical principles for addressing the new sites of pedagogy, see Jeffrey R. Di Leo, Walter Jacobs, and Amy Lee, "The Sites of Pedagogy," *symplokē* 10 (2003): 7–12.
12. William Greider, "The Right's Grand Ambition: Rolling Back the 20th Century," *The Nation* (May 12, 2003), 11.
13. One interesting analysis on the contingent nature of democracy and public space can be found in Rosalyn Deutsche, *Evictions: Art and Spatial Politics* (Cambridge: The MIT Press, 1998).
14. Cited in Robert Dreyfuss, "Grover Norquist: 'Field Marshal' of the Bush Plan," *The Nation* (May 14, 2001), 1.
15. Raymond Williams, *Communications* (New York: Barnes & Noble, 1967), 15.
16. Benjamin R. Barber, "A Failure of Democracy, Not Capitalism," *New York Times* (July 29, 2002), A23.
17. Bob Herbert, "The Art of False Impression," *New York Times* (August 11, 2003), A17.
18. W. E. B. Du Bois, *Against Racism: Unpublished Essays, Papers, Addresses, 1887–1961*, ed. Herbert Aptheker (Amherst: University of Massachusetts Press, 1985).
19. Cornelius Castoriadis cited in Zygmunt Bauman, *The Individualized Society*, 127.
20. Michele Barrett, *Imagination in Theory* (New York: New York University Press, 1999), 161.

21. Zygmunt Bauman and Keith Tester, *Conversations with Zygmunt Bauman* (Malden, MA: Polity Press, 2001), 32.
22. I take up this issue in great detail in Giroux, *Public Spaces, Private Lives: Democracy Beyond 9/11*.
23. See Robert W. McChesney and John Nichols, *Our Media Not Theirs: The Democratic Struggle Against Corporate Media* (New York: Seven Stories Press, 2002).
24. See Zygmunt Bauman, *In Search of Politics* (Stanford, CA: Stanford University Press, 1999).
25. Williams, *Communications*, 15, 16.
26. Williams, *Communications*, 14.
27. See Raymond Williams, *Marxism and Literature* (New York: Oxford University Press, 1977), and Raymond Williams, *The Year 2000* (New York: Pantheon, 1983).
28. See Williams, *Marxism and Literature*.
29. Tony Bennett, *Culture: A Reformer's Science* (Thousand Oaks, CA: Sage, 1998), 223.
30. Antonio Gramsci, *Selections from the Prison Notebooks* (New York: International Press, 1971), 350.
31. Cornelius Castoriadis, "Democracy as Procedure and Democracy as Regime," *Constellations* 4 (1997), 10.
32. Cornelius Castoriadis, "The Problem of Democracy Today," *Democracy and Nature* 8 (April 1996), 19.
33. Cornelius Castoriadis, *Philosophy, Politics, Autonomy: Essays in Political Philosophy* (New York: Oxford University Press, 1991), 124–142.
34. Cornelius Castoriadis, *The World in Fragments*, ed. David Ames Curtis (Stanford, CA: Stanford University Press, 1997), 91.
35. Cornelius Castoriadis, "Culture in a Democratic Society," in *The Castoriadis Reader*, ed. David Ames Curtis (Malden, MA: Blackwell, 1997), 343, 341.
36. Cornelius Castoriadis, "The Crisis of the Identification Process," *Thesis Eleven* 49 (May 1997), 87–88.
37. Cornelius Castoriadis, "The Anticipated Revolution," *Political and Social Writings*, Volume 3, ed. David Ames Curtis (Minneapolis: University of Minnesota Press, 1993), 153–154.
38. John Binde, "Toward an Ethic of the Future," *Public Culture* 12 (2000), 65.
39. Cornelius Castoriadis, *Philosophy, Politics, Autonomy*, 102.
40. Castoriadis, *Philosophy, Politics, Autonomy*, 144–145.
41. Castoriadis, *Philosophy, Politics, Autonomy*, 15. It is crucial here to note that Castoriadis develops both his notion of democracy and the primacy of education in political life directly from his study of ancient Greek democracy.
42. Castoriadis, *Philosophy, Politics, Autonomy*, 24.
43. Bauman and Tester, *Conversations with Zygmunt Bauman*, 131.
44. See Susan Sontag, "Courage and Resistance," *The Nation* (May 5, 2003): 11–14.
45. Zygmunt Bauman, *Society under Siege* (Malden, MA: Blackwell: 2002), 170.
46. See Jacques Derrida, "Intellectual Courage: An Interview," *Culture Machine* 2 (2000): 1–15.
47. Bauman, *The Individualized Society*, 54–55.
48. Gerald Graff appears to have made a career out of this issue by either misrepresenting the work of Paulo Freire and others, citing theoretical work by critical educators that is outdated and could be corrected by reading anything they might have written in the last five years, creating caricatures of their work, or by holding up as an example of what people in critical pedagogy do (or more generally, anyone who links pedagogy and politics) the most extreme and ludicrous examples. For more recent representations of this position, see Gerald Graff, "Teaching Politically Without Political Correctness," *Radical Teacher* 58 (fall 2000): 26–30; and Gerald Graff, *Clueless in Academe* (New Haven: Yale University Press, 2003).
49. Lani Guinier, "Democracy Tested," *The Nation* (May 5, 2003), 6. Guinier's position is in direct opposition to that of Graff and his acolytes. For instance, see Lani Guinier and Anna Deavere Smith, "Rethinking Power, Rethinking Theater," *Theater* 31 (winter 2002): 31–45.
50. George Lipsitz, "Academic Politics and Social Change," in *Cultural Studies and Political Theory*, ed. Jodi Dean (Ithaca: Cornell University Press, 2000), 81–82.

51. For a more detailed response to this kind of watered down pedagogical practice, see Stanley Aronowitz, *The Knowledge Factory* (Boston: Beacon Press, 2000); and Henry A. Giroux, *The Abandoned Generation: Democracy Beyond the Culture of Fear* (New York: Palgrave, 2003).

52. Julie Ellison, "New Public Scholarship in the Arts and Humanities," *Higher Education Exchange* (2002), 20.

53. Amy Gutmann, *Democratic Education* (Princeton, NJ: Princeton University Press, 1998), 42.

54. Bauman and Tester, *Conversations with Zygmunt Bauman*, 63.

CHAPTER 2

Education, Social Class, and the Sites of Pedagogy

STANLEY ARONOWITZ

> . . . the crisis in American education, on the one hand, announces the bankruptcy of progressive education and, on the other hand, presents a problem of immense difficulty because it has arisen under the conditions and in response to the demands of a mass society.
>
> —Hannah Arendt, "The Crisis in Education"

Introduction

Americans have great expectations of their schools. We tend to invest them with the primary responsibility for providing our children with the means by which they may succeed in an increasingly uncertain work-world. If the child "fails" to be inducted, through academic discipline, into the rituals of labor, we blame teachers and school administrators. Indirectly schools have been burdened with addressing many of the world's ills. Along with two world wars, and revolutions, the twentieth century witnessed great hopes for democracy, but experienced its demise in the wake of the rise of the dictatorships. We knew that education was the key to technological transformation that became the main engine of economic growth. Schooling was a bulwark of secularism, but has buckled under the onslaught produced by the revival of religious fundamentalism. And, in almost every economically "developed" country, we count on schools to smooth the transition of huge populations from rural to urban habitats, from "foreign" languages and cultures to English and Americanism.

At the dawn of the new century, no American institution is invested with a greater role to bring the young and their parents into the modernist regime than public schools. This charge is underscored by the vast wave of Latin American, Asian and East European immigration of the last twenty-five years, which rivals in numbers, and in economic and social significance, even the great European immigration of the turn of the twentieth century. The public school is charged with the task of preparing children and youth for their dual responsibilities to the social order: citizenship and, perhaps its primary task, learning to labor. As schools gradually dispense with the tasks of encouraging critical, independent thinking and transmitting the jewels of past literate culture from the curriculum, the point of schooling is increasingly to prepare students for work-world. The curriculum must justify itself by this single criterion.

In the wake of these awesome tasks, fiscal exigency as well as a changing mission have combined to leave public education in the United States in a chronic state of crisis. For some, the main issue is whether schools are failing to transmit the general intellectual culture, even to the most able students. Hannah Arendt goes so far as to ask whether we "love the world" and our children enough to devise an educational system capable of transmitting to them the salient cultural traditions. Other critics complain that schools are failing to fulfill the promise of equality of opportunity for good jobs for working-class students—Black, Latino and White. The two positions, both with respect to their goals and to their implied educational philosophies, may not necessarily be contradictory but their simultaneous enunciation produces considerable tension, for the American workplace has virtually no room for dissent and individual or collective initiative not sanctioned by management. The corporate factory, which includes sites of goods and symbolic production alike, is perhaps the nation's most authoritarian institution. But any reasonable concept of democratic citizenship requires an individual who is able to discern knowledge from propaganda, is competent to choose among conflictual claims and programs, and is capable of actively participating in the affairs of the polity. Yet, the political system offers few opportunities, beyond the ritual of voting, for active citizen participation.[1]

The progressives, who misread John Dewey's educational philosophy to mean that the past need not be studied too seriously, have offered little resistance to the gradual vocationalizing, and dumbing-down of the mass education curriculum. In fact, historically they were advocates of making the curriculum less formal, reducing requirements and, on the basis of a degraded argument that children learn best by "doing," promoted practical, work-oriented programs for high school students. Curricular *deformalization* was often justified on interdisciplinary criteria, which resulted in watering-down of course content and deemphasizing writing. Most

American high school students, in the affluent as well as the "inner city" districts, may write short papers which amount to book reviews and auto-biographical essays, but most graduate without ever having to perform research and write a paper of considerable length. Moreover, in an attempt to make the study of history more "relevant" to students' lives, since the late 1960s the student is no longer required to memorize dates; he may have learned the narratives but was often unable to place them in a specific chronological context. Similarly, economics has been eliminated in many schools or taught as a "unit" of a general social studies course. And, if philosophy is taught at all, it is construed in terms of "values clarification," a kind of ethics in which the student is assisted to discover and examine her own values.

In Black and Latino working-class districts, schools are, for many students, way stations to the military or to prison even more than to the civilian paid labor force. As Michelle Fine observes: "visit a South Bronx high school these days and you'll find yourself surrounded by propaganda from the Army, Navy, and Marines . . . look at the 'stats' and you'll see that 70% of the men and women in prison have neither a GED or a diploma; go to Ocean Hill-Brownsville, Brooklyn 40ish years later, and you'll see a juvenile justice facility on the very site that they wanted to build their own schools."[2] In the current fiscal crisis afflicting education and other social services, there is an outstanding exception: prisons continue to be well-funded and despite the decline of violent crimes in the cities, drug busts keep prisons full and rural communities working.

Beyond schooling, young people learn, for ill as well as good, from popular culture, especially music, from parents and family structure, and perhaps most important, from their peers. Schools are the stand-in for "society" and for the prevailing culture. In the American vein, society is equated with the aggregation of individuals who, by contract or by coercion, are subject to governing authorities in return for which they may be admitted into the world albeit on the basis of different degrees of reward. To the extent they signify solidarity and embody common dreams, popular culture, parents, and peers are quasi-communities which are often more powerful influences on their members.

Media and Popular Culture

The ubiquity and penetration of the products of the culture industry by means of visual media and electronic aural equipment into the home has called into question the separation of the public and private spheres, and challenged the notion that autonomous private life any longer exists. This has prompted writers such as Hannah Arendt to insist on the importance of maintaining their separation.[3] When taken together with the advent, in the technical as well as metaphoric sense, of "big brother" where the government now announces openly its right to subject every telephone and computer to surveillance, it is difficult to avoid the conclusion that media are a crucial source of education and may, in comparison to schools, exercise a greater influence on children and youth. Many claim that television, for example, is the prime source of political education, certainly the major source of news for perhaps a majority of the population. And, there is a growing academic discourse of the importance of popular culture, especially music and film in shaping the values, but more to the point, the cultural imaginary of children and adolescents. Many writers have noted the influence of media images on dream work, on children's aspirations, on their measurement of self-worth, both physically and emotionally. Debate rages as to what is learned. The implied frameworks, for example, that are masked by the face of objectivity presented by television news, and by fiction which, as everybody knows, is suffused with ethical perspective on everyday relations.[4]

Nor does every critic accept the conventional wisdom that, in the wake of the dominance of visual media in everyday life, we are, in the phrase of a leading commentator, "amusing ourselves to death," or that the ideological messages of popular music, sitcoms and other TV fare are simply conformist.[5] But, it must be admitted that since the 1920s and 1930s, when critics argued that the possibility of a radical democracy in which ordinary people participated in the great and small decisions affecting their lives was undermined by the advent of the culture industry, popular culture has, to a large degree, become a weapon against, as well as for, the people. As a general rule, in periods of upsurge, when social movements succeed in transforming aspects of everyday life as well as the political landscape art, in its "high" as well as popular genres, has expressed popular yearning for a better world. In this vein, a vast literature, written largely by participants in the popular culture since the 1960s, rejects the sharp divide between high and low art. While many contemporary cultural theorists acknowledge their debt to the work of the Critical Theory of the Frankfurt School, they find a subversive dimension in rock and roll music. It may be that the 1960s phrase, "sex, drugs and rock 'n' roll" no longer resonates as a universal sign of rebellion. Yet, when evaluated from the perspective of a society still obsessed with drug use among kids and pre-marital sex, and frequently "blames" the music for this non-conformity, the competition between school and popular culture still rages. From anthems of rebellion to musical expressions of youth rejection of conventional sexual and political morality, critics have detected signs of resistance to official mores.[6]

Of course, even as punk signaled the conclusion of a sort of "golden age" of rock 'n' roll and the succeeding genres—heavy metal, alternative, techno among others—were confined to market niches, hip-hop took on some of the trapping of a universal oppositional cultural form which, by the 1990s, had captured the imagination of White as well as Black kids. Out of the ruins of the South Bronx came a new generation of artists whose music and poetry enflamed the embers of discontent. Figures such as Ice-T, Tupac Shakur, Biggie Smalls and many others articulated the still vibrant rebellion against what George Bernard Shaw had once called "middle class morality," and the smug, suburban confidence that the cities could be safely consigned to the margins. Like Bob Dylan, some of the hip-hop artists were superb poets; Tupac Shakur had many imitators and eventually the genre became fully absorbed by the culture industry, a development which, like the advent of the Velvet Underground, the Who and other avant-garde rock groups of the early 1970s gave rise to an underground. And, just as rock 'n' roll was accused of leading young people astray into the dungeons of drugs and illicit sex, the proponents of hip-hop suffered a similar fate. Some record producers succumbed to demands they censor artistic material, radio stations refuse to air some hip-hop, and chain record stores, especially in suburban malls, are advised to restrict sales of certain artists and records.

What White kids learn from successive waves of rock 'n' roll and hip-hop music is, in contrast to the overwhelming barrage of propaganda in favor of careerism and the glorious pursuit of commodities and money, it is alright to defy these conventions. After the mid-1950s, the varied genres of rock, rhythm and blues and hip-hop steadily challenged the class, racial and sexual constructs of this ostensibly egalitarian, but puritanical culture. Bored and dissatisfied with middle-class morality, White suburban teenagers flood the concerts of rock and hip-hop stars, smoke dope and violate the precepts of conventional sexual morality, to the best of their abilities. Many adopt Black rhetoric, language and disdain for mainstream values. Of course, middle-class kids are obliged to lead a double life: since their preferred artistic and cultural forms are accorded absolutely no recognition in the worlds of legitimate school knowledge, and for these reasons they are in a double bind. Since the 1960s, their shared music and the messages of rebellion against a racist, conventional, suburban, middle-class culture have constituted a quasi-counter community. Yet, on penalty of proscription, they must absorb school knowledge without invoking the counter-knowledge of popular culture.

The products of visual culture, particularly film and television, are no less powerful sources of knowledge. Since movies became a leading form of recreation early in the twentieth century, critics have distinguished schlock from "film," produced both by the Hollywood system and by a beleaguered corps of independent filmmakers. In the 1920s, elaborating the dynamic film technique pioneered by D. W. Griffith, the Soviet filmmakers—notably, Sergei Eisenstein and Zhiga Vertov—fully comprehended the power of visual culture in its ornamental, aesthetic sense, and gave pride of place to film as a source of mass education.[7] Vertov's *Man With a Movie Camera* and Eisenstein's *October* were not only great works of art, they possessed enormous didactic power. Vertov evoked the romance of industrial reconstruction in the new Soviet regime, and the imperative of popular participation in building a new technologically directed social reality. In most of his films, Eisenstein was the master of revolutionary memory. The people should not forget how brutal was the ancient regime and that the future was in their hands, and he would produce the images that created a new "memory" even among those who had never experienced the heady days of the revolution. Griffith conveyed a different kind of memory. In his classic *Birth of a Nation,* he deconstructed the nobility and romance of the American Civil War and the Reconstruction period by depicting them a corrupt alliance of Blacks and northern carpetbaggers, the epithet applied to the staff of the Freemen's Bureau and the military, which had been dispatched to guarantee the newly won civil rights of millions of African Americans.

In 1950, anthropologist Hortense Powdermaker termed Hollywood "the dream factory." While we were entertained by the movies, she argued, a whole world of hopes and dreams was being manufactured that had profound effects on our collective unconscious.[8] Rather than coding these experiences as "illusion," she accorded them genuine social influence. With the work of critics such as Andre Bazin, Pauline Kael, Christian Metz, and Laura Mulvey,[9] the study of movies as an art form—and also as a massive influence on what we know and how we learn—came into its own. Film, which was for Critical Theory and the minions of cultural taste in America just another product of the Culture Industry, is now taken seriously by several generations of critics and enthusiasts as a many-sided cultural force. Despite their ubiquity and vast influence, the kinds of knowledge derived from mass media and popular music remain largely unexamined within the secondary school curriculum. Through the production of iconography, film has shown its ability to manufacture politicians as well as cultural heroes as the successful political careers of George Murphy, Ronald Reagan, Sonny Bono and many others demonstrate.

In this respect, public education may be regarded as one of the last bastions of high cultural convention, and of the book. Perhaps more to the point, by consistently refusing to treat popular culture—television, film, music and video games—as objects of legitimate intellectual knowledge, schools deny the validity of student experiences, even if the objective would be to deconstruct them. Thus, a century after mass-mediated music and

visual arts captured our collective imagination, notwithstanding its unde-
niable commodification, popular culture remains subversive, regardless of
its content, because it continues to be outlawed in official precincts. By
failing to address this epochal phenomenon, even as its forms are overwhelmingly influential in everyday life, school knowledge loses its capacity
to capture the hearts and minds of its main constituents. And, if schools
cannot enter the students' collective imagination, other forms of knowledge
are destined to fill the vacuum.

Of course, the power of television in shaping the political culture is far
less well understood. If the overwhelming majority of the population receives news and viewpoints from television sources then—absent counter-
weights such as those that may be provided by social movements,
counter-hegemonic intellectuals, and independent media—the people are
inevitably subjected to the ruling common sense, in which alternatives to
the official stories lack legitimacy, even when they are reported on the back
pages or by a thirty second spot on the eleven o'clock news. Even journalists have discovered that the integration of the major news organizations
with the ruling circles inhibits their ability to accurately report the news.

Public issues are framed by experts, opinion surveys, and the media, which
faithfully feature them. That Saddam Hussein and his government constituted an imminent threat to United States security—a judgment that, neither
for the media nor for the Bush administration seemed to require proof—
was the starting point of virtually all of the contemporary media's coverage
of recent U.S. foreign policy. On many public television programs—where
experts mingle with the political directorate to discuss world and national
events—the question was almost never posed whether there is warrant for
this evaluation, but revolved instead around how to fight the terrorists,
for whom the Iraqi dictator was at least partially responsible. The taken-
for-granted assumption was that Saddam had viable "weapons of mass destruction" in his possession, which became the justification for war, whether
or not the United Nations inspectors dispatched by the U.N. Security Council
to investigate this allegation disconfirmed this U.S. government-manufac-
tured "fact." Since the Bush administration knows that there is nothing as
efficient as a war to unify the underlying population behind its policies,
and the media is complicit, citizens are deprived of countervailing assess-
ments unless they emanate from within the establishment. And even then,
there is only a small chance that these views will play prominently.

Note well, at its inception, some educators and producers touted the
educational value of television. Indeed, perhaps the major impact of the
dominance of visual culture on our everyday knowledge is that many now
believe "to be, is to be seen." Celebrity is a word that is reserved for people
whose names become "household" words. Celebrity is produced by the

repetition of appearances of an individual on the multitude of television talk shows—Oprah Winfrey, *Today*, Jay Leno, David Letterman, and others—in which personalities constitute the substance of the event. The point of the typical interview between the host and her or his subject is not what is said, or even that the guest in currently appearing in a film or television show—the ostensible purpose of the segment. The interview is a statement of who exists, and by implication, who does not. The event has little to do with economic or high-level political power, for these people are largely invisible, or, on occasion, may appear on *The Charlie Rose Show* on PBS or, formerly, on ABC's *Nightline*. The making of sports, entertainment, political or literary celebrities defines the horizon of popular hope or aspiration. The leading television celebrity talk shows are instances of the American credo that, however high the barrier, anyone can become a star. For this is not an instance of having charisma or exuding aura: the celebs are not larger than life, but are shown to be ordinary in an almost banal sense. Fix your nose, cap your teeth, lose weight, take acting lessons and, with a little luck, the person on the screen could be you.

The Labor and Radical Movements as Educational Sites

The working-class intellectual as a social type precedes and parallels the emergence of universal public education. At the dawn of the public school movement in the 1830s, the ante bellum labor movement (that consisted largely of literate skilled workers) favored six years of schooling in order to transmit to their children the basics of reading and writing, but opposed compulsory attendance in secondary schools. The reasons were bound up with their congenital suspicion of the state that they believed never exhibited sympathy for the workers' cause.

Although opposed to child labor, the early workers' movements were convinced that the substance of education—literature, history, philosophy—should be supplied by the movement itself. Consequently, in both the oral and the written tradition, workers' organizations often constituted an alternate university to that of public schools. The active program of many workers' and radical movements, until World War II, consisted largely in education through newspapers, literacy classes for immigrants where the reading materials were drawn from labor and socialist classics, and world literature. These were supplemented by lectures offered by independent scholars who toured the country in the employ of lecture organizations commissioned by the unions and radical organizations.[10]

The shop floor was also a site of education. Skilled workers were usually literate in their own language and in English, and many were voracious readers and writers. Union and radical newspapers often ran poetry and stories written by workers. Socialist-led unions, such as those in the needle trades, machineries, breweries, and bakeries, sponsored educational programs; in the era when the union contract was still a rarity, the union was not so much an agency of contract negotiation and enforcement as an educational, political and social association. In his autobiography, Samuel Gompers, the founding AFL (American Federation of Labor) president, remembers his fellow cigar makers hiring a "reader" in the 1870s, who sat at the center of the work-floor and read from literary and historical classics as well as more contemporary works of political and economic analysis such as the writings of Marx and Engels.[11] Reading groups met in the back of a bar, in the union hall, or in the local affiliate of the socialist wing of the national federations. Often these groups were ostensibly devoted to preparing immigrants to pass the obligatory language test for citizenship status. The content of the reading was, in addition to labor and socialist newspapers and magazines, often supplemented by works of fiction by Shakespeare, the great nineteenth century novelists and poets, and of Marx and Karl Kautsky. In its anarchist inflection, Kropotkin, Moses Hess, and Bakunin were the required texts.

In New York, Chicago, San Francisco and other large cities where the Socialist and Communist movements had considerable membership and a fairly substantial periphery of sympathizers, the parties established adult schools that not only offered courses pertaining to political and ideological knowledge, but were vehicles for many working- and middle-class students to gain a general education. Among them, in New York, the socialist-oriented Rand School and the Communist sponsored Jefferson School (formerly the Workers' School) lasted until the early 1950s when, due to the decline of a left intellectual culture among workers as much as the contemporary repressive political environment, they closed. But, in their respective heydays, from the 1920s to the late 1940s, for tens of thousands of working-class people— many of them high school students and industrial workers—these schools were alternate universities, with offerings beyond those that promoted the party's ideology and program. Many courses concerned history, literature and philosophy and, at least at the Jefferson school, students could study art, drama and music, as could their children. The tradition was revived, briefly, by the 1960s New Left that, in similar sites, sponsored free universities where the term "free" designated not an absence of tuition fees but signaled they were ideologically and intellectually unbound to either the traditional left parties or to the conventional school system. I participated in organizing New York's Free University and two of its successors. While not affiliated with the labor movement or socialist parties, it succeeded in attracting more than a thousand students in each of its semesters—mostly young—and offered a broad range of courses which were taught by people of divergent intellectual and political orientations, including some free market libertarians who were attracted to the school's non-sectarianism.

When I worked in a steel mill in the late 1950s, some of us formed a group that read current literature, labor history and economics. I discussed books and magazine articles with some of my fellow workers in bars as well as on breaks. Tony Mazzocchi, who was at the same time a worker and union officer of a Long Island local of the Oil, Chemical and Atomic Workers, organized a similar group, and I knew of several other cases where young workers did the same. Some of these groups evolved into rank and file caucuses that eventually contested the leadership of their local unions; others were mainly for the self-edification of the participants and had no particular political goals.

But beyond formal programs, since the industrializing era, the working-class intellectual, although by no means visible in the United States, has been part of shop-floor culture. In almost every workplace, there is a person or persons to whom other workers turn for information about the law, the union contract, contemporary politics or, equally important, as a source of general education. This individual (or these individuals) may not be schooled, for schools were not the primary source of their knowledge. Moreover, until the late 1950s, few had gone to college. They were, and are, largely self-educated. In my own case, having left Brooklyn College after less than a year, I worked in a variety of industrial production jobs. When I worked the midnight shift, I got off at 8:00 in the morning, ate breakfast, and spent four hours in the library before going home. I mostly read American and European history and political economy, particularly the physiocrats Adam Smith, David Ricardo, John Maynard Keynes and Joseph Schumpeter. I read Marx's *Capital* in high school and owned the three volumes.

My friend, Russell Rommele, who worked in a nearby mill, was also an autodidact. His father was a first generation German-American brewery worker, with no particular literary interests. Russell had been exposed to reading a wide range of historical and philosophical works as a high school student at Saint Benedict's Prep, a Jesuit institution. The priests singled out Russell for the priesthood and mentored him in theology and social theory. The experience radicalized him, and he decided not to answer the call, but to enter the industrial working class instead. Like me, he was active in the union and Newark Democratic party politics. Working as an educator with a local union in the auto industry recently, I have met several active unionists who are intellectuals. The major difference between them and those of my generation is that they are college graduates, although none claims to have acquired their love of learning or their analytic perspective from schools. One is a former member of a radical organization and another learned his politics from participation in a shop-based study group/union caucus organized by a member of a socialist grouplet that dissolved in the mid-1990s when the group lost a crucial union election. In both instances, with the demise of their organizational affiliations, they remain habituated to reading, writing and union activity.

Parents, Neighborhood, Class Culture

John Locke observes that, consistent with his rejection of innate ideas, even if conceptions of good and evil are present in divine or civil law, morality is constituted by reference to our parents, relatives, and, especially, the "club" of peers to which we belong:

> He who imagines commendation and disgrace not to be strong mo-
> tives to men to accommodate themselves to the opinions and rules of
> those with whom they converse, seems little skilled in the nature or
> history of mankind: the greatest part whereof we shall find govern
> themselves, chiefly, if not solely, by this *law of fashion*; and so they do
> what keeps them in reputation with their company, little regard for
> the laws of God, or the magistrate.[12]

William James put the manner equally succinctly: "A man's social self is the recognition which he gets from his mates."[13]

That the social worlds of peers and family are the chief referents for the formation of the social self, neither philosopher had a doubt. Each in his own fashion situates the individual in a social context, which provides a "common *measure* of virtue and vice," even as they acknowledge the ultimate choice resides with the individual self.[14] These, and not the institutions, even those that have the force of law, are the primary sources of authority.

Hannah Arendt argues that education "by its very nature cannot forego either authority or tradition," nor can it base itself on the presumption that children share an autonomous existence from adults.[15] Yet, schooling ig-nores the reality of the society of kids at the cost of undermining its own authority. The society of kids is, in virtually all classes, an alternative and opposition site of knowledge and moral valuation. Paul Willis has shown how working-class kids get working-class jobs by means of their rebellion against school authority.[16] Since refusal and resistance is a hallmark of the moral order, the few who will not obey the invocation to fail or to perform indifferently in school often find themselves marginalized or expelled from the community of kids. While they adopt a rationality that can be justified on eminently practical grounds, the long tradition of rejection of academic culture has proven hard to break, even in the wake of evidence that those working-class jobs to which they were oriented no longer exist. What is at stake in adolescent resistance is their perception that the blandishments of the adult world are vastly inferior to the pleasures of their own. In the first place, the new service economy offers few inducements: wages are low, the job is boring, and the future bleak. And, since the schools now openly present themselves as a link in the general system of control, it may appear to some students that cooperation is a form of self-deception.

If not invariably, then in many households, parents provide to the young a wealth of knowledge: the family mythologies that feature an uncle or aunt, a grandparent or an absent parent. These are the stories, loosely based on some actual event(s) in which the family member has distinguished her or himself in various ways that (usually) illustrate a moral virtue or defect, the telling of which constitutes a kind of didactic message. Even when not attached to an overt narrative, parable, or myth, we learn from our parents by their actions in relation to us and others: How do they deal with adversity? How do they address ordinary, everyday problems? What do they learn from their own trials and tribulations, and what do they say to us? What are our parents' attitudes towards money, joblessness, and everyday life disruptions such as sudden, acute illness or accidents? What do they learn from the endless conflicts with their parent(s) over issues of sex, money and household responsibilities?

The relative weight of parental to peer authority is an empirical question that cannot be decided in advance; what both have in common is their location within everyday life. The parents are likely to be more susceptible to the authority of law and of its magistrates and, in a world of increasing uncertainty, will worry that if their children choose badly they may be left behind. But, the associations with our peers we make in everyday life provide the recognition that we crave, define what is worthy of praise or blame, and confer approbation or disapproval on our decisions. In making a choice that runs counter to that of "their company" or club, the individual must form, or join, a new "company" to confer the judgement of virtue on her or his action. This company must, of necessity, consist of "peers," the definition of which has proven fungible.

Religion, the law, and, among kids, school authorities, face the obstacles erected by the powerful rewards and punishments meted out by the "clubs" to which people are affiliated. At a historical conjunction when, beneath the relentless pressure imposed by capital to transform all labor into wage labor, thereby forcing every adult into the paid labor force, the society of kids increasing occupies the space of civil society. The neighborhood, once dominated by women and small shopkeepers, has all but disappeared, save for the presence of children and youth. As parents toil for endless hours to pay the ever-mounting debts incurred by home ownership, perpetual car and appliance payments, and the costs of health care, kids are increasingly on their own, and these relationships have consequences for their conceptions of education and life.

Some recent studies and teacher observations have discovered a not in-considerable reluctance among Black students in elite universities to per-form well in school, even those of professional/managerial family backgrounds. Many seem indifferent to arguments that show that school performance is a central prerequisite to better jobs and higher status in the larger work-world. Among the more acute speculations is the conclusion that Black students' resistance reflects an anti-intellectual bias, and a hesi-tation, if not refusal, to enter the mainstream corporate world. Perhaps the charge of anti-intellectualism is better understood as healthy skepticism about the chance that a corporate career will provide the well-publicized satisfactions. There are similar indications among some relatively affluent white students as well. Although by no means a majority, some students are less enamored by the work-world to which they, presumably, have been habituated by school, especially by the prospect of perpetual work. In the third-tier universities, state and private alike, apparently forced by their parents to enroll, many students wonder out loud why they are there. Skep-ticism about schooling still abounds even as they graduate high school and enroll in post-secondary schools in record numbers. According to one col-league of mine who teaches in a third-tier private university in the New York Metropolitan area, many of these mostly suburban students "sleep-walk" through their classes, do not participate in class discussions, and are lucky to get a "C" grade.

In the working-class neighborhoods—White, Black and Latino—the word is out: given the absence of viable alternatives, you must try to obtain that degree, but this defines the limit of loyalty to the enterprise. Based on testimonies of high school and community college teachers, for every stu-dent who takes school knowledge seriously, there are twenty or more who are time-servers. Most are ill-prepared to perform academic work and, since the community colleges and state four-year colleges and "teaching" univer-sities simply lack the resources to provide the means by which their school performance can improve, beyond the credential there is little motivation among students to try to get an education.

In some instances, those who break from their club and enter the regime of school knowledge make a decision that risks being drummed out of a lifetime of relationships with their peers. What has euphemistically been described as "peer pressure" bears, among other moral structures, on the degree to which kids are permitted to cross over the line into the precincts of adult authority. While being a success in school is not equivalent to squeal-ing on a friend or to the cops, or transgressing some sacred moral code of the society of kids, it comes close to committing an act of betrayal. This is comprehensible only if the reader is willing to suspend prejudice that school-ing is tantamount to education and is an unqualified "good" as compared to the presumed evil of school failure, or the decision of the slacker to rebel by refusing to succeed.

To invoke the concept of "class" in either educational debates or any other politically charged discourse generally refers to the White working-class. Educational theory and practice treats Blacks and Latinos, regardless of their economic positions, as unified, bio-identities. That Blacks kids from professional, managerial, and business backgrounds share more with their White counterparts than with working-class Blacks is generally ignored by most educational writers. Similarly, "Whites" are undifferentiated in race discourse, since the word "race"—which refers in slightly different registers to people of African origin and those who migrated from Latin countries of South America and the Caribbean—is treated as a unified category. The narrowing of the concept limits our ability to discern class at all. I want to suggest that, although we must stipulate ethnic, gender, race and occupational distinction among differentiated strata of wage labor, with the exception of children of salaried professional and technical groups, where the culture of schooling plays a decisive role, class education transcends these distinctions. No doubt there are gradations among the strata that comprise this social formation, but the most privileged professional strata (physicians, attorneys, scientists, professors), and the high-level managers are self-reproducing, not principally through schooling but through social networks. These include: private schools, some of which are residential; clubs and associations; and, in suburban public schools, the self-selection of students on the basis of distinctions. Show me a school friendship between the son or daughter of a corporate manager and the child of a janitor or factory worker, and I will show you a community service project to get into one of the "select" colleges or universities such as Brown, Oberlin, or Wesleyan.

Schooling selects a fairly small number of children of the class of wage labor for genuine class mobility. In the first half of the twentieth century, having lost its appeal among middle-class youth, the Catholic Church turned to working-class students as a source of cadre recruitment. In my neighborhood of the East Bronx two close childhood friends, both of Italian background, entered the priesthood. As sons of construction workers, the Church provided their best chance to escape the hardships and economic uncertainties of manual labor. Another kid became a pharmacist because the local Catholic college, Fordham University, offered scholarships. A fourth was among the tiny coterie of students who passed the test for one of the city's special schools, Bronx Science, and became a science teacher. Otherwise almost everybody else remained a worker or, like my best friend, Kenny, went to prison.

Despite the well publicized claim that anyone can escape their condition of social and economic birth—a claim reproduced by schools and by the media with numbing regularity—most working-class students, many of whom have some college credits, but often do not graduate—end up in low and middle-level service jobs that do not pay a decent working-class wage. Owing to the steep decline of unionized industrial production jobs, those who enter factories increasingly draw wages that are substantially below union standards. Those who do graduate find work in computers, although rarely at the professional levels. The relatively low paid become K–12 teachers and health-care professionals, mostly nurses and technicians, or enter the social service field as case workers, medical social workers or line social welfare workers. The question I want to pose is whether these "professional" occupations represent genuine mobility.

Since the 1960s, many of these professionals have asserted working-class values and social position. This may have been strategic, indeed it inspired the largest wave of union organizing since the 1930s. But, together with the entrance of huge numbers of women and Blacks into the public and quasi-public sector workforces, it was as well a symptom of the proletarianization of the "second-tier" professions. Several decades later, salaried physicians made a similar discovery; they formed unions and struck against high malpractice insurance costs as much as the onerous conditions imposed on their autonomy by Health Maintenance Organizations and government authorities bent on cost containment, often at their expense. More to the point, the steep rise of public employees' salaries and benefits posed the question of how to maintain services in times of fiscal austerity, which might be due to economic downturn or to pro-business tax policies. The answer has been that the political and public officials told employees that the temporary respite from the classical trade union trade-off was over. All public employees have suffered relative deterioration in their salaries and benefits. Fiscal crises, which began in the mid-1970s in New York City, have brought about layoffs for the first time since the depression. Their unions have been on a continuous concessionary bargaining mode for decades. In the politically and ideologically repressive environment of the last twenty-five years, the class divide has sharpened. Ironically, in the wake of the attacks by legislatures and business against their hard-won gains in the early 1980s, the teachers unions abandoned their militant, class posture and reverted to the doctrine of professionalism and to a center-right political strategy.

In truth, schools are learning sites of intellectual knowledge, even if only for a handful. In the main, they transmit the instrumental logic of credentialism, together with their transformation from institutions of discipline to those of control, especially in working-class districts. Even talented, dedicated teachers have more difficulty reaching kids and convincing them that the life of the mind may hold unexpected rewards, even if the career implications of critical thought are not apparent. The breakdown of the mission of public schools has produced varied forms of disaffection; if school violence has abated in some places, it does not signify the decline of gangs and other "clubs" that signify the autonomous world of youth. The society of kids is more autonomous because, in contrast to 1960s, official authorities no longer offer hope; instead, in concert with the doctrine of control, they threaten punishment that includes, but is not necessarily associated with, incarceration. Although the large number of drug busts of young Black and Latino men should not be minimized, with over a million Blacks, more than 3 percent of the African American population—most of them young—within the purview of the criminal justice system, the law may be viewed as a more or less concerted effort to counter by force the power of peers. This may be regarded in the context of the failure of schools.[17]

Conclusion

What are the requisite changes that would transform schools from credential mills and institutions of control to a site of education that prepares young people to see themselves as active participants in the world? The fundamental condition is to abolish high stakes standardized tests that dominate the curriculum and subordinate teachers to the role of drillmasters and subject students to stringent controls. By this proposal, I do not mean to eliminate the need for evaluative tools. The essay is a fine measure of both writing ability and of the student's grasp of literature, social science and history. While it must be admitted that math and science as much as language proficiency require considerable rote learning, the current curriculum and pedagogy in these fields includes neither a historical account of the changes in scientific and mathematical theory, nor a meta-conceptual explanation of what the disciplines are about. Nor are courses in language at the secondary level ever concerned with etymological issues, comparative cultural study of semantic differences, and other topics that might relieve the boredom of rote learning by providing depth of understanding. The broader understanding of science in the modern world—its relation to technology, war and medicine, for example—should surely be integrated into the curriculum; some of these issues appear in the textbooks, but teachers rarely discuss them because they are busy preparing students for the high stakes tests in which knowledge of the social contexts for science, language and math are not included.

I agree with Arendt that education "cannot forgo either authority or tradition." But authority must be earned rather than assumed, and the transmission of tradition needs to be critical rather than worshipful. If teachers were allowed to acknowledge student skepticism, incorporated kids' knowledge into the curriculum by making what they know the object of rigorous study, especially popular music and television, they might be treated with greater respect. But there is no point denying the canon; the more egregious condition of subordination is the failure of schools to expose students to its best exemplars, for people who have no cultural capital are thereby condemned to social and political marginality, and deprived of some of the pleasures to be derived from encounters with genuine works of art, whether in the high or popular canons. When the New York City Department of Education mandates that during every semester students in high school English classes read a Shakespearean play and one or two works of nineteenth century English literature, but afford students little or no access to the best Russian novels of the nineteenth century, to Indian, Chinese, Latin American literature and others, it does not create opportunities to examine some of the most influential works of Western and Eastern philosophy, and provides no social and historical context for what is learned; tradition is observed in the breach more than in its practice. And, when under budgetary pressures, elementary and secondary schools cut music and art from the curriculum, they deprive students of the best sources for cultivating the creative imagination.[18]

Having proposed these changes, we need to remain mindful of the limitations of schooling and the likelihood that youth will acquire knowledge that prepares them for life—where to find jobs, how to bond with other people, how to fight, how to love and hate—outside of schools. The deinstitutionalization of education does not require abandoning schools. Schools should be rendered benign, removed as much as possible from the tightening grip of the corporate, warfare state. In turn, teachers must resist becoming agents of the prison system, of the drug companies, of corporate capital. In the last instance, the best chance for education resides in the communities, in social movements, and in the kids themselves.

Notes

1. See Hannah Arendt, "The Crisis in Education," in *Between Past and Future: Six Exercises in Political Thought* (New York: Penguin Books, 1961).
2. Personal communication with the author.
3. See Hannah Arendt, *The Human Condition* (Chicago: University of Chicago Press, 1958).
4. See Max Horkheimer and Theodor Adorno, *Dialectic of Enlightenment: Philosophical Fragments* (Palo Alto, CA: Stanford University Press, 2002); Dwight Macdonald, *Against the American Grain* (New York: Da Capo Press, 1983); and Marshall McLuhan, *Understanding Media: The Extensions of Man* (New York: McGraw-Hill, 1964).
5. See Neil Postman, *Amusing Ourselves to Death: Public Discourse in the Age of Show Business* (New York: Viking, 1986).
6. See Griel Marcus, *Mystery Train: Images of America in Rock 'N' Roll Music* (New York: E. P. Dutton, 1975); and Robert Christgau, *Any Old Way You Choose It: Rock and Other Pop Music, 1967–1973* (New York: Cooper Square Press, 2000).
7. See Siegfried Kracauer, *The Mass Ornament: Weimar Essays* (Cambridge: Harvard University Press, 1995).

8. See Hortense Powdermaker, *Hollywood, the Dream Factory: An Anthropologist Looks at the Movie-Makers* (Boston: Little Brown, 1950).

9. See Andre Bazin, *What is Cinema?* (Berkeley: University of California Press, 1968); Pauline Kael, *I Lost It at the Movies: Film Writings, 1954–1965* (New York: Marion Boyers, 1965); Christian Metz, *Film Language: A Semiotics of the Cinema* (New York: Oxford University Press, 1974); and Laura Mulvey, "Visual Pleasure and Narrative Cinema," in *Feminism and Film Theory*, ed. Constance Penley (New York: Routledge: 1988).

10. See Kenneth Teitelbaum, *Schooling for "Good Rebels": Socialism, American Education, and the Search for Radical Curriculum* (New York: Teachers College Press, 1995).

11. See Samuel Gompers, *Seventy Years of Life and Labor: An Autobiography* (New York: E. P. Dutton, 1925).

12. John Locke, *An Essay Concerning the Human Understanding,* Volume 1 (New York: Dover Editions, 1959), 479.

13. William James, *Principles of Psychology* (New York: Henry Holt, 1890), 351.

14. Locke, *An Essay Concerning the Human Understanding,* 477.

15. Arendt, "The Crisis in Education," 180–81.

16. See Paul Willis, *Learning to Labor: How Working Class Kids Get Working Class Jobs* (New York: Columbia University Press, 1981).

17. See Henry Giroux, *Stealing Innocence: Youth, Corporate Power, and the Politics of Culture* (New York: St. Martin's Press, 2000).

18. See chapter seven in Stanley Aronowitz, *The Knowledge Factory: Dismantling the Corporate University and Creating True Higher Education* (Boston: Beacon Press, 2000).

CHAPTER 3

Interrupting the Right
On Doing Critical Educational Work in Conservative Times

MICHAEL W. APPLE

Culture Counts

Over the past decade, I have been engaged in a concerted effort to analyze the reasons behind the rightist resurgence—what I call "conservative modernization"—in education and to try to find spaces for interrupting it.[1] My aim has not simply been to castigate the right, although there is a bit of fun in doing so. Rather, I have also sought to illuminate the dangers, and the elements of good sense, not only bad sense, that are found within what is an identifiable and powerful new hegemonic bloc—the various factions of the rightist alliance of neoliberals, neoconservatives, authoritarian populist religious conservatives, and some members of the managerial new middle class. I have a number of reasons for doing so. First, people who find certain elements of conservative modernization relevant to their lives are not puppets. They are not dupes who have little understanding of the "real" relations of this society. This smacks of earlier reductive analyses that were based in ideas of "false consciousness." My position is very different. I maintain that the reason that some of the arguments coming from the various factions of this new hegemonic bloc are listened to is because they *are* connected to aspects of the realities that people experience. The tense alliance of neoliberals, neoconservatives, authoritarian populist religious activists, and the professional and managerial new middle class only works because there has been a very creative articulation of themes that resonate deeply with the experiences, fears, hopes, and dreams of people as they go about their daily lives. The right has often been more than a little manipulative in its articulation of these themes. It has integrated them within racist nativist discourses, within economically dominant forms of understanding, and within a problematic sense of "tradition." But, this integration could only occur if they were organized around people's understanding of their real material and cultural lives.

The second reason I have stressed the tension between good and bad sense—aside from my profound respect for Antonio Gramsci's writings about this—has to do with my belief that we have witnessed a major educational accomplishment over the past three decades in many countries. All too often, we assume that educational and cultural struggles are epiphenomenal. The real battles occur in the paid workplace—the "economy." Not only is this a strikingly reductive sense of what the economy is (its focus on paid, not unpaid, work; its neglect of the fact that, say, cultural institutions such as schools are also places where paid work goes on, etc.),[2] it also ignores what the right has actually done. Conservative modernization has radically reshaped the common sense of society. It has worked in every sphere—the economic, the political, and the cultural—to alter the basic categories we use to evaluate our institutions and our public and private lives. It has established new identities. It has recognized that to win in the state, you must win in civil society. The accomplishment of such a vast educational project has many implications. It shows how important cultural struggles are. And, oddly enough, it gives reason for hope. It forces us to ask a significant question. *If the right can do this, why can't we?*

I do not mean this as a rhetorical question. As I have argued repeatedly in my own work, the right has shown how powerful the struggle over meaning and identity can be. While we should not want to emulate their often cynical and manipulative processes, the fact that they have had such success in pulling people under their ideological umbrella has much to teach us. Granted there are real differences in money and power between the forces of conservative modernization and those whose lives are being tragically altered by the policies and practices coming from the alliance. But, the right wasn't as powerful thirty years ago as it is now. It collectively organized. It created a decentered unity, one where each element sacrificed some of its particular agenda to push forward on those areas that bound them together. Can't we do the same?

I believe that we can, but only if we face up to the realities and dynamics of power in unromantic ways. As I argued in *Educating the "Right" Way*, the romantic possibilitarian rhetoric of some of the writers on critical pedagogy is not sufficiently based on a tactical or strategic analysis of the current situation, nor is it sufficiently grounded in its understanding of the reconstructions of discourse and movements that are occurring in all too many places. Here I follow Cameron McCarthy, who wisely reminds us, "We must think possibility within constraint; that is the condition of our time."[3]

We need to remember that cultural struggles are not epiphenomenal. They *count*, and they count in institutions throughout society. In order for dominant groups to exercise leadership, large numbers of people must be convinced that the maps of reality circulated by those with the most economic, political, and cultural power are indeed wiser than other alternatives. Dominant groups do this by attaching these maps to the elements of good sense that people have and by changing the very meaning of the key concepts and their accompanying structures of feeling that provide the centers of gravity for our hopes, fears, and dreams about this society. The right has been much more successful in doing this than the left, in part because it has been able to craft—through hard and lengthy economic, political, and cultural efforts—a tense but still successful alliance that has shifted the major debates over education and economic and social policy onto its own terrain.

Evidence of this is all around us in the terms we use, in the arguments in which we engage, indeed even in many of the cultural resources we employ to imagine alternative futures. For example, as I completed the writing of my latest book, one of the top selling books on the *New York Times* fiction list was Tim LaHaye (yes, the Tim LaHaye of extremely conservative evangelical leadership) and Jerry Jenkins's *The Indwelling*, the seventh of a series of books about "true believers" who confront the "Antichrist."[4] The imagined future is a time of "rapture" where the good are taken up to heaven and the bad are condemned to eternal damnation. Who each of these groups are is predictable. In a number of ways, then, the authoritarian populist "outside" has moved to become the inside. It has creatively learned how to use the codes of popular adventure and science fiction novels to build an imaginative space of possibility, and a "muscular" yet sensitive Christianity that gives meaning to people's daily lives and hopes.[5]

Just as these spaces create imagined futures, so too do they help create identities. Neoliberalism creates policies and practices that embody the enterprising and constantly strategizing entrepreneur out of the possessive individualism it establishes as the ideal citizen. Neoconservatism creates imagined pasts as the framework for imagined and stable futures, futures in which identities are based on people knowing the knowledge and values that neoconservatives themselves have decided "have stood the test of time." Authoritarian populist religious conservatives also have an imagined past where a society, based on God's knowledge and values, has pre-given identities that enable women and men to rearticulate the neoliberal ideology of "choice" and to act in what are seen as godly ways toward bringing society to God. And managerialism establishes new identities for the professional and managerial middle class, identities that give new meaning to their lives and enable them to recapture their feelings of worthiness and efficacy. Out of all of these multiple spaces and identities, and the conflicts, tensions, and compromises that their interactions generate, policies evolve. These policies are almost never purely from only one of these elements within this bloc. Rather they often embody a rich mix that somehow must accommodate as many themes as possible from within the multiple forces of conservative modernization—without at the same time alienating those groups believed to be significant who are not yet integrated under the hegemonic umbrella of the right but who the right would like to bring under its leadership in the future.

This is a truly difficult task and it is filled with contradictory impulses. Yet, even with its contradictions and tensions, it has moved the balance of forces significantly to the right. Educational policies have been part of that move. In fact, education has not only been drawn along by the pressure of these rightist waves, it has actually played a major role in building these waves. The conservative alliance has paid attention to education—both formal and informal—and it has paid off for them. Indeed, in most of the critical discussions in the academic and popular literature of the effects of neoliberal, neoconservative, and managerial policies and practices in education in a number of countries, it is *their* policies that have provided the outlines of the debates in which we engage—vouchers, markets, national standards, high stakes testing, and so on.

Contradictory Reforms

As I have demonstrated elsewhere, policies often have strikingly unforeseen consequences. Reforms that are instituted with good intentions may have hidden effects that are more than a little problematic. I have shown in *Educating the "Right" Way* that the effects of some of the favorite reforms of neoliberals and neoconservatives, for instance—voucher plans, national or state-wide curricula, and national or state-wide testing can serve as examples—quite often reproduce or even worsen inequalities. Thus, we should be very cautious about accepting what may seem to be meritorious intentions at face value. Intentions are too often contradicted by how reforms may function in practice. This is true not only for large scale transformations of educational policies and governance, but also about moves to change the ways curriculum and teaching go on in schools.

The framework I have employed to understand this is grounded in what in cultural theory is called the act of repositioning. It, in essence, says that the best way to understand what any set of institutions, policies, and practices does is to see it from the standpoint of those who have the least power.[6] That is, every institution, policy, and practice—and especially those that now dominate education and the larger society—establish relations of power in which some voices are heard and some are not. While it is not preordained that those voices that will be heard most clearly are also those who have the most economic, cultural, and social capital, it is most likely that this will be the case. After all, we do not exist on a level playing field. Many economic, social, and educational policies when actually put in place tend to benefit those who already have advantages.

These points may seem overly rhetorical and too abstract, but, unfortunately, there is no small amount of truth in them. For example, in a time when all too much of the discourse around educational reform is focused on vouchers and choice plans on the one hand and on proposals for national or state curricula, standards, and testing on the other, there is a good deal of international evidence now that such policies may actually reproduce or even worsen class, gender, and race inequalities. Thus, existing structures of economic and cultural power often lead to a situation in which what may have started out in some educators' or legislators' minds as an attempt to make things better, in the end is all too usually transformed into another set of mechanisms for social stratification. While much of this is due to the ways in which race, gender, class, and "ability" act as structural realities in this society, some of it is related to the hesitancy of policy makers to take seriously enough the complicated ways in which education is itself a political act.

Near the end of the introductory section of a recent volume on the politics of educational policies and practices, *Learning as a Political Act*, the editors state that as progressives they are committed to an "intellectual solidarity that seeks to lay bare the ideas and histories of groups that have been silenced in mainstream educational arenas."[7] There are a number of key concepts in this quote—intellectual solidarity, laying bare, silencing. Each speaks to a complicated history, and each phrase again says something about our understanding of democracy. They are "keywords." They come from a very different tradition than that provided by the linguistic mapping of markets. They also speak to a different politics of official knowledge.

Over the past decade, it has become increasingly clear that the school curriculum has become a battleground. Stimulated in large part by neoliberal complaints about "economically useless" knowledge, neoconservative laments about the supposed loss of discipline and lack of "real knowledge," and by religious authoritarian populists' relentless attacks on schools for their supposed loss of God-given "traditional" values, discussions of what should be taught in schools and how it should be taught are now as contentious as at any time in our history.

Evidence of this is not hard to find. In his repeated call for a return to a curriculum of "facts," E. D. Hirsch, Jr. argues in *The Schools We Need and Why We Don't Have Them*[8] that schools have been taken over by progressive educators from Rousseau to Dewey, a claim that has almost no empirical warrant at all and largely demonstrates how disconnected he is from the daily life of schools.[9] Most schooling in the United States is already fact-driven. In addition, school districts throughout the country are constantly looking over their shoulders, worried that their reading, social studies, or mathematics programs will be challenged by the forces of the authoritarian religious right—although as I demonstrate in *Cultural Politics and Education*,[10] sometimes schools systems themselves create the conditions for the growth of rightist anti-school movements in their own communities by being less than democratic in their involvement of the community. Other evidence of such contentiousness is visible in the fact that the contents of the mathematics curriculum was even recently debated in the editorial pages of *The New York Times*, where spokespersons for constructivist and traditional curricula went head to head. Many more instances might be cited. But it is clear that the debate over "What knowledge is of most worth" has taken on more than a few political overtones.[11]

Much of the debate over this goes on with little empirical substance. For example, the argument that we must "return" to teaching, say, mathematics in "traditional" ways is obviously partly an ideological one. (We need to restore discipline; students have too much freedom; "bad" knowledge has pushed "good" knowledge to the sidelines.) Yet it is also based on a claim that such a return will lead to higher achievement and ultimately to a more competitive economy. Here, neoliberal and neoconservative emphases are joined with authoritarian populist mistrust of child-centeredness. This is where Jo Boaler's *Experiencing School Mathematics*,[12] a richly detailed qualitative and quantitative comparison of mathematics curricula and teaching enters.

Boaler engages in a fine-grained analysis of two secondary schools with decidedly different emphases. While her book is based on data from England, its implications are again profound for debates over curriculum and teaching in the U.S. and elsewhere as well. Both schools are largely working class, with some minority and middle-class populations as well. Both sets of students had attended our equivalent of middle schools that were dominated by more traditional academic methods. And both had similar achievement profiles. One school overtly focused on preparing its students for national tests. Its program was almost totally teacher directed, organized around textbooks that were geared to the national tests, ability grouped, and run in such a way that speed and accuracy of computations and the learning of procedural rules for dealing with mathematical problems were highly valued—all those things that traditionalists here say that are currently missing in mathematics instruction. Furthermore, the boundary between mathematics and both the real world and other subjects was strong.[13] The other school did not group by ability. It was decidedly more "progressive" both in its attitude toward students (there was a more relaxed communication style between teachers and students; student input was sought on the curriculum) and in its mathematics program. In this second school, the instruction was project-based, with a minimum of textbook-based teaching and a maximum of cooperative work among the students. The boundary between mathematics and "real world" problems was weak.

The first school was quiet, on-task, well organized—the very embodiment of the dream of nearly all elements of conservative modernization. The second was more noisy, students were not always fully on-task, and had very flexible time schedules. Both schools had dedicated and hard working teachers. Yet the differences in the results were striking, both in terms of overall achievement and in terms of the differential effects of each orientation on the students themselves.

The more traditional school, with its driving concern for "covering material" that would be on the test, stressed textbook knowledge and moved relatively rapidly from topic to topic. The more student-centered approach of the second school sacrificed some coverage, but it also enabled students to more fully understand the material. By and large, students in the first school actually did less well on the standardized tests than the second, especially but not only on those parts of the tests that needed them to actually think mathematically, in large part because they could not generalize to new contexts as well as did those students who had used their mathematics in more varied (though more time-consuming) projects. Further— and of great importance for equity—young women in the second school did consistently better in a more cooperative atmosphere that stressed understanding and use rather than coverage. The same held true for social class. Working-class students were consistently disadvantaged in the more pressured and text- and test-based agenda of traditional mathematics instruction.

This is a complex situation and Boaler is talking about general tendencies here. But her overall conclusions are clear and are supported by a very nice combination of data. In sum, the claim that a return to (actually, given the fact that most mathematics instruction is still chalk and talk and textbook based, it would be much more honest to say the *continuation of*) the traditional mathematics programs that the critics are demanding neither increases students' mathematical competence nor their ability to use their mathematical knowledge in productive ways. While it may keep classrooms quiet and students under control, it may also systematically disadvantage young women—including, as Boaler shows, the brightest young women—

and economically disadvantaged students.[14] Finally, it may have one other effect, a strengthening of students' dislike of mathematics and their feelings that it is simply irrelevant for their future. If this is true for mathematics, it is worth considering the hidden negative effects of the more general policies being proposed by neoconservative reformers who wish to return to what they have constructed, rather romantically, as "the tradition" in all subjects.

If Boaler's conclusions are even partly generalizable, as I think they may very well be, the hidden effects of certain reform movements may not be what we had in mind. Tighter control over the curriculum, the tail of the test wagging the dog of the teacher and the curriculum, more pressure, more reductive accountability plans—all of this may lead to less equitable results, not more. Boredom, alienation, and increased inequalities are not the ideal results of schooling. Once again, looking outside of our usual all-too-limited and parochial boundaries can be more than a little beneficial. The careful research underpinning Boaler's volume needs to be taken seriously by anyone who assumes that in our unequal society there is a direct relationship between policy intentions and policy results. There isn't.

One of the most important tasks of critical education, therefore, is an empirical one. Just as Boaler did, we need to make research public not only on the negative effects of the policies of conservative modernization, but just as importantly on the positive effects of more socially and educationally critical alternatives. A good example of this is the SAGE program in Wisconsin where significantly reducing class size within schools that historically have served a larger portion of dispossessed people has had much more robust results than, say, marketization and voucher plans.[15] This is one form of interrupting dominant discourses and policies and much more of it needs to be done. However, in doing this we cannot simply rely on the dominant forms of what counts as evidence. In Linda Tuhiwai Smith's words, we need "decolonizing methodologies."[16]

Making Challenges Public

My arguments in the previous section of this paper have been at a relatively general level because I did not want us to lose sight of the larger picture. How else can these retrogressive movements be interrupted? Let me now get more specific and tactical, since I am convinced that it is important to interrupt rightist claims immediately, within the media, in academic and professional publications, and in daily life.

One crucial example of such interruption is found in the Educational Policy Project formed under the auspices of the Center for Education Research, Analysis, and Innovation. This involves the ongoing construction of an organized group of people who are committed to responding very rapidly to material published by the right. This group includes a number of well-known educators and activists who are deeply concerned that the right has successfully used the media to foster its own ideological agenda, just as it has devoted a considerable amount of resources to getting its message to the public. For example, a number of conservative foundations have full-time staff members whose responsibility it is, for example, to fax synopses of reports to national media, to newspapers, and to widely read journals of opinion and to keep conservative positions in the public eye. Progressives have been much less successful in comparison, in part because they have not devoted themselves to the task as rigorously or because they have not learned to work at many levels, from the academic to the popular simultaneously. In recognition of this, a group of socially and educationally critical educators met first in Milwaukee and has been continuously meeting to generate an organized response to conservative reports, articles, research, and media presentations.

A full-time staff member was hired by the Center to focus on conservative material, to identify what needs to be responded to, and to help edit responses written by individual members of the group. A website has been developed that publishes these responses and/or original publications of more progressive research and arguments. The project also focuses on writing "op-ed" pieces, letters to the editor, and other similar material and on making all of this available to the media. This requires establishing contacts with journals, newspapers, radio, and television, and so on. This is exactly what the right did. We can and must do similar things. It requires hard work, but the Educational Policy Project is the beginning of what we hope will be a larger effort involving many more people. The reader can see the kinds of things that have been done by going to the following website for the Educational Policy Project of the Center for Education Research, Analysis, and Innovation: http://www.uwm.edu/Dept/CERAI/project.html.

This is just one example of one strategy for bringing what we know to parts of the public in more popular forms. There are many other examples posted on the website and published as reports, responses in journals, letters to the editor, and op-ed pieces. While this project is relatively new, it shows considerable promise. In combination with the use of talk radio, call-in shows, and similar media strategies in *multiple* languages,[17] these kinds of activities are part of a larger strategy to bring both more public attention to what the dangers are in the "solutions" proposed by the right and to what the workable alternatives to them might be. Integrating the educational interventions within a larger focus on the media is absolutely crucial.[18]

Learning From Other Nations

During one of the times I was working in Brazil with Paulo Freire, I remember him repeatedly saying to me that education must begin in critical dialogue. Both of these last two words were crucial to him. Education both must hold our dominant institutions in education and the larger society up to rigorous questioning and at the same time this questioning must deeply involve those who benefit least from the ways these institutions now function. Both conditions were necessary, since the first without the second was simply insufficient to the task of democratizing education.

Of course, many committed educators already know that the transformation of educational policies and practices—or the defense of democratic gains in our schools and local communities—is inherently political. Indeed, this is constantly registered in the fact that rightist movements have made teaching and curricula the targets of concerted attacks for years. One of the claims of these rightist forces is that schools are "out of touch" with parents and communities. While there are elements of insight in such criticisms, we need to find ways of connecting our educational efforts to local communities, especially those members of these communities with less power, that are more truly democratic than those envisioned by the right.

There is a good deal of efficacy in turning to the experiences of other nations to learn about what the effects of neoliberal and neoconservative policies and practices actually are. Yet there are many more things that we can learn from other nations' struggles. For example, currently in Porto Alegre, Brazil, the policies of participatory budgeting are helping to build support for more progressive and democratic policies there in the face of the growing power of neoliberal movements at a national level. The Workers Party ("PT" as it is known there) has been able to increase its majority even among people who had previously voted in favor of parties with much more conservative educational and social programs *because* it has been committed to enabling even the poorest of its citizens to participate in deliberations over the policies themselves and over where and how money should be spent. By paying attention to more substantive forms of collective participation and, just as importantly, by devoting resources to encourage such participation, Porto Alegre has demonstrated that it is possible to have a "thicker" democracy, even in times of both economic crisis and ideological attacks from neoliberal parties and from the conservative press. Programs such as the "Citizen School" and the sharing of real power with those who live in *favelas* (slums) provide ample evidence that thick democracy offers realistic alternatives to the eviscerated version of thin democracy found under neoliberalism.[19] Just as important is the pedagogic function of these programs. They develop the collective capacities among people to enable them to continue to engage in the democratic administration and control of their lives.[20] This is time-consuming, but time spent in such things now has proven to pay off dramatically later on.

A similar story can be told about another part of Brazil. In Belem, a "Youth Participatory Budget" process was instituted. It provided resources and space for the participation of many thousands of youth in the deliberations over what programs for youth needed to be developed, how money should be spent, and the creation of a set of political forums that could be used by youth to make public their needs and desires. This is very different than most of the ways youth are dealt with in all too many countries, where youth are seen as a "problem" not as a resource.[21] A similar instance is found in New Zealand, where under the original leadership of the International Research Institute on Maori and Indigenous Education at the University of Auckland, multi-racial groups of youth are formed in communities to publicly discuss the ways in which youth see their realities and advance proposals for dealing with these realities. In this way, alliances that begin to cut across race, class, and age are being built. There are models, then, of real participation that we can learn from and that challenge the eviscerated vision of democracy advanced by neoliberals by putting in place more substantive and active models of actually "living our freedoms." The issue is not the existence of such models; it is insuring that they are made widely visible.

Thinking Heretically

In order to build counter-hegemonic alliances, we may have to think more creatively than before—and, in fact, may have to engage in some nearly heretical rethinking. Let me give an example. I would like us to engage in a thought-experiment. I believe that the right has been able to take certain elements that many people hold dear and connect them to other issues in ways that might not often occur "naturally" if these issues were less politicized. Thus, for instance, one of the reasons populist religious groups are pulled into an alliance with the right is because such groups believe that the state is totally against the values that give meaning to their lives. They are sutured into an alliance in which other elements of rightist discourse are then able to slowly connect with their own. Thus, they believe that the state is anti-religious. Others also say that the state seeks to impose its will on White, working-class parents by giving "special treatment" to people of color and ignoring poor White people. These two elements do *not* necessarily have to combine. But they slowly begin to be seen as homologous.

Is it possible that by taking, say, religion out of the mix that some parts of the religious community that currently find collective identities on the right would be less susceptible to such a call if more religious content was found in school? If religious studies had a more central place within the curriculum, is it less likely that people who find in religion the ultimate answers to why they are here would be less mistrustful of the state, less apt to be attracted to a position that public is bad and private is good? I am uncertain that this would be the case. But I strongly believe that we need to entertain this possibility.

Do not misunderstand me. I am decidedly not taking the position that we should use vouchers to fund private religious schools; nor am I saying that the authoritarian populist religious right should be pandered to. Rather, I am taking a position similar to that espoused by Warren Nord.[22] Our failure to provide a clear place for the study of religion in the curriculum makes us "illiberal." Yet, I do not want to end with Nord's position. Rather, I see it as a starting point. In earlier books, I have argued that at times people "become right" because of the lack of responsiveness of public institutions to meanings and concerns that are central to their lives. Teaching more *about*, not for, religion doesn't just make us more "liberal" in Nord's words. It may also help interrupt the formation of anti-public identities. This has important implications for it can point to strategic moves that can be made to counter the integration of large numbers of people under the umbrella of conservative modernization.

As I have demonstrated in *Cultural Politics and Education*, people often become right at a local level, not through plots by rightist groups but because of local issues and sentiments. Making schools more responsive to religious sentiments may seem like a simple step, but it can have echoes that are profound since it may undercut one of the major reasons some populist groups who are also religious find their way under the umbrella of rightist attacks on schools and on the public sphere.

I am not a romantic about this. I do think that it could be dangerous and could be exploited by the religious right. After all, some of them do have little interest in "teaching about" and may hold positions on Christianity and other religions that both construct and leave little room for the "Other." Yet the centrality of religious sentiments need not get pushed toward neoliberalism. It need not be connected to a belief that public schools and teachers are so totally against them that marketization and privatization are the only answers. Thus, I'd like us to think seriously—and very cautiously—about the possible ways members of some of the groups currently found under the umbrella of the conservative alliance might actually be pried loose from it and might work off the elements of good sense they possess. In saying this, I am guided by a serious question. In what ways can religious commitments be mobilized for socially progressive ends? Our (often justifiable) worries about religious influences in the public sphere may have the latent effect of preventing such a mobilization by alienating many people who have deep religious commitments and who might otherwise be involved in such struggles. If many evangelicals do commit themselves to helping the poor,[23] for example, in what ways can these sentiments be disarticulated from seeing capitalism as "God's economy" and from only helping the "deserving poor" and rearticulated toward greater social and economic transformation. It would seem well worth studying the recent histories of religious involvement in, say, the anti-WTO (World Trade Organization) struggles to understand this better. At the very least, we cannot act as if religious beliefs about social and educational justice are outside the pale of progressive action, as too many critical educators do. A combination of caution, openness, and creativity is required here.

Yet another example is to take advantage of the shared elements of good sense among groups who usually have very different agendas in order to work against specific policies and programs that are being instituted by other elements within the new hegemonic alliance. That is, there *are* real tensions within conservative modernization that provide important spaces for joint action.

This possibility is already being recognized. Because of this, for example, there are some truly odd political couplings emerging today. Both the populist right and the populist left are occasionally joining forces to make strategic alliances against some neoliberal incursions into the school. For instance, Ralph Nader's group Commercial Alert and Phyllis Schlafly's organization the Eagle Forum are building an alliance against Channel One.[24] Both are deeply committed to fight the selling of children in schools as a captive audience for commercials. They are not alone. The Southern Baptist Convention has passed a resolution opposing Channel One. Groups such as Donald Wildmon's American Family Association, and even more importantly, James Dobson's powerful conservative organization Focus on the Family, have been working with Nader's groups to remove Channel One from schools and to keep it out of schools where it is not already established. This tactical alliance has also joined together to support anti-gambling initiatives in a number of states and to oppose one of the fastest growing commercial technology initiatives in education—ZapMe! Corp. Though now financially troubled because of over-expansion, ZapMe! provided free computers to schools at the cost of collecting demographic data on students which it then uses to target advertising specifically at these children.

The tactical agreement is often based on different ideological positions. While the progressive positions are strongly anti-corporate, the conservative positions are grounded in a distaste for the subversion of traditional values, "the exploiting of children for profit," and a growing rightist populist tension over the decisions that corporations make that do not take into consideration the "real folks" in America. This latter sentiment is what the rightist populist and nativist Pat Buchanan has worked off of for years. In the words of Ron Reno, a researcher at Focus on the Family, we need to fight "a handful of individuals exploiting the populace of America to make a buck."[25]

This teaming up on specific causes is approached more than a little cautiously on both sides, as you would imagine. As Ralph Nader says, "You have to be very careful because you can start tempering your positions. You can be too solicitous. You have to enter and leave on your own terms. You tell them, 'Here's what we're doing, if you want to join us fine. If not, fine.'" Phyllis Schlafly portrays her own reasons this way. "[Nader and I] agree that the public schools should not be used for commercial purposes. A captive audience of students should not be sold for profit. I agree with that. I don't recall his objection to the content of the news, which is what stirs up a lot of conservatives."[26]

Schlafly's comments show the differences as well as similarities in the right-left division here. While for many people across the divide, there is a strong distaste for selling our children as commodities, divisions reappear in other areas. For one group, the problem is a "handful of individuals" who lack proper moral values. For the other, the structural forces driving our economy create pressures to buy and sell children as a captive audience. For conservatives, the content of the news on Channel One is too "liberal;" it deals with issues such as drugs, sexuality, and similar topics. Yet, as I have shown in my own analysis of what counts as news in the major media and in Channel One, even though there is some cautious treatment of controversial issues, the content and coding of what counts as news is more than a little conservative and predominantly reinforces dominant interpretations.[27]

These differences should not detract from my basic point. Tactical alliances are still possible, especially where populist impulses and anti-corporate sentiments overlap. These must be approached extremely carefully, however, since the grounding of much of the populism of the right is also in a racist nativism, a very dangerous tendency that has had murderous consequences. A recognition, though, of the anti-corporate tendencies that do exist here is significant, since it also points to cracks in the alliance supporting some aspects of conservative modernization in general and to similar fissures within the ranks of authoritarian populism itself. For example, the fact that Ralph Reed was hired as a consultant to burnish Channel One's image has also created a number of tensions within the authoritarian populist ranks.[28]

Another area that is ripe for such coalitions is that of national and state curricula and testing. Neither the populist right nor the populist left believe that such policies leave room for the cultures, histories, or visions of legitimate knowledge to which they are so deeply committed. While the specific content of such knowledge is decidedly dissimilar for each of these groups, the fact that there is agreement both on a generally anti-elitist position and on the fact that the very processes involved are anti-democratic provides room for tactical alliances not only against these processes but as a block against even further incursions of managerialism into schools. In addition, given the ideological segregation that currently exists in this society, working (carefully) with such groups has the advantage of reducing stereotypes that they may hold (and perhaps that we might also hold?). It increases the possibility that the populist right will see that progressives may in fact be able to provide solutions to serious issues that are so distressing in populist movements of multiple orientations. This benefit should not be minimized.

My position here, hence, embodies a dual strategy. We can and must build tactical alliances where this is possible and where there is mutual benefit—and where such an alliance does not jeopardize the core of progressive beliefs and values. At the same time, we need to continue to build on more progressive alliances between our core constituencies around issues such as class, race, gender, sexuality, ability, globalization and economic exploitation, and the environment. That such a dual strategy can be used to organize both within already existing alliances and to work across differences is made clear in the anti-WTO mobilizations in Seattle, Washington, Philadelphia, Genoa, Italy, and in a number of other cities throughout the world.

Once the issue of tactical alliances is raised, however, it is nearly impossible to ignore charter schools. For a number of people on both the left and the right, charter schools have been seen as a compromise that can satisfy some of the demands of each group. Here, though, I would urge even more caution. Much of the discussion of these schools has been more than a little romantic. It has accepted the rhetoric of "de-bureaucratization," experimentation, and diversity as the reality. Yet, as Amy Stuart Wells and her colleagues have demonstrated, charter schools can and do often serve less meritorious ends. They can be manipulated to provide public funding for ideologically and educationally problematic programs, with little public accountability. Beneath the statistics of racial equality they supposedly produce, they can exacerbate white flight and can be captured by groups who actually have little interest in the culture and futures of those whom they assume are the "Other." They are used as the "constitutive outside" in attacks on public schooling for the majority of children in schools throughout the United States, by deflecting attention to what must be done there. Thus, they often can and do act to deflect attention from our lack of commitment to provide sufficient resources and support for schools in urban and rural areas. And in a number of ways they threaten to become an opening wedge for voucher plans.[29]

Having said this, however, I do not believe that charter schools will go away. Indeed, during the many periods of time when I have lectured and engaged in educational and political work in countries in, say, Latin America and Asia, it has become ever more clear to me that there is considerable interest in the charter school movement. This is especially the case in those nations that have a history of strong states and strong central control over the curriculum, teaching, and evaluation and where the state has been inflexible, highly bureaucratic, and unresponsive. Given this situation, it is absolutely crucial that the terrain of charter schools *not* be occupied by the forces within the conservative alliance. If charter schools become, as they threaten to, primarily a site where their function is to deflect attention from schools where the vast majority of students go, if they are allowed to be used as vouchers "in cognito," if they serve to legitimate concerted attacks on teachers and other educators, then the effects will not be limited to the United States. This will be a world-wide tragedy. For these very reasons, it is crucial that some of our empirical, educational, and political energy goes into guaranteeing that charter schools are a much more progressively inclined set of possibilities than they are today. We need to work so that the elements of good sense in the movement are not lost by it being integrated under the umbrella of conservative modernization.

Making Critical Educational Practices Practical

You will notice that I said "some" of our energy in the previous paragraph. Once again we need to be extremely cautious that by focusing our energies on "alternatives" such as charter schools we are not tacitly enhancing the very real possibility that progressives will spend so much of their attention on them that action in the vast majority of schools will take a back seat. While all of the tactical and strategic foci I have mentioned are important, there is one area that I believe should be at the center of our concerns as educators—providing real answers to real practical problems in education. By showing successful struggles to build a critical and democratic education in real schools and real communities with real teachers and students today, attention is refocused on action not only in charter schools but on local elementary, middle, and secondary schools in communities much like those in which most of us spend our lives. Thus, publicizing such "stories" makes critical education seem actually "doable," not merely a utopian vision dreamed up by "critical theorists" in education. For this very reason, political/educational interventions such as the popular and widely translated book

Democratic Schools[30] and the increasingly influential journal *Rethinking Schools* become even more important. This is crucial if we are indeed to interrupt the right. Since the right does have an advantage of speaking in "common sense" and in "plain-folks Americanism"[31]—and peoples' common sense *does* have elements of good and bad sense within itself—we can also use these progressively inclined elements to show that it is not only the right that has answers to what are real and important issues of educational practice.

For example, the specific vocational and academic programs in which curricula and teaching are linked to paid work and to the economy in socially progressive ways in the Rindge School of Technical Arts in the Boston area powerfully demonstrate that those students and parents who are (justifiably) deeply concerned about their economic futures do *not* have to turn to neoliberal policies to find practical answers to their questions.[32] I can think of little that is more important than this. The forces of conservative modernization have colonized the space of practice and of providing answers to the question of "What do I do on Monday?" in part not because the right has all the answers, but in part due to the fact that the left has too often evacuated that space.

Here again, we have much to learn from the right. While we do not need progressive imitators of, say, E. D. Hirsch, we do need to be much more active in actually attempting to provide answers to teachers, community members, and an increasingly skeptical public that questions such as *what* will I teach, *how* will I teach it, *how* will I evaluate its success—in essence, all those practical questions that people have a right to ask and to which they are entitled to get sensible answers—are taken very seriously. In the absence of this, we are left standing on the sidelines while the right reconstructs not only common sense but the schools that help produce it.

This is where the work engaged in by a number of critically inclined practicing educators has proven to be so important. Debbie Meier and her colleagues at Central Park East School in New York and at Mission Hill School in Boston; Bob Peterson, Rita Tenorio, and their colleagues at Fratney Street School in Milwaukee; the staff at Rindge School; and many other educators in similar schools throughout the country provide critical models of answering the day-to-day questions that I noted above. They also directly respond to the arguments that are made by neoliberals, neoconservatives, and authoritarian populists. They do this not only by defending the very idea of a truly public school—although they are very good at marshaling such a defense[33]—but also by demonstrating workable alternatives that are based both on high expectations for their diverse students and on a deep-seated respect for the cultures, histories, and experiences of these students and their parents and local communities.[34] Only in this way can the neo-liberal, neoconservative, and managerial factions of the new alliance be undercut at the level of the school.

Hope as a Resource

Much more could be said about interrupting the right and about building workable alternatives. I have written this paper and the book on which it is based—*Educating the "Right" Way*—to contribute to an ongoing set of crucial debates about the means and ends of our educational institutions and about their connections to larger institutions and power relations. Keeping such debates alive and vibrant is one of the best ways of challenging "the curriculum of the dead." Building and defending a truly democratic and critical education is a collective project. We have much to learn from each other.

Let me end with something that I always want to keep in the forefront of my own consciousness when times are difficult. Sustained political and cultural transformations are impossible "without the hope of a better society that we can, in principle and in outline, imagine."[35] All of us hope that our work will contribute to the larger movement that is struggling to loosen the grip of the narrow concepts of "reality" and "democracy" that have been circulated by neoliberals and neoconservatives in education and so much else over the past decades. Historically, there have been alternatives to the limited and increasingly hypocritical conception of democracy that unfortunately even social democratic parties (under the label of the "third way") in many nations have come to accept. In the words of Panitch and Leys, we need "to insist on a far fuller and richer democracy than anything now available. It is time to reject the prevailing disparagement of anything collective as 'unrealistic' and to insist on the moral and practical rightness, as well as the necessity, of egalitarian social and economic arrangements."[36] As they go on to say, this requires "the development of popular democratic capacities and the structures that nurture rather than stifle or trivialize them."[37] The movements surrounding conservative modernization may be "wrong," not "right." They may in fact "stifle or trivialize" a vision of democracy that is based on the common good. But they certainly don't have trivial effects on millions of people all over the world. Our children, our teachers, and our communities deserve something better.

Notes

1. See especially, *Official Knowledge*, 2nd ed. (New York: Routledge, 2000), and *Educating the "Right" Way* (New York: Routledge, 2001).
2. See my *Teachers and Texts* (New York: Routledge, 1988).

3. Cameron McCarthy, unpublished lecture, International Sociology of Education Conference, University of Sheffield, England, January 2000.

4. Tim LaHaye and Jerry Jenkins, *The Indwelling* (New York: Tyndale, 2000).

5. Of course, people read all kinds of fiction and are not compelled to follow its precepts. Thus, people can read hard-boiled detective novels in which women and men detectives often engage in violent acts of retribution. This does not necessarily mean that the readers are in favor of such acts. The politics of pleasure follows its own relatively autonomous logic. Most people engage in what have been called "guilty pleasures" and reading books like *The Indwelling* may fall under that category for many readers. However, the fact that it is a national best seller still has considerable importance.

6. See Sandra Harding, *Whose Science, Whose Knowledge?* (Ithaca, NY: Cornell University Press, 1991); and György Lukács, *History and Class Consciousness* (Cambridge: MIT Press, 1971).

7. Jose Segarra and Ricardo Dobles, eds., *Learning as a Political Act*, No. 33 (Cambridge: Harvard Educational Review Reprint Series, 1999), xiii.

8. E. D. Hirsch, Jr., *The Schools We Need and Why We Don't Have Them* (New York: Doubleday, 1996).

9. See Kristen Buras, "Questioning Core Assumptions," *Harvard Educational Review* 69 (1999): 67–93.

10. Michael W. Apple, *Cultural Politics and Education* (New York: Teachers College Press, 1996).

11. Of course, in actuality the content and form of curricula and teaching have always been political issues. See my *Ideology and Curriculum*, 3rd ed. (New York: Routledge, 2004). On some of the recent curriculum struggles in England and Wales, see Richard Hatcher and Ken Jones, eds., *Education After the Conservatives* (Stoke-on-Trent, England: Trentham Books, 1996).

12. Jo Boaler, *Experiencing School Mathematics* (Philadelphia: Open University Press, 1998).

13. See also Basil Bernstein, *Class, Codes, and Volume Control III*, 2nd ed. (London: Routledge and Kegan Paul, 1977).

14. The focus on keeping youth "under control" is connected to a long history of the fear of youth and of seeing them as constantly in need of regulation. For an insightful discussion of this history, see Nancy Lesko, *Act Your Age!* (New York: Routledge, 2001).

15. Alex Molnar, et al., "Evaluating the SAGE Program," *Education Evaluation and Policy Analysis* 21 (1999): 165–77.

16. Linda Tuhiwai Smith, *Decolonizing Methodologies* (New York: Zed Books, 1999). See also Andrew Gitlin, *Power and Method* (New York: Routledge, 1994).

17. For example, in one of the "teach-ins" in which I participated in preparation for the anti-WTO mobilizations in Seattle and Washington, DC, very few people had thought about the integration of Spanish language newspapers, television, radio, and websites in building support for the movement. Yet, these are among the fastest growing media in the United States and they reach an audience that is suffering deeply from the effects of globalization and economic exploitation.

18. See Ellen Ratner, *101 Ways to Get Your Progressive Ideas on Talk Radio* (Washington, D.C.: National Press Books, 1997); Pierre Bourdieu, *Acts of Resistance* (Cambridge: Polity Press, 1998); Robert McChesney, et al., eds., *Capitalism and the Information Age* (New York: Monthly Review Press, 1998); and Douglas Kellner, *Media Culture* (New York: Routledge, 1995).

19. Luis Armando Gandin and Michael W. Apple, "Challenging Neoliberalism, Building Democracy," *Journal of Education Policy* 17 (April 2002): 259–79.

20. Diane Elson, "Socializing Markets, Not Market Socialism," in *Necessary and Unnecessary Utopias*, ed. Leo Panitch and Colin Leys (New York: Monthly Review Press, 1999).

21. Nancy Lesko, *Act Your Age!*

22. Warren Nord, *Religion and American Education* (Chapel Hill: University of North Carolina Press, 1995).

23. Christian Smith, *American Evangelicalism* (Chicago: University of Chicago Press, 1998).

24. Ruth Coniff, "Left-Right Romance," *The Progressive* (May 2000): 12–15.

25. Coniff, "Left-Right Romance," 13.

26. Coniff, "Left-Right Romance," 13.

27. Apple, *Official Knowledge*.

28. Coniff, "Left-Right Romance," 13.
29. Amy Wells, et al., "Charter Schools as Postmodern Paradox," *Harvard Educational Review* 69 (1999): 172–204.
30. Michael W. Apple and James A. Beane, eds., *Democratic Schools* (Alexandria, VA: Association for Supervision and Curriculum Development, 1995).
31. See Justin Watson, *The Christian Coalition* (New York: St. Martin's Press, 1997); and Linda Kintz, *Between Jesus and the Market* (Durham, NC: Duke University Press, 1997).
32. Larry Rosenstock and Adria Steinberg, "Beyond the Shop," *Democratic Schools*, ed. Michael W. Apple and James A. Beane, *op cit.*, 41–57.
33. See Deborah Meier, et al., *Will Standards Save Public Education?* (Boston: Beacon Press, 2000); Robert Lowe and Barbara Miner, eds., *False Choices* (Milwaukee: Rethinking Schools, 1992); and Robert Lowe and Barbara Miner, *Selling Out Our Schools* (Milwaukee: Rethinking Schools, 1996).
34. See Apple and Beane, eds., *Democratic Schools*; Gloria Ladson-Billings, *The Dreamkeepers* (San Francisco: Jossey-Bass, 1994); and L. Janelle Dance, *Tough Fronts: The Impact of Street Culture on Schooling* (New York: Routledge, 2002).
35. Leo Panitch and Colin Leys, eds., *Necessary and Unnecessary Utopias* (New York: Monthly Review Press, 1999), vii.
36. Panitch and Leys, *Necessary and Unnecessary Utopias*, viii.
37. Panitch and Leys, *Necessary and Unnecessary Utopias*, viii.

CHAPTER 4

Critical Pedagogy in a Time of Permanent War

PETER McLAREN

NATHALIA E. JARAMILLO

The Crisis of the Educational Left in the United States

Critical educators today are struggling assiduously to defend the public sphere from its integration into the neoliberal and imperialist practices of the state and the behemoth of globalized capitalism. While no one is seriously talking about seizing the state on behalf of workers struggling against the "petrolarchs" in Washington, D.C., there are promising indications that social movements in the United States will become more active in the days ahead. With administration hawks such as Defense Secretary Donald Rumsfeld, Vice President Dick Cheney, Deputy Defense Secretary Paul Wolfowitz, Undersecretary of State John Bolton, and Defense Policy Board member Richard Perle leading the White House charge for "preventative war," it is clear that their fanatical allegiance to the imperialist Project for the New American Century is fuelled by U.S. triumphalism, unipolar political consolidation and dominion, and the conquest of new markets. The bacchanalia of patriotism that has overtaken cities and towns throughout the country has blinded U.S. citizens to the thousands of innocent civilians killed in the "liberation" of Iraq. The slogan dripping red and black from anti-war posters that reads "No Blood for Oil" has, if anything, increased in relevance since the U.S. military invasion of Iraq. As it stands, OPEC resides outside the ambit of complete U.S. control. Total U.S. influence over the vast untapped oil reserves would demonstrably change the power equation.

Iraqi opposition to the U.S. "free market" looting of their country was a major factor in the Bush administration's decision to invade Iraq. The drive to obtain "free markets" and to open up investment for U.S. corporations is now accompanied by the most formidable military presence ever known to humankind, one that is fundamentally unopposed. Iraq is now "liberated" for U.S. corporate investment and control, having been "pacified" as a client state. Judging from recent U.S. history, the future will no doubt require that millions more will die in the oil-rich Middle East and elsewhere around the planet on behalf of the U.S. empire. The Bush junta has serious lessons to learn. You can't bomb democracy into being. You can bomb a country into pieces but you cannot bomb a country into peace. Democracy's universal egalitarian values require the reciprocal acceptance of mutual perspectives, not a ham-fisted unilateralist imposition of capitalist principles and practices.

In a social universe pockmarked by the ravages of capitalism's war against the working class and people of color, there are few places in which to retreat that the global market does not already occupy. Clearly, the United States has not faced up to capitalism's addiction to injustice, and its politicians have provided little space in educational debates for teachers to question the structurally dependent relationship between the standard of living in developed countries and misery and poverty in the underdeveloped ones. Early in the twentieth century, this country failed to heed the advice of one of its greatest philosophers, John Dewey, who, mindful of "the extended meaning which has been given to the Monroe Doctrine," warned: "The natural movement of business enterprise, combined with Anglo-American legalistic notions of contracts and their sanctity, and the international custom which obtains as to the duty of a nation to protect the property of its nationals, suffices to bring about imperialistic undertakings."[1]

Employing a politics that counts on the stupefaction of a media-primed electorate, the Bush administration has marshaled the corporate media in the service of its foreign policy such that the environment is literally suffused with its neoliberal agenda, with very little space devoid of its ideological cheerleading. Where classrooms once served as at least potentially one of the few spaces of respite from the ravages of the dominant ideology, they have now been colonized by the corporate logic of privatization and the imperial ideology of the militarized state. Teachers are left suspended across an ideological divide that separates reason and irrationality, consciousness and indoctrination, as they are reminded by their administrators and government officials that to bring "politics" into the classroom is unpatriotic. Consider the case of Bill Nevins, a high school teacher in New Mexico who faced an impromptu paid leave of absence following a student's reading of "Revolution X," a poem that lends a critical eye toward the war in Iraq.

If the President is to be believed, it was Jesus who first approved of the current Pentagon plan to expand the U.S. empire into the Middle East, as Bush *hijo* shamelessly exploits his policy objectives with frequent Biblical references and overtures of solidarity to Christian evangelical fundamentalists. Through direct presidential orders that circumvent congressional debate and bypass public debate, the White House has launched faith-based initiatives which provide millions of dollars in state funds to right-wing Christian groups who run job-training programs requiring a "total surrender to Christ," or who oversee childcare programs or chemical-dependency recovery programs, or who offer spiritual and moral regeneration to troubled families.

All of this has not gone unnoticed by critical educators. Though they have become used to the academic marginalization that often follows in the wake of attacks by the more churlish and reactionary conservative educationalists among us, proponents and practitioners of critical pedagogy have long feared being cast into the pit of academic hell for being perceived not only as dangerously irrelevant to United States democracy but also as politically treasonous. At this current historical juncture in U.S. history, when fighting a "permanent war" against terrorism, and expanding the American empire while we're at it, one would think that such a fear is duly warranted. This is partly due to the fact that critical pedagogy earned its early reputation as a fierce critic of U.S. imperialism and capitalist exploitation. However, times have changed. Today critical pedagogy is no longer the dangerous critic of free market liberal education that it once was. Rather, it has become so absorbed by the cosmopolitanized liberalism of the postmodernized left that it no longer serves as a trenchant challenge to capital and U.S. economic and military hegemony.[2]

Of course, we believe that this can change. There are numerous developments on our campuses related to the anti-war and anti-globalization movements that give us hope that the voices of our youth—and among them, those who will be attending our teacher education programs—will be much more politicized or open to what Freire called "conscientization" than in previous years. No doubt this has been encouraged by the worldwide mobilization against Bush and his de facto military/oil junta. There will be pressure on critical educators (who in the United States are mostly liberal, not revolutionary) to respond to the voices of a new generation of politicized student teachers. But it won't be a simple case of preaching to the converted. There are now more than 80 right-leaning newspapers and magazines circulating on college and university campuses throughout the country. Clearly, there is a concerted effort by conservative organizations to silence progressive voices. There is a need for teacher educators to bring a more radical discourse into the educational literature as well as directly into their teacher education programs. Even in the field of critical pedagogy these attempts have been disappointing.

Written as a counterpoint to the onslaught of neoliberal globalization and its "civilizing mission" for the oppressed of developed and developing countries alike, this chapter is both a commentary on the domestication of critical pedagogy, and a challenge for revivifying its political roots and role in the civil societarian left. It is meant to initiate a dialogue and conversation among progressive educators. Especially for those of us living in *las entrañas de la bestia* in *gringolandia*, we are inhabiting a time when citizenship has become marked by a lived historical presence blindingly uncritical of its own self-formation, when residents inhabiting the nation's multifarious geoscapes are racially marked so as to render them educationally segregated, and when the working class has become deputized by capital to uphold the neoliberal market ideology of the ruling class against any and all other alternatives—all of which legitimates the subordinate status of the working class within the existing division of labor.

This chapter is written at a time of permanent war, which is not only a war against the enemies of the United States (which today seems like just about every other country or dissenting organization/persons) but also a war against the working class, people of color and women (a war that dates back to the violent founding of the country itself). This is not to say that times haven't changed. For instance, Bush *hijo*, our boy emperor, a beneficiary of the so-called "good breeding" of the "Episcopacy," made it into Yale in the days when "character" (read as the cultural capital of rich, White, "silver spoon" families) was a singular badge of merit. Today, increasingly egregious forms of "testocracy"—scores from scientifically invalid and unreliable aptitude tests that correlate well with social class, race and linguistic background—serve as the primary route to the academy. The overt racism and class privilege of the ruling elite now enables the bourgeoisie to shirk off the notion of "good breeding" and hide themselves beneath the "objectivity" of high school test scores and university entrance criteria at a time in which meritocracy is presumed to have been secured. This is reflected in Bush *hijo*'s condescending and patronizing attitude towards ethnic populations, both at home and abroad. As William Saletan has pointed out, President Bush likes to use the term "gifted" when addressing the Iraqi people on their TV screens.[3] "You are a good and gifted people," he conveyed to them while Arabic subtitles appeared below his face during a broadcast that followed in the wake of the destruction of Baghdad. Saletan notes that Bush has used the term "gifted" seven times during his presidency, once to refer to Bill Cosby, once to Martin Luther King Sr., and four times to Iraqis and Palestinians. The other time was when he was reading from a script at an arts award ceremony. He has referred to Iraqis and Latinos as "talented" people. The Chinese have been referred to by Bush as "talented, brilliant, and energetic" while Russians are singled out as possessing "entrepreneurial talent." Irish Americans betray an "industry and talent" while Cubans display "determination and talent." Saletan correctly notes that such description is tantamount to the obscenely patronizing and condescending discourse that white people often use to refer to "ethnic" people who need to be told that they are capable. Saletan remarks:

> If you're black, Hispanic, or a member of some other group often stereotyped as incompetent, you may be familiar with this kind of condescension. It's the way polite white people express their surprise that you aren't stupid. They marvel at how "bright" and "articulate" you are. Instead of treating you the way they'd treat an equally competent white person—say, by ignoring you—they fuss over your every accomplishment.[4]

At this current historical juncture, as the right seizes every chance it gets to replace the social wage with the free market system, as conservative think tanks game out plans for privatizing what remains of the devastated public sphere, thousands of teachers and teacher educators throughout the country look to the left for guidance and leadership. Stunned by the results of a *New York Times*/CBS News survey that revealed that 42 percent of the American public believes that Saddam Hussein is directly responsible for the attacks of September 11, and that 55 percent of Americans believe Saddam Hussein directly supports Al Qaeda, U.S. educators are feeling powerless against the hegemonizing force of the rightwing corporate media. Clearly the corporate media constitute an uncritical "perpetual pedagogy" that shapes public opinion in the direction of the ruling ideology.

Under cover of democracy, Bush's lingo about saving civilization from the terrorist hordes rings the air. Americans old enough to remember the anti-Communist propaganda of the late 1940s and 1950s are experiencing a political *deja vu*. Millions read books with titles like *Is This Tomorrow: America Under Communism!*, *Blood is the Harvest*, and *Red Nightmare*. In 1948, the Chamber of Commerce of the United States published *A Program for Community Anti-Communism*, which contained a phrase eerily reminiscent of a remark that President Bush made weeks after the attacks of September 11: "You know that they hate us and our freedom." Those too young to remember the McCarthy era get to experience the sequel first hand. Some see this as democracy in practice. Not everybody is fooled.

But even when we are detoxicated of the shadowed obscurity surrounding the current war on terrorism and disabused of the calls for the primitive patriotism of flags and bumper stickers that is part of Bush *hijo*'s petulant crusade for a decent America (i.e., an America devoid of its critics), there still remains a glaring absence within the liberal academy of challenging capital as a social relation. While there exists plenty of talk about income redistribution, surprisingly little is said about setting ourselves against the deviances and devices of capital's regime of profit-making other than prosecuting the CEOs of the latest round of corporate offenders. The stunted criticism of the Bush administration's fascist assault on democracy is not so much a refusal of political will among liberal educators as a realization that if we persist with an internationalized market economy, the introduction of effective social controls to protect the underclass create overwhelming comparative disadvantages for the nation state or the economic bloc that seeks to institute such policies. If, as liberal educators (begrudgingly) and conservative educators (demagogically) insist, there effectively is no alternative to working within institutionalized market economy, then admittedly neoliberal policies that champion free market capitalism and that undermine what is left of the welfare state make sense. And while surely the punishment exacted against the poor can be staggered by parceling out the conditions for mass poverty in more discreet—yet no less lethal—policies and practices, there remains the question of how to cope with the havoc that will eventually be wreaked on the poor and the powerless in the absence of a socialist alternative. It is in this context—of breadlines, overcrowded hospitals, and unemployment lines longer than those at the polling stations—that the question of organization becomes imperative for the left in a search for a socialist alternative.

The Politics of Organization

The thorny question of organization has been a problem that has exercised both the revolutionary left and the progressive left for over a century. Max Elbaum notes that organisations are crucial in the struggle for social justice. He writes that "[w]ithout collective forms it is impossible to train cadre, debate theory and strategy, spread information and analysis, or engage fully with the urgent struggles of the day. Only through organisations can revolutionaries maximise their contribution to ongoing battles and position themselves to maximally influence events when new mass upheavals and opportunities arise."[5] Yet at the same time, Elbaum warns that we must avoid what he calls "sectarian dead-ends" in our struggle for social justice.

Reflecting on his experiences with the New Communist Movement of the 1970s, he explains that when a movement becomes a "self-contained world" that insists upon group solidarity and discipline, this can often lead to the suppression of internal democracy. The rigid top-down party model is obviously a problem for Elbaum. On the one hand, social activists need to engage with and be accountable to a large, active, anti-capitalist social base; on the other hand, there are pressures to put one's revolutionary politics aside in order to make an immediate impact on public policy. There is the impulse to "retreat into a small but secure niche on the margins of politics and/or confine oneself to revolutionary propaganda."[6] Elbaum cites Marx's dictum that periods of socialist sectarianism obtain when "the time is not yet ripe for an independent historical movement."[7]

Problems inevitably arise when "purer-than-thou fidelity to old orthodoxies" are employed to maintain membership morale necessary for group cohesion and to compete with other groups. Elbaum reports that the healthiest periods of social movements appear to be when tight knit cadre groups and other forms are able to coexist and interact, while at the same time considering themselves part of a common political trend. He writes that "diversity of organizational forms (publishing collectives, research centers, cultural collectives, and broad organising networks, in addition to local and national cadre formations) along with a dynamic interaction between them supplied (at least to a degree) some of the pressures for democracy and realism that in other situations flowed from a socialist-oriented working class."[8] It is important to avoid a uniform approach in all sectors, especially when disparities in consciousness and activity are manifold. Elbaum notes that Leninist centralized leadership worked in the short run but the leaders "lacked any substantial social base and were almost by definition hostile to all others on the left; they could never break out of the limits of a sect." The size of membership has a profound qualitative impact on strategies employed and organizational models adopted. Elbaum warns that attempts to build a small revolutionary party (a party in embryo) "blinded movement activists to Lenin's view that a revolutionary party must not only be an 'advanced' detachment but must also actually represent and be rooted in a substantial, socialist-leaning wing of the working class." Realistic and complex paths will need to be taken which will clearly be dependent on the state of the working-class movement itself. Critical pedagogy has much to learn from Elbaum's sage analysis.

It is axiomatic for the ongoing development of critical pedagogy that it be based upon an alternative vision of human sociality, one that operates outside the social universe of capital, a vision that goes beyond the market, but also one that goes beyond the state. It must reject the false opposition between the market and the state. Massimo De Angelis writes that "the historical challenge before us is that the question of alternatives . . . not be separated from the organizational forms that this movement gives itself."[9] Given that we are faced globally with the emergent transnational capitalist class and the incursion of capital into the far reaches of the planet, critical educators need a philosophy of organization that sufficiently addresses the dilemma and the challenge of the global proletariat. In discussing alternative manifestations of anti-globalization struggles, De Angelis itemizes some promising characteristics as follows: the production of various counter-summits; Zapatista *Encuentros*; social practices that produce use values beyond economic calculation and the competitive relation with the other and inspired by practices of social and mutual solidarity; horizontally-linked clusters outside vertical networks in which the market is protected and enforced; social co-operation through grassroots democracy, consensus, dialogue, and the recognition of the other; authority and social cooperation developed in fluid relations and self-constituted through interaction; and a new engagement with the other that transcends locality, job, social condition, gender, age, race, culture, sexual orientation, language, religion and beliefs. All of these characteristics are to be secondary to the constitution of communal relations. He writes:

> The global scene for us is the discovery of the "other," while the local scene is the discovery of the "us," and by discovering the "us," we change our relation to the "other." In a community, commonality is a creative process of discovery, not a presupposition. So we do both, but we do it having the community in mind, the community as a mode of engagement with the other.[10]

But what about the national state? According to Ellen Meiksins Wood, "the state is the point at which global capital is most vulnerable, both as a target of opposition in the dominant economies and as a lever of resistance elsewhere. It also means that now more than ever, much depends on the particular class forces embodied in the state, and that now more than ever, there is scope, as well as need, for class struggle."[11] Sam Gindin argues that the state is no longer a relevant site of struggle if by struggle we mean taking over the state and pushing it in another direction. But the state is still a relevant arena for contestation if our purpose is one of transforming the state:

> Conventional wisdom has it that the national state, whether we like it or not, is no longer a relevant site of struggle. At one level, this is true. If our notion of the state is that of an institution which left governments can "capture" and push in a different direction, experience suggests this will contribute little to social justice. But if our goal is to transform the state into an instrument for popular mobilization and the development of democratic capacities, to bring our economy under popular control and restructure our relationships to the world economy, then winning state power would manifest the worst nightmares of the corporate world. When we reject strategies based on winning through undercutting others and maintain our fight for dignity and justice nationally, we can inspire others abroad and create new spaces for their own struggles.[12]

John Holloway's premise is similar to that of Gindin. He argues that we must theorize the world negatively as a "moment" of practice as part of the struggle to change the world. But this change cannot come about through transforming the state through the taking of power but rather must occur through the dissolution of power as a means of transforming the state and thus the world. This is because the state renders people powerless by separating them from "doing" (human activity). In our work as critical educators, Holloway's distinction between power-to do (*potentia*) and power-over (*potestas*) is instructive. Power-to is a part of the "social flow of doing," the collective construction of a "we" and the practice of the mutual recognition of dignity. Power-over negates the social flow of doing thereby alienating the collective "we" into mere objects of instruction.[13]

Holloway advocates creating the conditions for the future "doing" of others through a power-to do. In the process, we must not transform power-to into power-over, since power-over only separates the "means of doing" from the actual "doing" which has reached its highest point in capitalism. In fact, those who exercise power-over separate the done from the doing of others and declare it to be theirs. The doers then become detached from the origin of thought and practice, dehumanized to the level of instructed "objects" under the command of those that have assumed power-over. Power-over reduces people to mere owners and non-owners, flattening out relations between people to relations between things. It converts doing into a static condition of being. Whereas doing refers to both "we are" (the present) and "we are not" (the possibility of being something else), being refers only to "we are." To take away the "we are not" tears away possibility from social agency. The rule of power-over is the rule of "this is the way things are," which is the rule of identity. When we are separated from our own doing, we create our own subordination. Power-to is not counter-power (which presupposes a symmetry with power), but anti-power.

Holloway reminds us that the separation of doing and done is not an accomplished fact but a process. Separation and alienation is a movement against its own negation, against anti-alienation. That which exists in the form of its negation—or anti-alienation (the mode of "being" denied)—really does exist, in spite of its negation. It is the negation of the process of denial. Capitalism, according to Holloway, is based on the denial of "power-to," of dignity, of humanity, but that does not mean power-to (counter-capitalism) does not exist. Asserting our power-to is simultaneously to assert our resistance against subordination. This may take the form of open rebellion, of struggles to defend control over the labor process, or efforts to control the processes of health and education. Power-over depends upon that which it negates. The history of domination is not only the struggle of the oppressed against their oppressors, but also the struggle of the powerful to liberate themselves from their dependence on the powerless. But, there is no way in which power-over can escape from being transformed into power-to because capital's flight from labor depends upon labor (upon its capacity to convert power-to into abstract value-producing labor) in the form of falling rates of profit.

We are beginning to witness new forms of social organization as a part of revolutionary praxis. In addition to the *Zapatistas*, we have the important example of the participatory budget of the Workers Party in Brazil. And in Argentina, we are seeing new forms of organized struggle as a result of the recent economic collapse of the country. We are referring here to the examples of the street protests of the *piqueteros* (the unemployed) currently underway and which first emerged in May and June of 1997 in the impoverished communities in the provinces. More recently, new neighborhood *asambleas* (assemblies) have arisen out of local street corner protests. Numbering around 300 throughout the country, these assemblies meet once a week to organize *cacerolas* (protests) and to defend those evicted from their homes, or who are having their utilities shut off, etc. The *asambleistas* (assembly members) also coordinate soup kitchens to feed themselves and others. This anti-hierarchical, decentralized, and grassroots movement consisting of both employed and unemployed workers, mostly women, has taken on a new urgency since December 2002, when four governments collapsed in quick succession following Argentina's default on its foreign debt. Canadian activist Naomi Klein captures the spirit surrounding the creation of the *asambleas* when she writes:

> In Argentina, many of the young people fighting the neo-liberal policies that have bankrupted this country are children of leftist activists who were "disappeared" during the military dictatorship of 1976–1983. They talk openly about their determination to continue their parents' political fight for socialism but by different means. Rather than attacking military barracks, they squat on abandoned land and build bakeries and homes; rather than planning their actions in secret, they hold open assemblies on street corners; rather than insisting on ideological purity, they value democratic decision-making above all. Plenty of older activists, the lucky ones who survived the terror of the '70s, have joined these movements, speaking enthusiastically of learning from people half their age, of feeling freed of the ideological prisons of their pasts, of having a second chance to get it right.[14]

A recent report in *News & Letters* adds to this description:

> What is remarkable is how ferociously opposed the *asambleas* are to being controlled, and to any hint of a vertical, top down hierarchy. They insist on independence, autonomy, self-determination,

encouraging all to learn how to voice their opinions and rotating responsibilities. They are explicitly for individual, personal self-development at the same time as they are for fighting the powers that be with everything they've got at their disposal.[15]

The larger *asambleas interbarriales* (mass meetings of the various *asambleas*) elect rotating delegates from the *asambleas* to speak and vote on issues that their local communities generate. In addition, workers have occupied a number of factories and work sites such as Brukman, Zanon, and Panificadora Cinco. Workers have also occupied a mine in Rio Turbio. Clearly, new revolutionary forms of organization are appearing. As Ernesto Herrera notes:

> The experiences of the piquetero movement and neighborhood assemblies allow the possibility of the construction of a revolutionary movement, a democratic popular power with a socialist perspective. The "great revolt" has put on the agenda the question of a strategy that links resistance and the struggle for power, representative democracy and/or the principle of revocability, the "saqueos" as acts of self-subsistence in food.[16]

Brukman, a garment factory composed of fifty-five female workers, aged 45–50, has proved symbolic in the struggle against the Argentine state. Brukman workers are demanding public ownership of the factory, setting a dangerous precedent for the bourgeoisie. In fact, approximately twenty-five other factories in Argentina are occupied by workers who are also demanding public ownership. Workers in approximately 250 other factories are demanding some kind of state intervention for a type of workers' control (such as forming cooperatives, etc.). They have formed a popular front to resist assault from the state. However, assaults from the state continue.[17]

Of course, the *asambleas* confront many problems in that they are composed of members of different class factions, with their many different political agendas. Yet all of the *asambleas* hold the re-stratification of recently privatized industries as a top priority (even as they reject vanguardist parties). At the same time, in this new rise of popular mobilization, as subjectivities become revolutionized under the assault of capitalism, there needs to occur a programmatic proposal for a political regroupment of the radical and anti-capitalist forces. There must be more options available for organizers of the revolutionary left. Herrera writes:

> In Mexico, the Zapatista movement could not translate its capacity of mobilization in the Consultas and Marches into a political alternative of the left. There was no modification of the relationship of forces. The theory of the "indefinite anti-power" or "changing the world without

taking power" has produced neither a process of radical reforms, nor a revolutionary process.[18]

We are more optimistic about the possibilities of the Zapatista movement than Herrera, but we do believe that whatever shape the struggle against imperialism and capitalist globalization will take, it will need to be international. We believe in a multiracial, gender-balanced, internationalist, and anti-imperialist struggle. What appears promising are the rise of the Bolivarian Circles in Caracas, Venezuela, a mass mobilization of working-class Venezuelans on behalf of President Hugo Chavez. The Bolivarian Circles (named after Simón Bolívar) serve as watchdog groups modeled after Cuba's Committee for the Defense of the Revolution and function as liaisons between the neighborhoods and the government as well as fomenting support for Chavez. They are important in combating business leaders and dissident army generals who, with U.S. support, are trying to overthrow the Chavez government. Members of the Bolivarian Circles bang on hollow electricity poles to warn against mobilizations by the opposition and to rally supporters across the city's working-class neighborhoods. They are an example of self-determination for sovereignty as evidenced by the Bolivarian declaration "*Nuestra America: una sola patria*" (Our America: one motherhood) which rejects an ideological loyalty to "America" as an America defined by a capitalist-laden value system that favors imperialism and exploitation for increased profit margins. According to "Nuestra America," the people will not succumb to neoliberal modernity at the expense of becoming "scavengers of the industrial extravagance."[19] This movement is a clear signal that the present can be rewritten, that there is an alternative, and that the people can search for their own "America." In the spirit of this declaration we urge critical educators to pressure the International Monetary Fund (IMF) and World Bank to open their meetings to the media and to the public and to cancel the full measure of the debt they claim from underdeveloped countries, since such debts were accrued by dictators who used their IMF and World Bank loans to oppress their own people in the service of capital accumulation.

We argue that what needs to be emphasized and struggled for is not only the abolition of private property, but also a struggle against alienated labor. The key point here is not to get lost in the state (nationalized capital) versus neoliberalism (privatized capital) debate. As the resident editorial board of *News & Letters* have made clear, the real issue that must not be obscured is the need to abolish the domination of labor by capital. Capital needs to be uprooted through the creation of new human relations that dispense with value production altogether. This does not mean that we stop opposing neoliberalism or privatization. What it does mean is that we should not stop there.

Critical Pedagogy and the Civil Societarian Left

This brings us to a crucial question: How can critical educators reinvigorate the civil societarian left precisely at a time when we are creating a world where elites are less accountable to civil society than ever before? Takis Fotopoulos writes: "This new world order implies that, at the center, the model that has the greatest chance of being universalized is the Anglo-Saxon model of massive low-paid employment and underemployment, with poverty alleviated by the few security nets that the '40 percent society' will be willing to finance, in exchange for a tolerable degree of social peace which will be mainly secured by the vast security apparatuses being created by the public and private sectors."[20]

If we persist with an internationalized market economy, the introduction of effective social controls to protect the underclass and the marginalized will create overwhelming comparative disadvantages for the nation state or the economic bloc that seeks to institute such policies. Additionally, if we accept that there is no alternative to working within the institutionalized market economy, then the neoliberal policies of the ruling class make sense to the elites and under these circumstances there is a logic in rejecting the imposition of social controls by the civil societarian left. The only answer is one from without—we need to make our choice between socialism or barbarism. If we choose the latter, then we truly have no alternative than to sleep in the neoliberal bed that we have made for ourselves. If we choose socialism, then we must never abandon a vision for the radical transformation of society. As critical revolutionary educators who seek to transform the existing capitalist state into a socialist alternative, we can begin by revisiting our notions of democracy, by extending the traditional public realm to include the economic, ecological and social realms as well as the political realm. Democracy here is seen as a process of self-institution, where there exists no divinely or objectively defined code of human conduct.

A number of positions illuminated by Takis Fotopoulos on the creation of a revolutionary transition to socialism proves exceedingly instructive here for reconquering the notion of democracy and providing a politically robust concept of social justice.[21] According to Fotopoulos, we need to develop a deeper conception of political democracy or direct democracy that includes economic, political, cultural, social, and ecological democracy. This falls under the rubric of what Fotopoulos calls "confederal inclusive democracy" and refers to the equal sharing of power among all citizens through the self-institution of society. This means that democracy is grounded in the choice of its citizens, mandating the dismantling of oligarchic institutionalized processes and eliminating institutionalized political structures embodying unequal power relations. Economic democracy must be institutionalized by giving over macro economic decisions to the citizen body, whereas micro decisions at the workplace and household are taken over by the individual production or consumption unit. Here, the focus is on the needs of the community, and not growth per se; where satisfaction of community needs does not depend upon the continuous expansion of production to cover the needs that the market creates.

Within this model of deep democracy, unequal economic power relations are structurally eliminated by assuring that the means of production and distribution are collectively owned and controlled by a multiracial citizen body. Democracy in the social realm refers to an equality of social relations in the household and in the social realm in general such as the workplace and the educational establishment. Cultural democracy means the creation of community controlled art and media activity. Democracy must also be ecologically sensitive, developing an expanded level of ecological consciousness which will work to create the institutional preconditions for radical change with respect to society's attitude toward nature, making it less instrumentalist and less likely to see nature as an instrument for growth within a practice of power creation.

In sum, Fotopoulos' notion of inclusive democracy implies a new conception of political citizenship and the return to the classical concept of direct democracy; where economic citizenship involves new economic structures of "demotic" ownership and control of economic resources; where social citizenship involves self-management structures at the workplace, democracy in the household, and new welfare structures; where all basic needs are democratically determined and served by community resources; where cultural citizenship allows every community worker to develop his or her intellectual and cultural potential. Here Fotopoulos combines democratic and anarchist traditions with radical Green, feminist, and liberation traditions. In our view, such a reworked notion of citizenship is compatible with building independent working-class political action involving teachers and students and other cultural workers. As the basis of the self-organization of the working class, this transitional stage would include the confederation of workplace assemblies as part of a broader democratic movement directly linked to communities. Clearly, what is needed is a form of representative democracy based on a council democracy or forms of direct democracy.

For critical revolutionary educators, the struggle for inclusive democracy stipulates working with students to build revolutionary consciousness and collective action as a means whereby we can resist our insinuation in the ugly truth of capital: that it is designed to separate the laborer from her labor. The fetishization and unequal distribution of life chances produced by capitalist social relations of production must be challenged by dialectical praxis. The center-left liberal covenant which enshrines resource distribution as the site of resistance, and seeks to calibrate social transformation according to how easily it can be integrated into a more "compassionate" capitalism with a human face, must be directly challenged by a coherent philosophy of praxis that directly confronts globalized capital with a socialist alternative. Such a war of position must fight for the social power of the popular classes that will enable them to challenge both the state and civil society simultaneously. It can pitch this challenge within the framework of an intergenerational, multiracial, transnational and anti-imperialist social movement. This will not be an easy task, especially at this current moment of political despair that has infected much of the educational left. It will require radical hope. It is a hope grounded in the conviction that the working class possesses the greatest revolutionary potential in overcoming the ongoing destruction by the whirlwind that capitalism has sown.

Hope is the freeing of possibility, with possibility serving as the dialectical partner of necessity. When hope is strong enough, it can bend the future backward towards the past, where, trapped between the two, the present can escape its orbit of inevitability and break the force of history's hubris, so that what is struggled for no longer remains an inert idea frozen in the hinterland of "what is," but becomes a reality carved out of "what could be." Hope is the oxygen of dreams, and provides the stamina for revolutionary struggle. Revolutionary dreams are those in which the dreamers dream until there are no longer dreamers but only the dreams themselves, shaping our everyday lives from moment to moment, and opening the causeways of possibility where abilities are nourished not for the reaping of profit, but for the satisfaction of needs and the full development of human potential.

The days ahead will witness furious attempts by the petrolarchs of the Bush administration to justify its political and military occupation. They will say that they are making the world safe for freedom and democracy and providing opportunities for other countries to benefit from "the American Way of Life." This will be accompanied by attempts by the Bush administration to get a whole new generation of nuclear weapons into production in order to meet their expanded "national security objectives." And they will have most of the evangelical Christian communities behind these initiatives. It looks as though the American public will be left out of the debate. Why should Bush care about what the American people think? They didn't vote for him.

Currently the most important front against capitalism is stopping the U.S. from invading more countries, since the administration's National Security Strategy of the United States of America establishes an irrevocable connection between U.S. global domination and the neoliberal Washington consensus. Callinicos warns:

If the U.S. is victorious in Iraq, then it is more likely to go on the offensive in Latin America, the zone in the south where resistance to neoliberalism is most advanced. Even if the B-52s and Special Forces aren't directly deployed against Brazilian landless laborers or Argentinean piqueteros, victory for U.S. military power will weaken the struggle against poverty and hunger everywhere.[22]

Commenting on imperialistic sentiment of the American people (with specific historical reference to Mexico), John Dewey wrote that "it is only too easy to create a situation after which the cry 'stand by the President,' and then 'stand by the country,' is overwhelming. . . . Public sentiment, to be permanently effective, must do more than protest. It must find expression in a permanent change of our habits."[23] Addressing U.S. imperialism since September 11, 2001, Gilbert Aschar portentously warns: "The real, inescapable question is this: is the US population really ready to endure even more September 11s, as the unavoidable price of a global hegemony that only benefits its ruling class?"[24]

Perhaps it's time to give consideration to comments coming not from the theater of war, but the theater of playwrights and actors. Recently, Peter Ustinov observed: "Terrorism is the war of the poor, and war is the terrorism of the rich."[25]

We reject the notion, advanced by Foucault and other poststructuralists, that posing a vision of the future only reinforces the tyranny of the present. Similarly, we reject Derrida's insistence that the fetish is not opposable.[26] It is self-defeating in our view to embrace the advice of many postmodernists: that all we can do is engage in an endless critique of the forms of thought defined by commodity fetishism. In contrast, we believe that we can do more than enjoy our symptoms in a world where the subjects of capitalism have been endlessly disappearing into the vortex of history. Such defeatism arises as long as critics believe that value production within capitalism is natural and immutable. We believe that the value form of mediation within capitalism is permeable and that another world outside of the social universe of capital is possible. We are also committed to the idea that revolutionary critical pedagogy can play a role in its realization. We agree with Jameson's perceptive account of utopia as possessing a negative function of demonstrating our confinement in a non-utopian present bereft of historicity and futurity and revealing the faultlines of our ideological entrapment in a votex of social relations linked to racism, patriarchy, and class exploitation.[27] Our utopian impulses work through the negation of our opposed utopian longings such that each one persists in its negation of the other, refusing to arrive at a final or grand synthesis. We reject coaxing critical agency into existence within the precincts of a nauseously puritanical idealism or discovering it in some otherworld gnosticism as an effulgent, indwelling spirit force fed by the muses. Similarly, we do not wish to revel in the inevitability of the shopsoiled nature of the human condition. That our agency is neccessarily sullied by the self-interest of others doesn't mean that we can't work for a common good; that it is unmasterable does not mean that it is impervious to change; that it is durable does not mean that it is imperishable. To admit that we are condemned to live within the interstices of contradictions is not to say we cannot overcome them. Whatever organizational forms our agency takes will need to address a global audience who similarly share the radical hope that another world outside the social universe of capital is possible. [28]

Notes

1. John Dewey, "Imperialism is Easy," *The New Republic* 50 (March 23, 1927). Available online: http://www.boondocksnet.com/ai/ailtexts/dewey.html.
2. See Peter McLaren, "Critical Pedagogy and Class Struggle in the Age of Neoliberal Globalization: Notes from History's Underside," *Democracy & Nature* 9.1 (2003): 65–90.
3. See William Saletan, "The Soft Bigotry of Loose Adulation," *Slate* (April 10, 2003). Available online: http://slate.msn.com/id/2081213/html.
4. Saletan, "The Soft Bigotry of Loose Adulation."
5. Max Elbaum, *Revolution in the Air: Sixties Radicals turn to Lenin, Mao, and Che* (London and New York: Verso, 2002), 335.
6. Elbaum, *Revolution in the Air*, 334.
7. Karl Marx, cited in Elbaum, *Revolution in the Air*, 334.
8. Elbaum, *Revolution in the Air*, 335. The next two quotations are also from page 335.
9. Massimo De Angelis, "From Movement to Society," *The Commoner* 4 (May 2002), 5. Available online: http://www.commoner.org.uk/01-3groundzero.htm.
10. De Angelis, "From Movement to Society," 14.
11. Ellen Meiksins Wood, "Contradictions: Only in Capitalism," in *A World of Contradictions: Socialist Register 2002*, ed. Leo Panitch and Colin Leys (London: Merlin, 2001), 291.
12. Sam Gindin, "Social Justice and Globalization: Are They Compatible?" *Monthly Review* 54 (June 2002): 1–11.
13. See John Holloway, "Twelve Theses On Changing the World Without Taking Power," *The Commoner* 4 (May 2002). Available online: http://www.commoner.org.uk/04holloway2.pdf
14. Naomi Klein, "Demonstrated Ideals," *Los Angeles Times* (April 20, 2003). Available online: http://www.alternet.org/story.html?StoryID=15737.
15. The Resident Editorial Board, *News & Letters* 47 (July 2002), 6.
16. Ernesto Herrera, "Latin America: The Current Situation and the Task of Revolutionaries," in *Fourth International Press* (July17, 2002), 10.
17. Over 25,000 people surrounded the Brukman factory in April 2003 to defend workers that had been expelled by the police, leading to numerous injuries and arrests.
18. Herrera, "Latin America," 13.
19. See "Nuestra America: una sola patria" (2003), available online: http://www.unasolapatria.org/documento.html.
20. Takis Fotopoulos, *Towards an Inclusive Democracy: The Crisis of the Growth Economy and the Need for a New Liberatory Project* (London: Cassell, 1997), 358.
21. See Fotopoulos, *Towards an Inclusive Democracy*.
22. Alex Callinicos, "War Under Attack," *Socialist Review* 273 (April 2003). Available online: http://www.swp.org.uk/SR/273/SR2.htm.
23. Dewey, "Imperialism is Easy."
24. Gilbert Aschar, *The Clash of Barbarisms: September 11 and the Making of the New World Disorder* (New York: Monthly Review Press, 2002), 81.

25. Cited in John Berger, "Fear Eats the Soul," *The Nation* 276 (May 12, 2003), 34.
26. Peter Hudis, "The Future of Dialectical Marxism: Towards a New Relation of Theory and Practice." A paper presented at the Rethinking Marxism Conference, November 2003.
27. Fredric Jameson, "The Politics of Utopia," *New Left Review* 25(Jan/Feb, 2004), 35–54.
28. This chapter is a revised version of "Critical Pedagogy as Organized Praxis" that appeared in *Educational Foundations* 16.4 (Fall, 2002), 5–32.

Re-Ruling the Classroom

The Possibilities of Places

CHAPTER 5

The U.S. Holocaust Memorial Museum as a Scene of Pedagogical Address

ELIZABETH ELLSWORTH

Introduction

Soon after it opened to the public in 1993, the U.S. Holocaust Memorial Museum [Washington, D.C.] was hailed as "one of the late twentieth century's most profound architectural statements." It houses a permanent exhibit that Leon Wieseltier has called "a pedagogical masterpiece." He declares: "The building itself teaches."[1]

Under any circumstances, the making of profound architectural statements and the achievement of pedagogical masterpieces are no small feats. But the accomplishments of the architect and exhibit designers of the Memorial Museum seem all the more profound given the philosophical and pedagogical problems that challenge any attempt to teach or memorialize the Holocaust.

In a recent analysis of the Memorial Museum, an architectural critic listed some of those challenges. How might exhibit designers "elucidate without lapsing into entertainment?" How might they "give form to the act of memory?" How might their designs hold the lack, the absence, of millions of European Jewry even as the Memorial Museum is filled by artifacts, text, photographs, films?[2]

The challenges for teachers and students of "traumatic historical events" are similar to those faced by the Memorial Museum's designers. Teaching and representing such traumatic histories brings educators up against the limits of our theories and practices concerning pedagogy, curriculum, and the roles of dialogue, empathy, and understanding in teaching about and across social and cultural difference. If, as Michael Berenbaum asserts, "children have to learn about the untrustworthiness of the world as they learn to trust the world," how might teachers teach distrust?[3] Such questions have become more urgent in the wake of recent anniversaries of events connected with the Holocaust, the wars in Bosnia and Kosovo, and the attacks of September 11, 2001. Just how should teacher educators respond to mandates such as the Wisconsin Department of Public Instruction's requirement that student teachers learn about slavery, genocides and the Holocaust?

As a concrete materialization of a particular pedagogical approach, the permanent exhibit of the Memorial Museum provides a rich context for studying key challenges and opportunities involved in teaching the Holocaust in particular, and in teaching about and across social and cultural difference in general.

An analysis of specific moments and scenes of pedagogical address in the Memorial Museum's permanent exhibit provides strong support for the following assertion: the power of the address of this museum's pedagogy lies in its indeterminacy. This museum, with its primary objective of education, paradoxically embraces the ways that histories of the Holocaust throw the pedagogical relation between teacher and student into crisis. I suspect that the usefulness of the pedagogy of the Memorial Museum to teachers lies in the ways that it embraces the dilemmas and impossibilities that confront teachers and witnesses of the Holocaust. Far from leading to paralysis or despair, an analysis of this museum's pedagogical address reveals concrete instances of how the paradoxes of teaching and learning can be productive, and can assist teachers and students in accessing moral imperatives without absolutes.

The Pedagogical Problem

In cultural studies, literary criticism, and philosophy, scholars debate theoretical aspects of the seemingly insurmountable dilemmas faced by designers of the permanent exhibit. Some argue that the Holocaust exceeds representation, it is unrepresentable.[4] Others argue that the Holocaust exceeds understanding, it is unteachable.[5] According to some teachers of the Holocaust such as Claude Lanzmann, director of the film *Shoah*, any attempt to "understand" the Holocaust is "obscene."[6] Writing about the production of *Shoah*, Lanzmann declares that the question "Why have the Jews been killed?" reveals right away its obscenity. He writes: ". . . not to understand was my iron law during all the eleven years of the production of Shoah . . . [it was] the only way to not turn away from a reality which is literally blinding."[7]

A teacher of literary responses to the Holocaust, Shoshana Felman, argues that the paradox of knowledge is that there are only misunderstandings. The testimonies contained within the Memorial Museum do not consist of "understandings" of the Holocaust. Rather, they are "bits and pieces of a memory that has been overwhelmed by occurrences that have not settled into understanding or remembrance, acts that cannot be construed as knowledge nor assimilated into full cognition, events in excess of our frames of reference."[8]

And yet, representations, memorials, museums, Web sites, and videotaped testimonies of the Holocaust proliferate. No longer rare, Holocaust memorials and museums "form a specific genre of architecture . . . indeed there may even be a certain world-weary resistance to their proliferation."[9] As Wieseltier observed, the Holocaust is the "subject of astonishing mass curiosity, it doesn't seem to diminish with the years, it gets larger."[10] He goes on:

> This is affecting, and this is revolting. It certainly makes the fear that the Holocaust will be forgotten seem faintly ridiculous. And worse, it ensures that if the Holocaust is forgotten, or if it is pushed to the peripheries of consciousness and culture, then it will be partly owing to the memorials themselves, which will have made the horror familiar and thereby robbed it of its power to shock and to disrupt . . . Too little memory dishonors the catastrophe; but so does too much memory. In the contemplation of the death camps, we must be strangers; and if we are not strangers, if the names of the killers and the places of the killing and the numbers of the killed fall easily from our tongues, then we are not remembering to remember, but remembering to forget.[11]

The proliferation of efforts to represent the unrepresentable, to understand that which exceeds all frames of cognition, threatens to trivialize.

The recent debate over Roberto Benigni's *Life is Beautiful* puts such tensions in stark relief. The film has been charged with offering up "Holocaust lite," or "Holokitch." Art Spiegelman, creator of *MAUS*, commented in an NPR interview that *Life is Beautiful* contributes to the Zeitgeist shift toward using the Holocaust with impunity as a metaphor. Spiegelman concedes that he too used metaphors in *MAUS*, his Pulitzer Prize-winning "comic book" about the Holocaust. But, he said, he used metaphors to try to approach the actualities that can never be met directly or finally. "I see that as a rather different project than taking the Holocaust and using it as a metaphor for a bummer."[12]

Arguments, debates, and analyses about the politics of representation, the social construction of knowledge, the space of difference between history and memory, or the uses of metaphor to gesture toward the unspeakable, could hardly remain abstract or academic during the design of the museum's exhibits. In fact, these issues and dilemmas were integral to the design of the Memorial Museum.[13]

And that is what, for me as an educator, makes my own encounter with the Memorial Museum so productive. In its architecture and in the design of the permanent exhibit, this museum materializes the ongoing social and cultural struggle about if, how, why to represent the Holocaust. "It is from these very issues that the architecture of the museum stems."[14]

The Permanent Exhibit

How, then, have the architects and exhibit designers addressed these pedagogical issues?

The permanent exhibit of the Memorial Museum has a potential of five hours of reading material and an additional five hours of audiovisual material. It presents artifacts, documents, poetry, letters, drawings, narrational text, film, photographs, and video. The visitors' routes through the permanent exhibit follow a corkscrew pattern, from the fourth floor, to the third, to the second floor, using both wings of the building. Visitors cross from one wing to the other through steel-framed glass bridges, suggestive of both camp observation systems and ghetto walkways. The visitor's experience of the exhibit is made up not only of artifacts and documents, but also of space, time, and a sequential montage of elements.

With characteristics such as these, one could almost call the permanent exhibit a multimedia exhibit. But that would be like calling Art Spiegelman's *MAUS* a comic book. The brilliant cultural achievement of *MAUS* lies in the ways Spiegelman explodes conventions and banalities of representation by exploding the form, style, and structure of the comic book. Similarly, designers of the permanent exhibit set out to explode conventions of pedagogy by refusing the obscenity of presuming to know or to understand the Holocaust.

As reported in the official description of the Memorial Museum, it was the view of the designers of the museum that the educational work of this museum must take place in the *space of difference* between history and memory, the concrete and the abstract, the unique and the universal. Only by locating its pedagogical address in such spaces-between could the museum's educational mission be realized. Michael Sorkin writes: "Perhaps the only way to approach the unrepresentable is to represent the impossibility of representing it, turning representation inside out to confront this horrific sublime."[15]

In his architectural critique, Dannatt describes the Memorial Museum's design as forming "a grammar of history"[16]—except it is a grammar composed of deliberate ambiguity, a confusion of potential metaphors and overlapping levels of signification. Its metaphors are "potential," not achieved. Details of shape, material, light and darkness never resolve into the reassuringly symbolic. Instead, they remain dangerously suggestive as they remain in the space between concrete and abstract. They "shimmer," "dissolve," "disappear," and "haunt."[17] The architecture, according to Dannatt, stages associations that "never force themselves but linger instead like a suggestive stain."[18] For example, the dominant skylight of exposed structural steel is "twisted and buckled, wrenched and turned . . . it is neither inside nor outside."[19] Such ambiguous, suggestive, irreconcilable architectural forms provide visitors with "a map of the Holocaust where all coordinates have been displaced or half-erased, a cartography more threatening than reassuring."[20] Navigating the physical space calls up confusion, lack of orientation, directional dilemmas.

If, as Herbert Muschamp writes in his review of the Memorial Museum, "a place is a form of knowledge,"[21] what does such a place know? How do its concrete materials suggest abstract conceptualizations of the Holocaust? If, as Wieseltier writes, the building itself teaches, if the Memorial Museum is a pedagogical masterpiece, then what is the genius of its pedagogy?

Refusing Narrative Closure: Analyzing the Pedagogical Address of the Permanent Exhibit

The terms of the permanent exhibit's pedagogical address to its student invites her not only into the activity of knowledge construction, but into the construction of knowledge from a particular social and political point of view. This makes "learning" not simply voluntary and idiosyncratic, but relational—an assumption of particular relations of self-to-self and between self, others, knowledge, and power.

According to this perspective, visitors experience not only the exhibit's style and story. They also experience and respond to how the exhibit's structure of address solicits a certain reading from them. The exhibit's narrative structure and visual design, for example, construct and "speak from" a particular position within the constellation of meanings surrounding the Holocaust and Holocaust pedagogy. And, not unlike the postal system, elements of the exhibit construct an address to/for the visitor. This address offers the visitor a "*structure*, a linguistic structure by which to relate himself to other human beings; a structure, therefore, in which meaning . . . can later be articulated."[22]

The pedagogical address of the permanent exhibit, therefore, invites its visitors into a relation. It articulates the relations of the objects in the Memorial Museum among themselves—and includes the visitor as one of the objects in the system. What makes the address of the exhibit "pedagogical," what a visitor "learns" from the terms of the exhibit's address, is to assume herself-in-relation to the symbolic constellation surrounding Holocaust history and memory. In other words, the visitor "learns" a relationship to Holocaust history and memory—a relationship into which meanings can later be articulated. The Memorial Museum's pedagogy addresses students and teachers in ways that invite them into a very particular symbolic constellation and, as a result, into the social relations articulated and inscribed in that constellation.

And this reveals the analytical importance of the notion of pedagogical address. The terms of the exhibit's address to its visitors, the terms of its invitation into a relationship with Holocaust history and memory, render certain meanings and relations possible and impossible, intelligible and unintelligible, within the symbolic constellation that it offers. The question: "Who does this exhibit think you are?" underscores the assertion that to "learn about" the Holocaust in the terms set forth by the exhibit, is to assume a relation within a system of meanings. And assuming a relation within a system of meanings is what permits the "learner" to relate symbolically to other humans.

Of course, no system of meanings can exhaust or contain all human relations, histories, and memories. Human experience and desire exceed any single system of meanings. All modes of address misfire one way or another. A student and a teacher never "is" the "who" that a pedagogical address thinks they are. And that brings us to the troubling scene of pedagogical address. How might a pedagogy address its students in ways that acknowledge and put into play the fact that the structure of relations being offered by any curriculum necessarily represses, denies, or ignores the very identities, ideas and events that would undo it?

The pedagogy of the U.S. Holocaust Memorial Museum makes that question pivotal to the permanent exhibit's design and educational approach. And this is what saves its pedagogy from being a closed system of exchange. By embracing the impossibility and undesirability of offering its visitors a fixed or knowable address within the constellation of meanings surrounding the Holocaust, the pedagogy of the exhibit opens the door onto the possibility for something else. It opens the door to the possibility, the paradoxical possibility, of a narrative without closure. It opens the door, in other words, to what Felman calls an "interminable learning."[23]

The pedagogy of the exhibit refuses narrative closure in at least two ways. First, it interrupts the logic of narrative structure throughout the exhibit, and especially, it refuses to provide an "ending." And second, any illusions of narrative completeness or adequacy are broken by metacommunicative layers imposed upon the narrative structure. In other words, the very narrative frame of the story being told is shattered by continual references to its own limits, by self-referential gestures at the impossibility of its own project—the impossibility, that is, of telling the story of the Holocaust.

According to the exhibit's catalogue, the Memorial Museum is a "narrative museum, because its display is organized along a story line."[24] And yet, the official description of the exhibit takes pains to explain that this is not a "traditional history museum," it is a "museum of a different kind."[25] Part of that difference lies in the way it addresses visitors.

> In the process of becoming exposed to the Museum's exhibitions and activities, visitors . . . find themselves positioned between two poles: between the concrete and the abstract, the historical and the metaphoric, the unique and the universal. The tension and discourse between these poles is inherent in the essence of the Museum and its educational work. One can say that, at any single moment, the educational process is taking place in the space between one pole and the other. To preserve the overwhelming power of the concrete event and, at the same time, the symbolic, universal implications inherent in it, there should never be an attempt at resolving the tension between the poles.[26]

In other words, the "story line" of the permanent exhibit is the line inscribed by visitors as they traverse *the space between* binaries. And how could it be otherwise? To address visitors in ways that invite them to take up positions at either one binary pole or the other, would be to invite them to assume positions within the very configuration of relations that perpetrated the Holocaust: insider/outsider, us/them, human/inhuman, victim/perpetrator, Aryan/non-Aryan. On the other hand, to promote a story that resolves the tensions between the poles would be to promote what Adam Phillips calls "the misleading idea that we are all in search of completion."[27] Phillips continues: "Bewitched by the notion of being complete, we become obsessed by notions of sameness and difference, by thoughts of what to include and what to reject in order to keep ourselves [and our stories] whole."[28] But, Phillips argues, "there is no cure for multiple plots."[29]

As visitors walk through the "story" of this narrative museum, they are literally positioned in the spaces between video monitors, life-size photographs, displayed artifacts, text, and audio recordings. Even though the texts presented are arranged in roughly chronological order along a corkscrew path, we do not read or hear or view a linear story line. Rather, we are placed physically in the spaces between the story's elements. We are entwined with the story elements. From the spaces between, there is no story line, only a three dimensional competition for our attention. Every visitor to the exhibit will "traverse [their] own path, crossing previous lines of locomotion."[30] No two paths or lines of attention compose the same story. Indeed, "the" story of the narrative exhibit is never stated.

Instead, there is a constant deferral of *the* story. There is a continual opening up of the space between resolved binary terms or resolved endings, knowings or understandings. This is accomplished, in part, by repeated interruption of any single line of attention, of any single sequential development of a story line out of the exhibit's separate elements.

For example, while elements are grouped into themes and events, such as "Nazi Propaganda" or "Resistance," there is no linear cause-effect explanation linking these groups. And within each grouping, elements can be encountered in any order, as when visitors come upon groupings of elements labeled "Nazi Propaganda," "Nazi Society," and "Search for Refuge" simultaneously. Even within the groupings, relations between elements within a group are seldom linear. On any given display panel, video testimonies or archival footage are not offered as direct illustrations of printed text. Nor does the text explain the video. Their association is not one of illustration or explanation. Rather, their association is topographical. Each element provides another facet, another perspective, another relation to the theme or event.

The display area labeled "To Safety" is one instance of this refusal of a single story line. The area is about how some Holocaust survivors were brought to "safety" in the United States. The video, photographs, narrational text, and artifacts each offer a different position in the space between the binary Safety/Danger. And despite the display's title: "To Safety," the various positions in the space between the poles "Safety" and "Danger" are never unproblematically resolved in favor of "safety." A heroic narrative of escape or rescue is not allowed to manage the elements of this grouping. For example, the first block of text reports that the U.S. Emergency Visitors' Visa Program was established to save "persons of exceptional merit" and "those of superior intellectual attainment." This is juxtaposed with text containing a quotation from Bertold Brecht: "I know, of course, it's simply luck that I've survived so many friends. But last night in a dream I heard those friends say of me: 'Survival of the fittest,' and I hated myself."

In another instance of interrupted narrative structure, visitors cross from one wing of the exhibit to another, passing along glass bridges. The present interrupts the exhibit's narration of the past: daylight, the weather, the

Washington Monument, the here and now of the nation's seat of democracy breaks the exhibit's narrative. But not heroically, not even reassuringly, as, simultaneously, the past interrupts the present. Inscribed on the glass walls of one bridge are the names of thousands of villages destroyed in the Holocaust. The names of obliterated villages interfere with the view of the Washington Monument. History interrupts the present and any attempts to use contemporary narratives to resolve the lost stories of these villages.

Ironically, the narrative structure of the permanent exhibit is further interrupted by the narrational text itself. If the narrational text of the exhibit were spoken, it would have the vocal qualities of a very poor storyteller. The voice of the written text is deadpan, devoid of inflection, drama, or embellishment—lacking any but the most colorless adjectives. For example: "These children's books were intended to indoctrinate young Germans in nationalism, love for Hitler, and obedience to his will. They include *The Poison Mushroom*, a collection of anti-Semitic stories, and *Read Along!*, an illustrated book of Nazi slogans." Or, "Roma (gypsies) were subjected to official discrimination well before 1933. After Hitler took power, long held prejudices were fueled by Nazi racism, although no comprehensive anti-Roma law was ever passed." Or, "Before the war, Warsaw was the center of Jewish life in Poland and contained the greatest concentration of Jews in Europe. Soon after the German conquest on September 39, 1933, Warsaw's 375,000 Jews were required to wear white armbands with a blue Star of David. A Jewish Council was appointed. The German authorities closed Jewish schools, confiscated Jewish owned property, and conscripted Jewish men. . . ."

These are not stories. Nor are they explanations. The voice of the exhibit's written text refuses to narrate, or to explain, what it tells. The text fragments its telling of the Holocaust into roughly chronological bits. By disrupting and dislocating "the apparent but misleading unities" of a story line unified and made coherent and understandable by cause/effect, question/answer relations, "the breakage of [the text] enacts the breakage of the world."[31]

Paraphrasing Adam Phillips, it is the conscious intention not to produce an exemplary story that frees the conversation. The story lines which students of the exhibit traverse have multiple beginnings and middles, and no knowable ends. It is this refusal of traditional forms of closure that distinguishes this exhibit's pedagogy from moral pedagogy.[32]

Constant interruption of narrative structure is one way that the exhibit becomes a narrative without closure. There is another way that the exhibit refuses closure. Repeatedly, it shatters its own narrative frame by making reference its own limits. The exhibit gestures, self-referentially, at the impossibility of its own project of narrating the Holocaust.

For example, a three-story tower displays photographs taken between 1890 and 1941 in Eishishok, a small town in what is now Lithuania. The photos describe a vibrant Jewish community that existed for 900 years. In two days in 1941, an SS mobile killing squad massacred the Jewish population. The design of this tower materializes the limits of teaching and knowing. Its construction makes it physically impossible for visitors to view all of the photos. The pedagogy of the tower's design, in other words, is one that actually withholds much of the "content material" of its curriculum. The staging of these photos enacts a pedagogy confronted by a loss of knowability—a loss of mastery of the subject, a loss of closure. Just as it is physically impossible to see all of the photos, it is impossible to recover and know the obliterated history of this town.

Perhaps the most profound moment of metacommunication by this museum about the limits of its own pedagogy, occurs at the "end" of the exhibition. Weiseltier describes the last element encountered by visitors:

> Its exhibition ends in a Hall of remembrance, a six-sided classically proportioned chamber of limestone . . . seventy feet high, unencumbered by iconography. . . . One of the achievements of the Holocaust Memorial Museum is that it leads its visitors directly from history to silence . . . the least that you can do, after seeing what you have just seen, is sit down and be still. . . . This, then, is the plot, the historical and spiritual sequence got right, of the infernal display on the Mall: memory, stiffened by history, then struck dumb.
> The museum is a pedagogical masterpiece.[33]

What are we educators to make of this declaration that it is a pedagogical achievement—it is the historical plot got right—that visitors be struck dumb? What are we to make of Wieseltier's suggestion that silence become a pedagogical goal?

The profound pedagogical achievement of the refusals of narrative closure that lead up to this silence is that this final gesture of silence cannot be taken as, simply, silence. All that comes before the silence at the "end" of the permanent exhibit frames it in a way that makes it a very particular silence.

It is a silence that teaches what pedagogy can never speak.

Given the structuring of all that comes before this last element of the exhibit, it would be a willful ignore-ance to call this silence a form of nihilism. Neither can it be read as a form of forgetting. Nor can it be taken as a melodramatic moment of overwhelming sentimentalism. Nor is it the silence of the witness, or the good listener. And it is not the silence of self-reflection. Like the exhibit's refusals of narrative continuity and closure, the silence with which the visitor is met at the end of the exhibit, a silence that asks to be met in turn by silence, is a communicative act after all. It is an act of metacommunication. This silence is a metacommunicative refusal of the rules of narrative closure. It is a self-referential refusal to offer an ending.

This silence that metacommunicates marks the limits of pedagogy. It marks the limits of knowledge. It is the silence of "passing through our own answerlessness."[34] It is the silence of the pedagogue who accepts that s/he does not, cannot, have the last word, and who embraces the pedagogical power of not providing the last word.

The Permanent Exhibit as a Scene of Pedagogical Address

The narrative of this museum is a narrative without closure. It is an interrupted narrative that metacommunicates about its own limits and explodes conventions of pedagogy by falling silent at the very moment a conclusion is expected. If such a narrative is at the heart of this pedagogical masterpiece—then what does its refusal of closure through interruption and silence teach?

But to answer this question would be to have the last word. To provide an answer for this question would be to provide closure, an ending to the exhibit's narrative, a meaning to the exhibit's ending. Such an answer would put an end to the exhibit's educational project—a project that teaches only to the extent that a conclusion is never reached. To answer the question: What does the exhibit's final gesture of silence "teach?" would be to participate in the obscenity of understanding.

This exhibit's pedagogy breaks from the address offered by many other Holocaust "curriculums." It does not create for us the virtual positions of victim, or perpetrator, or bystander and invite us to "occupy" those positions as a way of accessing understanding of the Holocaust. Nor does it address us as witnesses to the Holocaust (after all, as students of the exhibit, we do not witness the Holocaust. We witness representations of the Holocaust).

Rather, the pedagogy of the permanent exhibit addresses us as *implicated*. Implicated not in the guilt of perpetrators, bystanders, or victims, but rather, implicated in an ongoing narrative-in-the-making. Implicated not as "responsible for" or "guilty of," but implicated as entangled, intertwined, twisted together, wrapped up with, involved in.

> The witness is pursued, that is, at once compelled and bound by what, in the unexpected impact of the accident, is both incomprehensible and unforgettable. The accident does not let go: it is an accident from which the witness can no longer free himself.[35]

The design of the exhibit materializes the dynamic in which knowledge of a traumatic event both pursues the witness and the witness, in turn, pursues the traumatic event.[36] For example, one dominant structural motif throughout the exhibit positions video, artifacts, and photographs, as reaching out toward the visitor, meeting the visitor, pressing toward the visitor, closing in, as if in pursuit of the visitor. Yet at another point in the exhibit's sequential montage, a second structural motif causes text, video, and artifacts to recede from view. It is the visitor who must pursue the exhibit. The lighting throughout the exhibit contributes to this alternating invitation to pursue and to flee. Areas of palpable darkness interrupt areas illuminated by grainy light. Often, artifacts and text are displayed in near darkness, causing visitors to draw in very close, to lean in, to make a deliberate decision to pursue, uncover, recover what threatens to recede from view.

What the visitor must now do with the experience of the Memorial Museum cannot be prescribed. It cannot be written beforehand. That would be to take visitors out of the tense, volatile space of ongoing cultural production that exists *between* moral, political, or philosophical absolutes. It would be to position visitors instead in the very structure of relations that perpetrated the Holocaust—as occupying one or another moral, political, or philosophical absolute. Addressing visitors in the space between absolutes makes impossible any *specification of how* visitors should apply the metaphoric meaning of the Holocaust to their lives. At the same time, it is addressing visitors in the space between absolutes that opens up a mode of access to that imperative.[37]

In these ways, the permanent exhibit constructs a pedagogical space that invites the visitor to, as Felman puts it,

> *pursue the accident,* to actively pursue its path and its direction through obscurity, through darkness, and through fragmentation, without quite grasping the full scope and meaning of its implications, without entirely foreseeing where the journey leads and what is the precise nature of its final destination.[38]

Indeed, according to the museum's official description, the exhibit's educational goal is to make it possible for the visitor to pursue the accident without knowing where it will lead, without knowing the precise nature of its final destination:

> The museum's educational responsibility is to help visitors apply the metaphoric meaning embedded in Holocaust history to their contemporary experience as individuals and as members of society. . . . This is indeed what the Museum is all about: creating an encounter between the visitor and this moral imperative.[39]

And of course, paradoxically, the nature of the encounter between the visitor and this moral imperative *cannot be specified.*

If upon hearing the "news" of the Holocaust, as teachers and students, we cannot ground our responses in what we "know"—then what might be the ground for responsibility? If the actions we might take in response to encountering the Holocaust are not to be articulated to *cognition*—then to what? When we read the museum's pedagogy as a scene of address—rather than as an offering of security or of cognitive certainty—it becomes possible to imagine what Laclau calls "a hero of a new type who has still not been entirely created by our culture."[40] That non-heroic hero is "a figure who is at the same time profoundly heroic and tragic, someone who, when confronted with Auschwitz, has the moral strength to admit the contingency of her own beliefs, instead of seeking refuge in religious or rationalistic myths."[41]

Teaching Moral Imperatives Without Absolutes: The Ringelblum Milk Can

Just how does the Memorial Museum's pedagogical address open up access to the moral imperative that visitors apply their experience of the Museum to their contemporary lives, without specifying what the visitors should do?

I'm going to explore one more moment in the Museum's mobilization of narrative, visual design and point of view into a pedagogical address. It's a moment that inaugurates the psychic split between the self who is held hostage to the Museum's moral imperative, and the self who walks away into the daylight. It is the moment of coming upon a particular artifact: the Ringelblum milk can.

Designers of the permanent exhibit write:

> The Ringelblum milk can is perhaps the Memorial Museum's most important historic artifact. Under the leadership of Emmanuel Ringelblum, a university trained historian, several dozen writers, teachers, rabbis, and historians compiled an archive documenting life in the Warsaw ghetto.[42]

> On the eve of the final annihilation of the ghetto, Ringelblum buried all records and documents in metal containers and milk cans so they would be found after the war, after his death and the death of all other members of his historical society. So they would let the world know.[43]

> Ringelblum was shot by the Nazis in 1944; this can, one of those buried by Ringelblum and his colleagues, was discovered in 1950.[44]

Perhaps this milk can is the museum's most important artifact because of the scene of address that it stages. When I come upon the rusted milk can, I enter a scene of address. Unlike the pile of shoes and broken eyeglasses, unlike the railroad car, unlike the clothing and bunk beds—the Ringelblum milk can exceeds the representational. Instead, it performs an address. It is not simply an artifact that represents something elsewhere, at some other time. It exists in the moment, as an ongoing call. It is this call that inaugurates the "psychic split" that architecture critic Herbert Muschamp claims this museum recreates with "excruciating fidelity." It is the psychic split that Muschamp says he experienced while visiting Dachau when he stood inside a gas chamber, and walked out again. Muschamp writes:

> It is when you cross the threshold of that door that you grasp the reason for visiting Dachau. You walk out into daylight, but part of you does not leave. The doorway divides you. You feel lightheaded, as though you have broken the law, as indeed you have. Your passage through that door has violated the design. The room was not meant to be exited alive. This is a privileged moment. Not because you are free to walk out of the gas chamber, but because you are not. Because part of us remains behind, wondering how, since no one deserved to die here, we deserve to leave. A moral universe could arise from the imperative to answer the self we left behind.[45]

According to Muschamp, the architecture of the U.S. Holocaust Memorial Museum avoids any literal representation of Dachau or any of the other death camps. Nevertheless, he argues, it recreates with excruciating fidelity the psychic split that he experienced as he exited the gas chamber. In the description of his visit, Muschamp renders this split as a scene of address. The self left behind in the gas chamber addresses the self free to walk out. "No one deserved to die here. Why do you deserve to leave?" This question can be avoided, denied, repressed, ignored. But it also cannot be answered. It cannot, in other words, be escaped.

The Memorial Museum is not the gas chamber at Dachau. We do not violate its design by exiting its doors. Nevertheless, its pedagogical address is designed to hold us hostage in another sense—hostage to the call, the moral imperative, the address from the other, which we cannot escape. But this position of hostage is neither a paralyzing position of despair, nor a heroic position of empowerment that enables me to assume the role of rescuer. Neither does this address from the other that holds me hostage teach me prescribed responsibility. Rather, it stages responsibility as an indeterminate, interminable labor of response. This labor of response can only take place in the space of difference between the self who is held hostage to an imperative, and the self who is free to step out into the daylight.

The scene of address staged by this coming-upon-the-milk-can sets the stage for grasping how responsibility does not follow from understanding or knowledge. Rather, responsibility, Thomas Keenan argues, is the condition of a structure of address.[46] Paraphrasing Keenan, I come upon the milk can and I become hostage to a structure of address for which there is no escape, no end. The contents of this artifact are addressed—to me. I am the posterity for whom its contents were assembled and buried. And yet, as Keenan declares, "there is nothing special about me, no preordained election nominates me for responsibility—no matter how irreplaceable, I could be (I am) anyone."[47] He continues: "There is a cry for help, addressed not to me in particular, not to anyone in particular, but to me as anyone—anyone can help."[48]

I, walking alongside others in the exhibit, turn a corner and enter this scene of address staged by the Ringelblum milk can. Suddenly, no matter how crowded this public space might be, I am alone. The address to me is "a public address with a strangely singular destination. . . ."[49] Alone, singular, and yet replaceable; alone because replaceable, a substitute for anyone and the one for whom anyone can substitute. Quoting Blanchot, Keenan continues: "I am the one whom anyone at all can replace . . . but one for whom nonetheless there is no dispensation: I must answer to and for what I am not."[50]

Keenan argues that if I fail to identify or to acknowledge the address of the messages inside the milk can—this "in no way disqualifies me or indemnifies me—the cry . . . insures that I remain in place, even if it is not 'my' place."[51] It is the call of the address—not anything special or "heroic" about me—that becomes the condition of my response.

Paraphrasing Keenan, I have not been preordained by the writers of this artifact's contents as the one for whom they are intended. Nor do I assume responsibility by virtue of my virtues, much less my knowledge, my wisdom, or my experience. My responsibility is not constituted by anything "in me," such as my interests, desires, compulsions, ideology, or educated ability to reference rules of ethics or democracy. I simply happen to be there, without deserving it.[52]

How will I respond within the structure of the Ringelblum milk can's address? It is impossible to know or to understand the Holocaust fully, or finally. And so I cannot construct a response to the address of the contents of the milk can by successfully articulating what I know to what I do. Its address stages an impasse. I am the singular one addressed. And yet I am the replaceable no one in particular who is addressed. Who, then, "takes" responsibility in response to the address? The moment of meeting the address of the call is not a moment of responsible decision-making by one who "takes responsibility." There is no "taking" of responsibility. Keenan argues:

> I do not respond or find myself obligated because some self precedes mine and addresses me, but because I am always already involved and entangled with others, always caught up in answering, from the start: we begin by responding.[53]

Coming upon the Ringelblum milk can, I reach an impasse. I cannot pass by without inaugurating the psychic split that Muschamp described. Part of me does not leave. It is hostage to a structure of address for which there is no escape, no end. There is no final, responsible "answer" that I might give that would release me from this scene, as if in reward for learning the lessons of this museum.

The U.S. Holocaust Memorial Museum as a Scene of Address

Who does the pedagogy of this museum think I am? If this museum is a pedagogical masterpiece, it is because it does not address me "as" a victim, perpetrator, bystander, rescuer, or liberator of the Holocaust. It does not reinscribe the very positions and address that were the condition of the Holocaust in the name of preventing another. Rather, this museum is a pedagogical masterpiece because it stages a scene of address that is the condition of responsibility.

In that scene of address, the pedagogy of the Memorial Museum does not presume to know who I am or who I should become. Rather, this museum addresses me "as" the no one who is always already hostage to its ongoing scene of address. By refusing to suggest, or rather, to teach me how I could or should respond, its pedagogy does not leave me "free" to make my own (informed) decisions. Rather, refusing to teach me my response, it refuses to release me from an ongoing predicament. It is the predicament of not being able to leave this scene of address. There is no responsible act that I could perform that would put an end to the Holocaust.

If the pedagogy of this museum is a masterpiece, in other words, it is because it knows the limits of pedagogy, and puts them to productive use. The pedagogy of the permanent exhibit—the position it offers its "students" within its structure of address—not only refuses to seek refuge in religious or rationalistic myths. It also refuses to seek refuge in educationalistic myths. Myths such as: "responsibility can be taught," "the Holocaust can be taught," "the needs of the student of the permanent exhibit can be known and met," "understanding leads to responsibility."

The terms of the address of the Ringelblum milk can to those who encounter it are not accidental, given, or arbitrary. They are staged. All elements of the Memorial Museum's exhibit work together to make it happen, to set it in place. They are not inspired by any particular educational theory or practice. Rather, they are a social and cultural achievement aimed precisely at staging responsibility as an indeterminate, interminable labor of response.

Refusing the "Last Word" in Teaching About and Across Social and Cultural Difference

The silence that meets the visitor at the end of the exhibit, and that in turn invites the visitor's own silence, is not simply the silence of a narrative without closure, a story without an ending. Rather, it is the silence at the end of a story that will never end. A story that is always in-the-making. Designers of the Memorial Museum use this silence to structure a pedagogical address that implicates visitors in a knowing that is never complete, never mastered. It implicates us in a knowing that contains within it an inescapable and profound not-knowing.

Far from being the not-knowing of willful ignore-ance or unconscious denial, the position of not-knowing offered to the visitors of this museum is a refusal to give the last word or to presume to know the last word. It is a refusal of the heroic position of mastery. Far from being a refusal of responsibility, it instead marks the struggle to construct a new subject position in relation to the Holocaust. Namely, the position of one who is implicated in the task of the Memorial Museum itself—the task of producing an ongoing social and cultural response to the Holocaust that never bewitches itself with the desire for, or illusion of, completeness.

The Memorial Museum has begun the cultural and pedagogical labor of creating this new type of hero. The structure of its pedagogical address is designed to implicate visitors in the contingency of knowledge and belief—even in the face of Auschwitz. Especially in the face of Auschwitz. Its structure of address implicates visitors in the inescapable task of producing an interminable response. By structuring its pedagogy through a silence that marks the limits of teaching and knowing, by refusing to be either master or mastered, this museum, paradoxically, gives access to an interminable teaching and learning.

As a genre of academic writing, research and criticism about pedagogical practice often drives toward concluding statements that offer "best practices," "effective teaching strategies," or prescriptions for "educational interventions." Such an ending would contradict this essay's own pedagogy and the pedagogical project of the Memorial Museum itself. Rather than offering an end to an interminable process through pedagogical prescriptions designed to "cure" ignore-ance or forgetting, the reading I offer of this pedagogical site attempts to provide questions and perspectives that can be carried over into other pedagogical sites, opportunities, and problems. Carried over, that is, with the clear imperative not to imitate, but to return a difference. Pedagogies inspired or informed by that of the Memorial Museum must necessarily depart from it if they are to address the unique possibilities and problems of new pedagogical challenges. The imperative is to work the questions and perspectives offered here, or in any "pedagogical text," in and through new sites so that the new sites teach and transform our settled pedagogical assumptions.

I believe that the value of readings like the one I have tried to offer is their ability to provide "inspirational data"—data that can stimulate educational imaginations and pedagogical design, rather than simply define a set of supposedly replicable pedagogical strategies. Readings that trace the structures of address that this museum's "pedagogical masterpiece" crystallizes in image, text, sequence, duration, space, juxtaposition, might apprentice us to the exquisite contextual responsiveness required if we are to shape pedagogical designs to their subjects and to their sites.[54]

Notes

1. Leon Wieseltier, "After Memory: Reflections on the Holocaust Memorial Museum," *New Republic* (May 3, 1993): 20.
2. Adrian Dannatt, *Architecture in Detail: United States Holocaust Memorial Museum* (London: Phaidon Press, 1995), 6.
3. Mark Goldberg, "The Holocaust and Education: An Interview with Michael Berenbaum," *Phi Delta Kappa* 79 (December 1997): 319.
4. Edward Linenthal, *Preserving Memory: The Struggle to Create America's Holocaust Museum* (New York: Viking Press, 1995).
5. Shoshana Felman and Dori Laub, "Education and Crisis, or the Vicissitudes of Teaching," in *Trauma: Explorations in Memory*, ed. Cathy Caruth (Baltimore: Johns Hopkins University Press, 1995); and Jean Copjec, ed., *Radical Evil* (New York: Verso, 1996).
6. Claude Lanzmann, "Hier is kein Warum," in *Au sujet de Shoah: Le film de Claude Lanzmann*, ed. Bernard Cuau, et al. (Paris: Belin, 1990).
7. Lanzmann, "Hier is kein Warum," 279.
8. Shoshana Felman, *Jacques Lacan and the Adventure of Insight: Psychoanalysis in Contemporary Culture* (Cambridge: Harvard University Press, 1987), 16.
9. Dannatt, *Architecture in Detail*, 5.
10. Wieseltier, "After Memory," 19.
11. Wieseltier, "After Memory," 19.
12. Art Spiegelman, interview on National Public Radio (April 1999).
13. Linenthal, *Preserving Memory*.
14. Dannatt, *Architecture in Detail*, 5.
15. Michael Sorkin, "The Holocaust Museum: Between Beauty and Horror," *Progressive Architecture* 2 (1993), 74.
16. Dannatt, *Architecture in Detail*, 6.
17. Dannatt, *Architecture in Detail*, 17.
18. Dannatt, *Architecture in Detail*, 18.
19. Dannatt, *Architecture in Detail*, 18.
20. Dannatt, *Architecture in Detail*, 14.

21. Herbert Muschamp, "Shaping a Monument to Memory," *The New York Times* (April 11, 1993): 22.
22. Felman, *Jacques Lacan and the Adventure of Insight*, 114.
23. Felman, *Jacques Lacan and the Adventure of Insight*, 88.
24. Jeshajahu Weinberg and Rina Elieli, *The Holocaust Museum in Washington* (New York: Rizzoli International Publications, 1995), 17.
25. Weinberg and Elieli, *The Holocaust Museum in Washington*, 17.
26. Weinberg and Elieli, *The Holocaust Museum in Washington*, 19.
27. Adam Phillips, *On Flirtation: Psychoanalytic Essays on the Uncommitted Life* (Cambridge: Harvard University Press, 1994), 122.
28. Phillips, *On Flirtation*, 122.
29. Phillips, *On Flirtation*, 75.
30. Dannatt, *Architecture in Detail*, 14.
31. Felman, *Jacques Lacan and the Adventure of Insight*, 32.
32. Phillips, *On Flirtation*, 144.
33. Wieseltier, "After Memory," 20.
34. Felman, *Jacques Lacan and the Adventure of Insight*, 53.
35. Felman, *Jacques Lacan and the Adventure of Insight*, 30.
36. Felman, *Jacques Lacan and the Adventure of Insight*, 30.
37. Felman, *Jacques Lacan and the Adventure of Insight*, 24.
38. Felman, *Jacques Lacan and the Adventure of Insight*, 31.
39. Weinberg and Elieli, *The Holocaust Museum in Washington*, 19.
40. Ernesto Laclau, *Emancipations* (New York: Verso, 1996), 123.
41. Laclau, *Emancipations*, 123.
42. Weinberg and Elieli, *The Holocaust Museum in Washington*, 108.
43. Weinberg and Elieli, *The Holocaust Museum in Washington*, 17.
44. Weinberg and Elieli, *The Holocaust Museum in Washington*, 108.
45. Muschamp, "Shaping a Monument to Memory," 32.
46. Thomas Keenan, *Fables of Responsibility: Aberrations and Predicaments in Ethics and Politics* (Stanford: Stanford University Press, 1997), 19–23.
47. Keenan, *Fables of Responsibility*, 21.
48. Keenan, *Fables of Responsibility*, 22.
49. Keenan, *Fables of Responsibility*, 57.
50. Keenan, *Fables of Responsibility*, 58.
51. Keenan, *Fables of Responsibility*, 23.
52. Keenan, *Fables of Responsibility*, 23.
53. Keenan, *Fables of Responsibility*, 32.
54. Research for this chapter was supported in part by a Research Grant from the Memorial Foundation for Jewish Culture.

CHAPTER 6

Pilgrimage to My Lai
Social Memory and the Making of Art

CAROL BECKER

Vietnam the War never ends. It lurks in the shadows of U.S. history and emerges at difficult moments to stir up a past thick with denial.

The Stain

On March 16, 1968, the men of the 11th Brigade entered the village of My Lai, which they called Pinkville, and brutally murdered 504 Vietnamese civilians in a period of four hours. This "search and destroy" mission (Gen. William Westmoreland's strategy of "flushing out" the Vietcong from their countryside "safe havens") soon transformed into a bloody massacre: "The killings took place, part maniacally, part methodically, over a period of about four hours," write Michael Bilton and Kevin Sim in *Four Hours in My Lai,* their chilling account of what happened on that day.[1] Several women were gang-raped and killed with unconscionable brutality. Infants were blasted with machine-gun fire. The troops, whose average age was just twenty, were known as Charlie Company. They were under the leadership of Lt. William Calley—a name that has become synonymous with the nightmare of the war. He took his orders from Capt. Ernest Medina, who received his commands from even higher up. Those names still have not been spoken.

Lt. Calley was said to have forced a group of 100 to 170 villagers into a ditch and, without hesitation, slaughtered them all himself. Because of the nature of the war and the U.S. Army's philosophy of killing "Vietcong in such large numbers that they could not be replaced,"[2] because of the pressure on unit commanders to produce enemy corpses, because it was so difficult for U.S. soldiers to "see the enemy" waging this guerrilla war, and because U.S. soldiers were being blown up constantly by land mines planted by this unseen enemy, "it is not surprising that some men acquired a contempt for human life and a predilection for taking it," observe Bilton and Sim. "In this sense," they continue, "My Lai was not an aberration of the war, but its apotheosis."[3]

This event was one of the turning points in U.S. citizens' perceptions of the extreme brutality of the war. American soldiers had entered an unarmed village firing, killing everyone and everything alive: women, old men, children, babies, and animals. They then torched each house and all the vegetation surrounding the village. Even though it was clear within minutes of the attack that there were no Vietcong in the village, that no one was armed and no one was returning fire, U.S. soldiers, having been told it was a Vietcong stronghold and that they were "to destroy everything in sight," did not desist from that directive.

"It was worse than a massacre," write Bilton and Sim. "Too many of Medina's men were taking sordid pleasure in sadistic behavior."[4] It was this added realization that deeply disturbed all who heard about the massacre.

In fact, it was only because soldiers had been bragging about what had occurred in My Lai for almost a year, that GI Ron Ridenhour, twenty-one years old, even heard about the massacre. He wrote letters to congressmen telling them that something awful and "bloody" had occurred. As a result of his insistence, a serious investigation took place. American army photographer Ronald Haeberle, who documented the massacre, was also key to this investigation. His photographs were used to substantiate the claim that only civilians had been murdered and in the most brutal ways. The following are among the accounts given by GIs to investigators:[5]

> An old papa-san was found hiding. His pants kept coming off. Two GIs dragged him out to be questioned. He was trying to keep his pants on. Captain Medina was doing the questioning. The old man didn't know anything. He rattled something off. Somebody asked Captain Medina what to do with Tehran, and Jay Roberts heard the captain say, "I don't care." Captain Medina walked away and Roberts heard a shot; the old man was dead.

> I remember . . . two small children, one boy and one girl, kept walking toward us on this trail. They just kept walking toward us, you know, very nervously, very afraid, and you could hear the little girl saying, "No, no," in the Vietnamese tongue. The girl was on the right

and the boy was on the left. All of a sudden, the GIs just opened up and cut them down.

Off to the right a woman's form, a head, appeared from some brush. All the other GIs started firing at her, aiming at her, firing at her over and over again. She had slumped over into one of those things that stick out of the rice paddies so that her head was a propped-up target. There was no attempt to question her or anything. They just kept shooting at her. You could see the bones flying in the air chip by chip. . . .

Women were gang raped; Vietnamese who had bowed to greet the Americans were beaten with fists and tortured, clubbed with rifle butts, and stabbed with bayonets. Some victims were mutilated with the signature "C Company" carved into the chest.

The men who participated in these brutalities had lost many fellow soldiers in the recent Tet Offensive—the massive attacks on cities throughout South Vietnam that took place at the time of *Tet*—the lunar New Year in Vietnam. They had been told there *would* be Vietcong in the village, that it would be "hot" and they could get their revenge. Somewhere in all this lunacy these men lost their humanity and became rogue animals out for the kill. To them the Vietnamese were not civilians. They were not even human. Even babies were no exception; all were simply "the enemy."

In the midst of this frenzy of objectification and revenge, however, there were some men who simply refused to participate. They saw what was happening and condemned it. Among them was Herbert Carter, an African-American soldier who shot himself in the foot; it is assumed because he did not want to take part in the massacre. There were helicopter pilot Hugh Thompson, door gunner Lawrence Colburn, and crew chief Glenn Adreotta, who landed their helicopter between rampaging American troops and the people of My Lai village. Thompson literally stood between the American troops and the bunker, shielding Vietnamese civilians with his body. He told his men in the helicopter; "If any of the Americans open up on the Vietnamese we should open up on the Americans." On March 6, 1998, thirty years later, two of these men received the Soldier's Medal from the U.S. government.

The American people did not know about the massacre at My Lai when it actually occurred. A year and a half later, discharged GIs who refused to let the story go brought it to the attention of the military, as well as to writers and journalists. In November 1969 Seymour M. Hersh wrote a piece called "Hamlet Attack Called 'Point-Blank Murder'" in which he quoted a sergeant interviewed who said, "A few days before the mission, the men's general contempt for Vietnamese civilians intensified when some GIs walked into a land mine, injuring nearly 20 and killing at least one member of the company."[6]

There is no doubt that once the horror of My Lai was understood outside the military, it changed the course of the war. Innocent Vietnamese civilians were dying. American soldiers were dying. And many of the American soldiers who were still living had become sadistic and monstrous. It was clear that the American people had been misled by their government and did not know the level of brutality that was occurring daily. But once those outside the military were informed, many could not in good conscience allow the war to continue. The specific horrors of My Lai helped accelerate a growing consciousness that the war simply had to end.

Thirty-Four Years Later: Going to My Lai

After my first visit to Vietnam in 1996, I knew I would return with students. The thought of visiting the sites of the war and examining America's complex historical relationship to this country, as well as the possibility of exploring the many anthropological and art museums in the major cities and the wealth of Buddhist art throughout Vietnam, was too great a pedagogical opportunity not to pursue.

I did return in January 2002, with other faculty members—filmmaker Jeffrey Skoller and art historian Stanley Murashige—and ten students. We organized many expeditions during this trip together, but perhaps the most significant to many of us was the journey to My Lai. We came to call it a pilgrimage. This essay is my response to that experience.

As faculty, our basic intention for the trip was to take students who may have had only a vague understanding of what occurred in Vietnam and afford them an experience of the war and the country through the specificity of site. We hoped such explorations would, by analogy, translate into contemporary situations and help the students gain awareness of the historical and ongoing contradictions of American foreign policy. Within the context of the daily bombing of Afghanistan, often resulting in civilian casualties documented by the media, U.S. foreign policy was once again deeply in question.

The students who accompanied us were a mixture of undergraduate and graduate. Most, in their twenties, were not even born when the war was taking place, yet each of them felt drawn to Vietnam and wanted to move from thinking of Vietnam as a war to understanding it as a country. They were adventurers. Some had already traveled to distant places, others had never left the U.S. None had been to Southeast Asia. Joining us as our research assistant was Vu Thu, a young artist I had met on my first visit to Hanoi. She subsequently came to the School of the Art Institute of Chicago as a post-baccalaureate student and was then accepted into the Master's program in painting. For her, the trip had a different meaning: she was going home.

By traveling with us, she was choosing to encounter Vietnam through the eyes of Americans, some still filled with guilt for themselves and their country. Although many Vietnamese do not want to dwell on the past, many Americans of my generation still suffer the pain of what happened during the war. When I told a Vietnamese woman in a shop in Hoi An that we had visited My Lai, she said, "Don't feel bad about what you saw. We know it was your government and not you."

Like most of the students, Vu Thu was born right after the war ended, although her experience, of course, had been extraordinarily different from those of our other students. Her early years were steeped in poverty, reflecting the struggle of her parents and her country to recover economically. She had never traveled to the places we were going, and she had never even been to Ho Chi Minh City—the former Saigon. For her, the trip was a revelation. She was experiencing the totality of her country for the first time. And because she was willing to see Vietnam through our eyes, we had an opportunity to see it through hers.

Our goal was to visit many of the places whose names became well known to Americans during the war. We wanted to experience those places now—to connect with what remains of the past in the present and to gain an understanding of what happened at those sites. In this spirit we visited Hanoi and Ho Chi Minh City. We boated down the Mekong River. We stopped at the DMZ (Demilitarized Zone) and drove to Khe Sahn and the coast of China Beach. We passed through Danang. We stayed in Hue. And of course we made a pilgrimage to My Lai, known to the Vietnamese now as Son My (pronounced *shun me*).

Of all the sites we visited over our three-week journey, no other had the psychological and emotional impact of My Lai. We absorbed the nightmare that had occurred there, and left transformed. Without thinking too much about the weightiness of the term, some of us began to call the visit to My Lai a "pilgrimage," probably choosing this word because of our awareness that we wanted to know the place not just through the mind, but more deeply, in the body. This is the type of secular experience many of us associated with pilgrimage and, in such thinking, we were not alone.

Freud Visits the Acropolis

Although we generally associate pilgrimage with a deeply religious notion of transformation through peripatetic movement, many pilgrimages induce unique effects—the result of physically going to a place of symbolic meaning.

In 1936, late in his life, Sigmund Freud wrote an essay called "A Disturbance of Memory on the Acropolis." It was a tribute to writer Romain Rolland on Rolland's seventieth birthday.[7] The essay recounts a trip Freud made with his brother to Athens some thirty years before and the multifarious meanings he extracted from that journey.

The essay begins with this narrative: Presented with the possibility of visiting Athens, Freud becomes both depressed and anxious. Although he has always wanted to visit the Acropolis, has always dreamed of what it would be like, for complex and remarkably neurotic reasons (such as not wanting to usurp his father), Freud cannot believe that he might actually have the opportunity to do so. When he finally does, a series of unexpected emotions dominates his response. But most significant in the context of our visit to My Lai, Freud realizes, once at the site, that he never fully believed the Acropolis existed, that it was in fact *there*, or *anywhere*.

"If I may make a slight exaggeration," Freud writes, "it was as if someone, walking beside Loch Ness, suddenly caught sight of the form of the famous Monster stranded upon the shore and found himself driven to the admission: So it really *does* exist—the sea-serpent we've never believed in!"[8] The fact of the "occurrence of this idea on the Acropolis" had precisely shown Freud that in his unconscious he "had *not* believed in it." Only by *going* did he come to understand, as he says, that he could acquire a "conviction" in its existence that "reached down to the unconscious."

At first his conscious and unconscious minds could not come together in an integrative fashion to accept the reality of place, even though he stood on the physical site and understood, at least in his mind, that he was at the most luminous place of antiquity—the sacred rock where one went to worship the gods, the *Acro-polis*—the place *above the city.*

Such feelings of dissociation often accompany our arrival at a much-anticipated place or experience of a long-awaited event, giving the sensation that we are not "all there," or that what is taking place is not "really happening." At more devastating moments, when consciousness splits and cannot accept the reality of what has occurred, this can lead to a sense of living in a bad dream from which one soon will awaken. Depression and anxiety result when one realizes that there is no awakening *from*, no place to awaken *to*, for one is already awake.

Another form of surprising dissociation can occur when what happens is, as we say, "too good to be true." Something we never imagined occurs. Because we are in disbelief that such a thing could happen to us, we assume it cannot be true. This occurrence may simulate a pleasant dream, but we might think it cannot possibly be *our* dream. Or if it is our dream, then we will soon awaken. This explains why we often fail to experience the best moments of our lives. The multiple bodies of consciousness are unable to completely internalize the event.

Traveling to places of great symbolic significance can embody all this complexity and more. One goes to know the place in the physical body, to have an experience of the place, and then to have that experience recorded somewhere in the body, so it then can be accessed as memory by the mind and the spirit. Such journeys are performative rituals. The *going to* and the *being there* require preparation and are dependent on the body for completion of the experience.

Perhaps this is why we called our journey to My Lai a pilgrimage. For those of us who lived through the Vietnam War, even the name sent a sick reverberation through the cells of our bodies. For the younger generation, there was a great deal to learn about the event before they could feel the impact of the name, the place, and the trauma that had occurred there. But by the end of the journey, we were all equally turned inside ourselves, creating a type of silence that occurs when humans struggle, in their bodies, to absorb an excess of pain.

The Nature of Pilgrimage

Various conditions are associated with the notion of pilgrimage. The most primary is the simple movement away from and toward place. Peter Harbison, in *Pilgrimage in Ireland,* writes: "What sparked the first Christian pilgrimage was the desire felt by St. Paul to stand on the same ground the Savior had trodden."[9]

One needs to leave the mundaneity of one's life and become a seeker of that which is sacred: in oneself, in the world, and in those metaphysical realms that cannot be known in this world. In order to set out on a pilgrimage, space must metamorphose into metaphor. Once the journey has begun, the ground one walks on, the distance one travels, becomes a mirror for the evolution of one's own spirituality. This is an important element of pilgrimage—while walking, journeying, traveling to a designated place, the act of getting there is as important as the arrival. During that time of travel, it is assumed that one will undergo a certain transformation of consciousness that cannot be achieved when one is immersed in daily life. Harbison continues, "The act of going on pilgrimage is common to many religions, not only Christianity but Islam, Hinduism, and Buddhism as well. Nomadic people feel no need for it, as they are on the move anyway. It is a phenomenon found only among settled communities, usually those which have a considerable cultural development behind them."[10]

The act of going on pilgrimage may derive from a desire to seek absolution, but it might also be an expression of pain and compassion. It might come from needing or wanting something for oneself or one's loved ones, or, as in the case of our visit to My Lai, it might be a symbolic gesture, not only for oneself, but also for one's country: an attempt to resolve what remains unresolved. Whatever the motivation, there is a purposefulness about such a journey that separates it from the randomness and pleasure-seeking of mundane travel. The intention of this type of journey is not to change the world, but to change oneself: to achieve a consciousness and spiritual transformation while connecting with the history of others who have trodden the same path.

The time of the journey (which for the pilgrims of the Middle Ages might have extended over years) becomes mythic. It moves us into another, more informal way of measuring time that is much more internal and upon which one places a great deal of symbolic meaning. If this meaning is shared by a large group of people, as it often is when connected to famous sites of pilgrimage such as Croagh Patrick in Ireland or Santiago de Compostela in Spain—then the journey takes place in mythic time and mythic space. In *Roads to Santiago,* Cees Nooteboom writes:[11]

> It is impossible to prove and yet I believe it: there are some places in the world where one is mysteriously magnified on arrival or departure by the emotions of all those who have arrived and departed before. . . .

> At the entrance of the cathedral in Santiago de Compostela there is a marble column with deep impressions of fingers, an emotional, expressionistic claw created by millions of hands . . . by laying my hand in the hollow one I was participating in a collective work of art. An idea becomes visible in matter. . . . The power of an idea impelled kings, peasants, monks to lay their hands on exactly that spot on the column, each successive hand removed the minutest particle of marble so that, precisely where the marble had been erased, a negative hand became visible.

This is the symbolic made manifest through gesture. You can only participate in this collective act by physically standing in the exact place others have stood: St. Paul's motivation to stand where Christ had stood.

One can speak of sites that have seen pilgrims for centuries, like Santiago de Compostela, but one can also speak of places that have become sacred overnight, like the former World Trade Center. At first the World Trade Center was a site of horrific devastation, but it quickly became a place of visitation and mourning for New Yorkers, and then for those who traveled to the city. Now there is a viewing platform from which people can observe the site of the buildings' collapse. There is no longer anything physical to see—just a gigantic absence—but nonetheless, people come to pay homage. And to see with their own eyes, to feel in their own bodies the tremendous emptiness that remains. At least for now, until there is new construction, this deep pit will be considered hallowed ground that memorializes the thousands who died there.

The authors of *Image and Pilgrimage in Christian Culture* write that "a tourist is half a pilgrim, if a pilgrim is half a tourist."[12] We might say that one difference between pilgrims and tourists is that for pilgrims, the road *to* the site, the process of getting there, is as important as the arrival. It is filled with the anticipation of some spiritual event that will occur as they travel, when they arrive, and while they are there. This of course can be true of tourism as well: one can anticipate the Cathedral at Cologne, the Pyramids, or even the Acropolis as did Freud, with a sense that after having experienced these phenomena, one will never be the same. The difference is that a great deal of tourism is about consumption and acquisition of culture, the natural landscape, or both. One seeks out certain places because it is believed that to be a cultured or worldly person, one must have the experience of visiting them: Venice, Paris, Istanbul, the Grand Canyon, Niagara Falls, the Nile. One visits, just to have seen them, just to know, in a sense, what all the fuss is about. In this acquisitive mode, all will photograph, and some will physically take something from the site: stones from the foundation of the Parthenon, pieces of the Berlin Wall, magazine cutouts of movie stars from the wall of Anne Frank's bedroom in the Annex; maybe fake, maybe stolen, ancient ceramic turtles, sold at the site of Monte Albán. Others would be horrified to remove anything from such sites and will want to alchemize the experience psychically. Pilgrims, in particular, journey for the spirit, seeking purification or the granting of a wish or a prayer, while most others who travel are attracted by the external phenomena they might encounter. Some even want to circumvent the *going* entirely. I was quite taken aback when my mother suggested, only a bit tongue-in-cheek, that my trip to and time spent in Bellagio, Italy, could have been avoided by simply visiting Bellagio, Las Vegas. "You don't really need to travel anymore. You have it all in Las Vegas," she said. Some will be satisfied with simulacra. Others will always have to go.

But why? What does one want from such experiences? For those who have studied art history, the thought of actually seeing the paintings of Fra Angelico in Florence in the cells and niches of the Dominican priory for which they were painted is comparable to a religious experience; not because of the content of the paintings per se, but because one is transformed by what Walter Benjamin refers to as "aura," the experience of the art, as it was meant to be had in its intended actual location. No matter how many replicas of the Acropolis we might find in Nashville, Tennessee, there is nothing like standing on the actual site: the air, the light, the position of the rock over the city embracing its totality from 360 degrees, and its arched posture looking down at the Agora, the place in which it has stood since antiquity, are transformative. The experience links the traveler, pilgrim, tourist with history and, in this case, with the evolution of Western Civilization. It makes the past present, transforms the present into the past. Walking up to the Acropolis or down from it, one imagines that the cicadas one hears have been there for centuries. Nothing you can read, no simulations you may see, can give you that experience. And why is that? Because the experience takes place only through the sensation of the flesh. It is the physical knowing that links us to the body of collective memory.

There is a moveable wall called *The Wall that Heals* that simulates the permanent Vietnam Veterans Memorial designed by Maya Lin. The portable wall, which is a half-scale replica made of powder-coated aluminum, can never embody the physical and spiritual gravity of the actual granite wall. It has not absorbed the pain of the millions who have come to the actual wall as mourners and supplicants for twenty years now, praying on behalf of those who died. And although many viewers find the portable wall powerful, it cannot hold the weight of the 58,000 Americans and all the Vietnamese who died or the faith in the United States that died for many with the pain and shame that accompanied the war. At the actual wall in Washington, D.C., one doesn't even need to see the wall to feel its presence. Walking towards it, one begins to internalize the palpable sadness of the thousands who have come before. The memorial has become a repository for all the complex emotions associated with the war. For many Vietnam veterans it has become a destination for pilgrimage.

Such space is the opposite of nonspace, mall-space, suburban space, corporate, generic, or interchangeable space—the spaces of postmodernity. The Vietnam Veterans Memorial is well-designed and conceptualized space that has become ritualized through the spontaneity of the masses. As the artist/architect of this project, Maya Lin could never have imagined how her design would be transformed.

The Vietnam Veterans Memorial was also immediately turned into a site of offering by all the visitors who brought things to it. Soon a museum will be built to house the collection of objects left at the wall. Similarly, handmade altars immediately marked the perimeter of Ground Zero: candles, flowers, photos, offerings.

Pilgrimages have always been democratic in just this way. For the Greeks, the long journey to Delphi was about locating the future, the travel to Eleusis about finding the Mysteries—the fate that would befall them after death. In Christianity such pilgrimages existed outside the hierarchy of the church and the domain of priests and clerics. They arose spontaneously. Their perpetuation built community. Seekers of all kinds became equal as they undertook the journey. Because every pilgrim who comes must walk up the very difficult mountain of shale to get to the top of Croagh Patrick, the journey becomes about the community that is formed each time by those making it. They all find, in turn, their own internal peace through the process. Historically, when seekers could not physically go on such journeys, there were simulated pilgrimages close to home, such as that designed for the cathedral of Chartres. One could walk the length of the pilgrimage "in time" in the cathedral's eleven-circuit stone labyrinth set in the nave. This could serve as a substitute for the actual pilgrimage to Jerusalem and as a result came to be known as *Chemin de Jerusalem* or Road to Jerusalem. But in the actual journeys, the going is far different than the return, or as Victor and Edith Turner write: "Indeed, even when pilgrims return by the way they came, the total journey may still be represented, not unfittingly, by an ellipse, if psychological factors are taken into account. For the return road is, psychologically, different from the approach road."[13] The purposefulness and focus of the *going* may be over, while the *returning* to one's own life is full of a new expectation—that one will somehow return transformed.

Why Did We Go? What Did We Find?

On the bus from Hue to My Song, the district in which My Lai is located, we were, as usual, rather active and boisterous—asking our guide where he was during the war, how his life had been during that time. Students were talking to each other, writing in their journals, listening to music, cramming as much information as they could about the place we were about to visit. Engaged with the magnificence of the landscape, faculty and students alike were also photographing or filming out the windows. But the road back, although physically the same (there is only one North/South route through Vietnam), was not the road previously traveled. On the journey back, there was silence.

What did we find at My Lai? Everything and nothing. Nothing, of course, remains of the village. There are now only headstones where houses once stood. Engraved into each are the names of those who died. The engraving might say, "Foundation of Mr. Phon Cong's house burnt by U.S. Soldiers, four of his family members were murdered. Phan Hong 65, Le Thi Duoc 36, Phan San 12, Phan Thi Tranh 6." "Foundation of Mr. Nguyen Cai's house burnt by U.S. soldiers. Three of his family members were murdered: Phung Thi Hiep 31, Nguyen Thi Hwe 12, Nguyen Thi Be 3." These were the people in the village when the Americans arrived—mothers, children, grandparents. At each stone where there was once a house, there is now a place to burn incense for the dead, provided for us at the entrance to the site. There is also the ditch, now overgrown with plants, but still unmistakable as the site into which between 100 and 170 people were pushed, then shot. Jasmine and hibiscus have overgrown this site, which is now as green and resplendent as the rest of the Vietnamese countryside.

There is one stucco structure, and in this building are large black-and-white and color photographs, very specific, about the massacre. After looking at several and reading the captions that appear next to them in Vietnamese and English, one realizes that for these photos to exist at all, someone had to be watching the massacre while it was occurring and, more astoundingly, documenting it. Then you read the text: The photographer taking the pictures was Ronald Haeberle, the official U.S. Army photographer assigned to that platoon on that day. The images taken for the army and those he took with his own camera for himself became important evidence in the investigation to prove that a massacre had actually occurred. After the war, a set of prints was given to the Vietnamese government. They comprise a great deal of the material in the memorial museum.

The documentation allows us to walk through the massacre moment by moment—people being rounded up, terror on their faces. Children crying, clutching at their mothers. Very old, bony men walking toward the camera with their arms in the air in gestures of surrender. Piles of bodies in the ditch, one thrown over the other randomly, reminiscent of the mounds of human remains found at Bergen-Belsen after the camps were liberated in 1945. In the midst of this bedlam are photos of Lieutenant Thompson with a special declaration to his bravery and humanity. Even though he was only able to save one life, his gesture of refusal has earned him heroic status in Vietnam.

Taking up an entire wall is a list of all those who died: 504 names with ages. The long list is reminiscent of Maya Lin's wall of the dead, which is organized by date. The Vietnamese have organized those killed during the massacre in family clusters: The oldest in each family is listed first. The children are always last. This wall became the focal point for a performance created by two students on our return.

Transubstantiation

Perhaps it was the humility and lushness of the place, its green serenity. Or that we had traveled so far to get to it and then back to Hoi An that night, allowing time for contemplation. Or it was that this part of the journey was focused on one horrific incident in one annihilated village. Or it was because we had a very specific purpose in going there: to stand on the ground where the massacre had occurred and to pay homage to those who died. Through the particularity, perhaps we could almost imagine the magnitude of the totality.

We did not go to My Lai to judge. The verdict on that event was determined long ago. As Hannah Arendt said, in an interview given to Günter Grass in 1964, in reference to the death camps in Germany: "*This ought not to have happened. Something happened there, to which we cannot reconcile ourselves. None of us ever can.*"[14] My Lai, once a village, now a memorial, was determined to have been the site of a massacre by 1970. Lt. Calley was sentenced to life in prison, but this sentence was soon commuted and he actually only served four and a half years in a very well-protected and comfortable prison. He now runs his father-in-law's jewelry shop in Columbus, Georgia, where he drives a Mercedes-Benz given to him by a supporter and hides from reporters and others asking about the war.

Among less fortunate Vietnam veterans there have been many suicides, murders, and men incapacitated for civilian life whose tragic situations are traced to their involvement in My Lai. "The massacre had become a matter for individual conscience alone," write Bilton and Sim.[15] Those who set the policies and gave the orders, and the country that engaged in this war, have retained their psychic freedom, while those who followed the orders laid out by others, and were thus driven to horrific acts, live under a weight of guilt they cannot abide. Some of these individuals continue to suffer for their actions every day and will do so for the rest of their lives.

In 1977, the ten-year-old son of Vietnam veteran Varnardo Simpson was killed while playing in his front yard. Teenagers across the road began arguing. One pulled out a gun and a wild shot inadvertently hit the boy in the head. Varnardo Simpson will never recover. For him, his son's death marks his punishment for brutally killing twenty-five people in My Lai when he was twenty-five years old. Paranoid, he no longer leaves his house. As Bilton and Sim say, for Simpson, "Remembering has become a compulsion."[16]

These authors understand such men to be scapegoats in the Old Testament sense. They are like the "chosen goat"

> who, having had laid upon his head all the sins and transgressions of the Children of Israel, was then led by a fit man "unto a land not inhabited." These original scapegoats did not merely take the blame for the sins of others; they were machines for forgetting, for transporting as far away as possible, out of sight and out of mind, the sins of the entire community. Only after they had bathed their flesh and washed their clothes were the men who led the scapegoats into the wilderness allowed back to camp. For the scapegoats themselves, however, there was no return.[17]

By journeying to such a place as My Lai, it was our hope to develop our own form of absolution. Bilton and Sim write, "National Consciousness consists of what is allowed to be forgotten as much as by what is remembered."[18] The philosopher Giorgio Agamben writes: "Human beings are human in so far as they bear witness to the inhuman."[19] We came to bear witness through remembering and reclaiming memory across generations. I was as young as some of our students when I first had to take responsibility for my relationship to the war: Had I been male, would I have gone? As a female, what actions might I take to stop the war? How much was I willing to risk?

The silence on the bus on our return journey was our way of absorbing into our individual psyches what can hardly ever be absorbed—and that is tragedy—the unorganizable chaos generated through human volition that can be given shape and structure only by the writing of history and the making of art, forms that provide temporary containment for the uncontainable and allow the unspeakable to be spoken without destroying either the speaker or the audience.

Why do artists and writers, in particular, need to go to the actual place of trauma? What is it they hope to find? A quality of light? Past images juxtaposed to contemporary life? Words used to describe an event that will trigger a reaction and allow them to assume their roles as custodians of memory? Agamben quotes the poet Friedrich Hölderlein's statement that "What remains is what the poets found. . . . The poetic word is the one that is always situated in the position of a remnant and that can therefore bear witness . . . found language as what remains, as what actually survives the possibility, or impossibility, of speaking."[20]

If artists and writers are unique in their relationship to such journeys, it is that they are willing to bear witness and to do it by using such remnants to create an event or physical entity to mark their experience: a work of art, be it an essay, a poem, a film, a performance. However ephemeral, they will find a way to alchemize their internalization of the event into a further manifestation, filtered through the particularity of individual consciousness. In this way *their* work becomes interpretation, a gesture of remembering. Such responses—which often locate the humanity in the inhumanity—are as much about the person seeing as about the place being seen.

This is the transformative potential of art, its ability to take what is left of the incomprehensibility of human action and find a way to re-present it back into the collective; not to hide it or to hide from it, not to avoid the personal responsibility of collective action, but to allow the humanness in the inhumanity to be seen and its meaning made manifest. Such is the responsibility and challenge many of us feel to keep alive that which some would like to see dead. We can only hope that we will all be so completely revolted by what we see that we will finally understand that war destroys not only its victims, but also its perpetrators.

* * *

When we returned from the trip two students—American-born Jessica Almy Pagan and Vietnamese-born Vu Thu—constructed a durational performance, at the core of which Thu teaches Jessica to repeat, in correct Vietnamese, every name on the list of the 504 civilians killed on that day. By the rules Jessica established, she can only move on to the next name when she has correctly pronounced the preceding one. Needless to say, this takes time. The names are the remnants, all that remain of those who died. Her struggle to learn these names and say them correctly allows her to bear witness to the lives they represent.

Jessica became absorbed by the history of My Lai and deeply motivated to make it the subject of her work when she realized that at the exact time the massacre was taking place, between 9:00 a.m. and 1:00 p.m. on the morning of March 16, 1968, across the world and the international date line, she was being born. This exercise became her way of acknowledging each life that was lost. Witnessing in such a way allowed her to establish a relationship to each person who was killed that day. Perhaps she chose such literal speech so as not to be completely silent and to inhabit that space Agamben describes for such testimony, a liminal zone between the sayable and the unsayable. If My Lai causes silence, as an artist, Jessica has found a way to speak. She is one of the witnesses, who are "neither the dead nor the survivors, neither the drowned nor the saved." She is, in Agamben's term, "what remains between them."[21]

Such are the responses of those who travel to respond—pilgrims who come armed with cameras, tape recorders, notebooks, all in preparation to creatively reuse the traumas of the past. Not to hide from them or to hide them from us, not to obscure, but to clarify knowledge by moving it through the body, allowing it to leave its mark on us, like that already drawn onto the history of the world, those circles carved into the inner trunk of a gigantic tree that record the tumultuousness of nature and the tree's struggle to survive each year. If we become adept at reading such marks and making them our own, we might say:

> This was a year of much rain. This was a year of drought, and this was a year when something happened that we just cannot explain. All we know is that events etched an erratic, disturbed ellipse on the tree's core. Growth stopped for a time. Branches surely withered; some fell. With a mirror we can reverse the order of this knowledge and play it back. Our minds begin to reconstruct what occurred and absorb its

meaning. We wish we could erase the mark, see it gone forever. But the inscription is indelible and at times inaudible—a silent, persistent stain. Taking the body of this history into our own, we transform it and, through those forms available to us, respond.

Notes

1. Michael Bilton and Kevin Sim, *Four Hours in My Lai* (New York: Penguin Books, 1992), 3.
2. Bilton and Sim, *Four Hours in My Lai*, 32.
3. Bilton and Sim, *Four Hours in My Lai*, 14.
4. Bilton and Sim, *Four Hours in My Lai*, 14.
5. The first three accounts are from Hal Wingo, "The Massacre at My Lai," *Life* 67 (December 5, 1969): 36–45. Available online: http://karws.gso.uri.edu/Marsh/Vietnam/mylait01.htm. The last account is from "Murder in the Name of War—My Lai," BBC News Online (July 20, 1998), http://news.bbc.co.uk/1/low/world/asia-pacific/64344.htm
6. Seymour M. Hersh, "Hamlet Attack Called 'Point-Blank Murder,'" in *Reporting Vietnam*, Volume 2 (New York: Library of America, 1998), 19.
7. See Sigmund Freud, "A Disturbance of Memory on the Acropolis: An Open Letter to Romain Rolland on the Occasion of His Seventieth Birthday," in *Standard Edition of the Complete Psychological Works of Sigmund Freud*, Volume 22 (London: Hogarth Press, 1964).
8. Freud, "A Disturbance of Memory on the Acropolis," 241.
9. Peter Harbison, *Pilgrimage in Ireland: The Monuments and the People* (London: Rarrie and Jenkins, 1997), 23.
10. Harbison, *Pilgrimage in Ireland*, 23.
11. Cees Nooteboom, *Roads to Santiago: A Modern Day Pilgrimage through Spain* (New York: Harcourt, 1997), 3.
12. Victor Turner and Edith Turner, *Image and Pilgrimage in Christian Culture: Anthropological Perspectives* (New York: Columbia University Press, 1978), 20.
13. Turner and Turner, *Image and Pilgrimage in Christian Culture*, 32.
14. Giorgio Agamben, *Remnants of Auschwitz: The Witness and the Archive* (New York: Zone Books, 1999), 71.
15. Bilton and Sim, *Four Hours in My Lai*, 36.
16. Bilton and Sim, *Four Hours in My Lai*, 7.
17. Bilton and Sim, *Four Hours in My Lai*, 361.
18. Bilton and Sim, *Four Hours in My Lai*, 4.
19. Agamben, *Remnants of Auschwitz*, 121.
20. Agamben, *Remnants of Auschwitz*, 161.
21. Agamben, *Remnants of Auschwitz*, 164.

CHAPTER 7

Professionalism

What Graduate Students Need

ANDREW HOBEREK

In what follows, I argue that we need to think more seriously about graduate education as professional training: that is, as training geared towards preparing students to perform the work of professional academics.[1] Implicit in my argument is, of course, the idea that we don't do this now. The closest we now come is when we think about preparing our students "for the market." The sadly appropriate resonances of cattle ranching in this phrase aside, such preparation assumes that our students disappear once they get that magical call from the chair of another department. In this way training solely for the market is complicit with the fact, as John Guillory notes, that getting an academic job has become itself "the culmination of a successful career."[2] More practically, it leaves graduate students largely unprepared for the actual work they'll do once they land a job. Of course, there are certain things that one can learn only on the ground, but right now we carry this situation to an extreme: the resulting game of catch-up is one of the main reasons why (as everybody knows) "you can't get any writing done your first year."

This is a big problem, for which there is no simple fix. In what follows I'll discuss graduate training in my own field of English, both because its theory and practice are what I know best, and because English exemplifies an academic mindset that sees graduate training as fundamentally different from professional training, rather than a version of such training. My proposal for one course of action is as follows: I think that every PhD student should receive at some point on the way to their degree a one-course teaching release and instead be paid for a semester's worth of administrative activity in their department. This could take the form of working on a journal, serving on a labor-intensive committee, mentoring other graduate students, or other activities depending on the particular department. If this seems like a foolish (or possibly irrelevant; what does administrative work have to do with professional training?) plan of action, this is because—as I will discuss below—the profession operates under a falsely constrained notion of what constitutes its work. Thus, my suggestion is not aimed at maintaining the status quo; on the contrary, it's meant to serve the long-term goal of effecting institutional and cultural change within our departments.

Anti-Pedagogy

No one can teach you anything, not at the core, at the source of it.
—Henry Cameron, *The Fountainhead*

Ayn Rand's 1943 novel *The Fountainhead* tells the story of architect Howard Roark's heroic and ultimately triumphant struggle against the forces of professional and social conformity. Near the book's beginning Roark, who has been expelled from the Architectural School of the Stanton Institute of Technology, is called into the Dean's office and given a final chance to redeem himself. During this scene we learn that although Roark has excelled in his math and engineering courses, he has repeatedly refused to complete the historical exercises required by his professor of design. "When you were given projects that left the choice of style up to you and you turned in one of your wild stunts," the Dean tells him,

—well, frankly, your teachers passed you because they did not know what to make of it. *But*, when you were given an exercise in the historical styles, a Tudor chapel or a French opera house to design—and you turned in something that looked like a lot of boxes piled together without rhyme or reason—would you say it was an answer to an assignment or plain insubordination?[3]

Roark replies simply, "It was insubordination." Turning down an offer to return to the institution after he has taken a year off "to grow up," he informs his befuddled former dean, "I see no purpose in doing Renaissance villas. Why learn to design them when I'll never build them?"[4]

As anyone familiar with Rand's novel (or the 1949 film adaptation starring Gary Cooper) knows, Roark's interview with the Dean establishes the pattern that the rest of the novel more or less undeviatingly follows. Time and again, Roark defends his artistic integrity against those—employers, Boards of Directors, government bureaucrats—who want to tell him how to design buildings. Placed on trial at the novel's climax for blowing up a housing project whose builders perverted his original plans, Roark defends the values that fuel his antisocial work ethic. In a speech that moves the jury to acquit despite the fact that Roark admits to destroying the building, he delivers a paean to the individual creators who have, despite the opposition of their less daring fellow men, single-handedly driven the engine of human progress. "[T]he mind is an attribute of the individual," Roark tells those assembled in the courtroom, and thus

> There is no such thing as a collective brain. There is no such thing as a collective thought. Any agreement reached by a group of men is only a compromise or an average drawn upon individual thoughts. It is a secondary consequence. The primary act—the process of reason—must be performed by each man alone.[5]

Hence Roark's proprietary attitude towards his mental labor expresses not an individual preference, but the novel's moral horizon: "[O]nly by living for himself," Roark explains, is the innovator "able to achieve the things which are the glory of mankind."[6]

As the early scene between Roark and the Dean makes clear, this ethos has a pedagogical component as well, one subsequently expressed in the words of Roark's true mentor Henry Cameron: "No one can teach you anything." Cameron immediately qualifies his advice, although the qualification itself serves to reinforce his pedagogical point. "What you're doing," he tells Roark, "—it's yours, not mine, I can only teach you to do it better. I can give you the means, but the aim—the aim's your own."[7] Cameron can, that is—like the math and engineering that Roark does work to acquire at Stanton, or the construction experience he picks up on his summer breaks—provide the (merely) technical expertise necessary to shape the direction of Roark's natural genius. The novel even calls this limited influence into doubt, moreover. For while it does suggest that Cameron critiques Roark's work, it offers only the most oblique and self-contradictory representations of this process:

> Roark had come to this room every morning, had done his task, and had heard *no word of comment.* Cameron would enter the drafting room and stand behind Roark for a long time, looking over his shoulder. It was as if his eyes concentrated deliberately on trying to throw the steady hand off its course on the paper. . . . Roark *did not seem to notice it.* He went on, his hand unhurried, he took his time about discarding a blunted pencil and picking out another. "Uh-huh," Cameron would grunt suddenly. Roark would turn his head then, politely attentive. "What is it?" he would ask. Cameron would turn

away *without a word*, his narrowed eyes underscoring contemptu-
ously the fact that *he considered an answer unnecessary*, and would
leave the drafting room. Roark would go on with his drawing.[8]

The emphasis on non-communication in this passage points, I would
argue, to the impossible status of professional pedagogy in Rand's worldview.
Committed to the contradictory logic of a mentor who believes that no one
can teach you anything, Rand literally cannot represent the learning process.

Rand's novel would hardly seem like a good barometer for the current
state of graduate education. Yet nothing more accurately captures our relationship to graduate pedagogy than the sort of confused silence about professional training on display in the passage above, and in *The Fountainhead*
more generally. Sharon Stockton and Michael Szalay have recently argued
for Rand's engagement with such characteristic prewar forms of brain work
as civil engineering and modernist writing, but if anything her account of
mental labor assumes even greater cultural resonance during the postwar
years.[9] The academy provides no exception, as David Damrosch makes clear
in his compelling institutional critique *We Scholars*. In this book Damrosch
argues that academia as a whole—but particularly in the humanities, and
to a slightly lesser extent in the social sciences—is beset with an ethos of
"archaic hyperindividualism."[10] He credits this situation to a history of disciplinary and sub-disciplinary specialization that, reinforced by the reward
system of academic life and the institutional structures of higher education, selects for and rewards scholars inclined towards habits of "isolation
and aggression" in their work lives. "[T]he university bureaucracy," he writes,
"really works as an antibureaucracy, whose ideal is to allow the greatest
possible number of individuals to pursue their own private interests with
the least possible interaction."[11] As a result, those with a Roarkian belief in
the fundamentally individual nature of intellectual achievement thrive in
the academy, to the detriment of both collegiality and—as Damrosch
stresses—other models of scholarly activity.

Damrosch too sees this as a pedagogical issue, stressing the role of the
dissertation—and the largely reclusive work necessary to produce it—as
the fundamental component of training for the PhD. "The more scholars
came to see themselves as isolated or even self-exiled," he writes, "the more
logical it became to view the Ph.D., with its culminating years of solitary
research, as the necessary precondition for university and even college employment."[12] Here again *The Fountainhead* provides a strikingly accurate
portrait of the current state of graduate education: Roark must move beyond the classes which, he has discovered, are irrelevant to his interests,
and find a single mentor who will let him be to find his own way. In a
chapter on graduate education, Damrosch offers a number of suggestions

for making the PhD less of a funnel towards isolated writing and research.[13] In particular, he promotes the idea of allowing students to write not a proto-book but a collection of articles, which he argues would help break down the individualizing patronage system embodied in the mentor-protégé relationship and also open up greater possibilities for collaborative work.

Damrosch's suggestions for rethinking graduate education are compelling, although it's interesting that, despite his desire to undermine the culture of the scholarly loner, most of them focus on research. As practicing academics know, this is only one part (albeit the most important one at tenure and review time) of the job. Damrosch would rightly see this aspect of academic work less driven by the Roarkian ideal of isolated achievement. But in suggesting that graduate students write less unitary dissertations, or opt for interdisciplinary work instead of the frequently irrelevant language requirement,[14] he implicitly reinforces research's role at the top of the academic hierarchy, to the exclusion of other, already less solitary aspects of academic work. These include, obviously, teaching. It's perhaps telling that— despite his sincere commitment to the mutually beneficial nature of teaching and research, and despite extensive discussion of the classroom elsewhere in his book—Damrosch chooses not to discuss teacher training in his chapter on graduate pedagogy. This has the effect of perpetuating the professional logic whereby everything *but* research becomes something one picks up on the fly, after one has landed a job.

Of course there's a huge body of literature on teaching, ranging from practical handbooks like the *The St. Martin's Guide to Teaching Writing*,[15] to memoirs by figures like Wayne Booth and Jane Tompkins,[16] to the political arguments of Freireans, feminists, and others. But in between this teaching literature and the jeremiads against the academy issued with mechanical regularity (and reproducibility) by the *éminence grises* of right, left, and center, there lies a real and perceived gap that relatively few have ventured to bridge.[17] The lingering presence of this gap in even as wide-ranging and catholic a polemic as Damrosch's attests to the intransigence of the individualizing conception of academic labor that he critiques. Here one need only think about what academics mean when they say "my work," as in "I can't wait till I'm done teaching so that I can get back to my work." Teaching doesn't count as work because, within the Randian logic ironically embraced by academics who readily dismiss her writing, its public and institutional nature renders it necessarily uncreative. One sign of this situation is the academic prestige system that too often places composition on the bottom rung of the status ladder.

If teaching is thus outbounded, so much the worse for that most alienated form of academic labor, administration or service. Yet as Damrosch implies, academic disdain for administrative work parallels, as both cause and effect, the cult of isolated scholarly labor. "Collaborative scholarly activity," he writes,

> is a matter of departmental work as well as of scholarship proper, and these forms of work influence one another deeply—negatively if not positively. If a more positive relation between these modes of work is to take hold, it will be necessary for people to take a greater interest in direct exchange than they often do now.[18]

As this passage suggests, changing the nature of academic work will require a changed attitude towards institutions and public exchange, one that no longer sees them as inherently at odds with "scholarship proper."

The Fountainhead inadvertently demonstrates the pedagogical liabilities of conflating a professional career with individual creative activity. Perhaps most importantly, the sense that "no one can teach you anything" accounts for the enormous opacity that surrounds Roark's relationship with his mentor Cameron. In this relationship, neither participant knows quite what the other one wants, or what they themselves want, or how to ask for it if they do know, and as a result their interaction takes the form of silence, resentment, and aggression. That is, it's got roughly the same affective range as graduate school. If graduate school can seem like a second dysfunctional family—it's infantilizing; it promotes intense ambivalence towards one's mentors and rivalry with one's peers; it's hard to figure out what the rules are—this is in no small measure so because we understand its goal of fostering intellectual creativity as necessarily hindered by any form of institutional explicitness. In "Crisis, Collegiality, and Cultural Studies," Lauren Berlant suggests how such institutional silences continue to structure professional life even after the period of official training in graduate school:

> We learn to be professionals as assistant professors, when we are institutionally at our weakest; we figure out institutional cultures and imitate those whom we like or who we think have institutional savvy; we follow our survival instincts; we figure out how not to feel constantly threatened by the possible disrespect of colleagues and students and how to read the meaning of their respect; we brood about the demons that chase us and the ones that we chase, or we don't brood about them and instead just act and react. Our dignity often seems to be on the line, but no one ever talks about institutional life as a debilitating collective nightmare, which it so often is.[19]

I would only add that it is necessarily a part of the problem that we don't learn how to be professionals *until* we become assistant professors. This is the case because we don't consider graduate education to be professional training.[20] Rather, we understand its role as fostering individual creativity.

In this scheme, our major pedagogical role becomes letting our students alone.

Anti-Professionalism

> Anti-professionalism is professionalism itself in its purest form.
> —Stanley Fish, "Anti-Professionalism"

Letting graduate students alone is precisely the pedagogical agenda of John Guillory's still influential 1996 minute on graduate education, "Preprofessionalism: What Graduate Students Want." Guillory, then a professor of English at Johns Hopkins (he has since moved to Harvard and, most recently, NYU) best known for bringing the work of French sociologist Pierre Bourdieu to the attention of American literary scholars, begins his essay by stating the obvious: "The question of my subtitle—what graduate students want—is simply answered at the present time: they want a job."[21] Of course, Guillory is not satisfied with this simple explanation, and seeks to provide a broader economic and historical framework for the discussion of the job crisis in English. Relating this crisis to the much larger crisis of employment in the global economy, Guillory attributes English departments' vulnerability to downsizing to a combination of two factors: their internalization, during the boom years of the fifties and sixties, of more mainstream professions' quantitative modes of measuring productivity; and the long-term downturn, since then, in the market value of literary study. Up to this point, at least, Guillory's account jibes with that of more radical analysts of the academic job crisis, who have stressed the corporatized academy's efforts to cut costs through such strategies as the replacement of tenure-track lines with graduate student and adjunct labor. And indeed, Guillory stresses the way in which "the norm of productivity" and the shrinking job market have combined to extract additional surplus labor from graduate students forced to compete for fewer and fewer jobs: "Students do everything that their teachers do—teach, deliver conference papers, publish—without the assurance that any of these activities will secure them a job."[22] Moreover, he draws attention to the way in which graduate students are doubly exploited in their role as not only workers but also consumers of the academy's surplus production. In a memorable phrase, he notes that "graduate education appears now to be a kind of pyramid scheme"[23] in which graduate students exist primarily to provide an audience for professors' scholarship.

Guillory's concern with such regimes of workplace speedup differs markedly, however, from that expressed by more radical critics such as the contributors to Cary Nelson's roughly contemporaneous anthology, *Will Teach for Food*.[24] Whereas Nelson and his contributors focus on the institutional exploitation of graduate labor, Guillory—despite his efforts to identify the larger institutional forces bearing on the job crisis—ultimately demonstrates a far more traditional and individualizing concern with the quality of academic intellectual production. Hence teaching, the central axis of graduate student labor exploitation, all but disappears from Guillory's analysis after the brief mention cited above. Instead, he concentrates on the increased pressure for research that he labels "preprofessionalism:" "a curious sort of on-the-job training" characterized by "the penetration of graduate education by professional practices formerly confined to later phases of the career."[25] This situation, which he sees embodied in such phenomena as graduate student conferences, "telescopes professional careers into the time period of graduate school and conflates graduate education with self-marketing."[26] The worst effects of this situation lie, for Guillory, not in the exploitation of graduate labor (let alone adjunct labor, which he never mentions) but rather in the production of second-rate scholarship which deploys politics as a commodified "knowledge-product" and "validation of professional identification." "Because graduate students suffer most from the consequences of the social marginality of the literary profession," Guillory argues, they are most likely to produce such "prematurely professional" and "reductively political" work.[27] Despite his reference to larger economic forces, then, Guillory's interest lies primarily not in these forces, but rather in the scholarly shortcomings that they simultaneously engender and open to criticism. If "[a]bout the global crisis of unemployment there is nothing that members of our profession can do," this crisis nonetheless provides "a reality check . . . and perhaps an opportunity" to rethink our political commitments "in order to clarify what is merely phantasmic in" them.[28]

Guillory here makes a strikingly Randian argument, tantamount to suggesting that the worst effect of the Depression (much of *The Fountainhead* takes place during the 1930s) is the proliferation of bad architecture. Or as Howard Roark tells another character, "I don't believe in government housing," but "[i]f it has to be built, it might as well be built right."[29] Guillory unintentionally echoes Rand not because he shares her particular politics, but rather because he shares her belief in the inherently individual nature of creative labor. Like her, he understands the institutional trappings of professional life—in "Preprofessionalism," conferences and journals—as necessarily corrupting influences that can only pervert individual creativity by drawing it into pre-formed, conformist molds. Indeed, Guillory takes this point to be so obvious as to require no explanation: presuming agreement, he writes, "Let us acknowledge that to demand publications from graduate students as a requisite for job candidacy seriously deforms the experience of graduate school."[30] The imagined distinction between graduate training and professional training is seldom this clear; in what other profession could a leading member of the field assert that the proper procedure for professional education is to shelter trainees from the work that they will do in the future? Guillory's essay thus offers, as its implicit pedagogical prescription, protecting graduate students from the conditions of institutional life so that their native talents can take root and flourish; in essence, letting them alone. Clearly, this account of graduate training depends on equating such training solely with research; teaching, as we have seen, appears almost as an afterthought in his essay.

Guillory's prescription is problematic for a number of reasons. For one thing, its narrow emphasis on research reflects the circumscribed perspective of the sorts of programs that can afford to give graduate research institutional priority (the sorts of institutions, that is, where Guillory has taught). Moreover, this emphasis offers graduate students, no matter what sort of institution they attend, a falsely limited sense of the work they will do if and when they do obtain a job. Finally, Guillory's anti-professionalism operates—as Stanley Fish's epigraph to this section might predict—in the service of the very professional structures that it seems to defy.[31] In a fascinating psychoanalytic reading of "Preprofessionalism," Gregg Lambert demonstrates Guillory's commitment to professional hierarchy, arguing that Guillory relegates graduate students' professional desires—to the extent that they are not backed up by institutionally certified positions—to the realm of the hysterical or the Imaginary.[32] Guillory's investment in professional hierarchy becomes even clearer in his follow-up essay, "The System of Graduate Education."[33] From one perspective, this later essay seems to challenge "Preprofessionalism's" emphasis on research, criticizing the status hierarchy between researchers and (composition) teachers and calling for "a reconsideration of the nature of research, and of the system of rewards in the profession."[34] Guillory continues to stress "the degradation of research" engendered by its overproduction, however.[35] Moreover, he now understands this as not solely an intellectual problem but a practical, professional one as well, in so far as the overproduction of research gluts the market and "threatens our very professional identity as producers of knowledge."[36] Guillory's project thus becomes one of crisis management in the name of "our professional identity." That this identity excludes graduate students becomes clear in Guillory's concluding argument that "we need to rethink the unofficial or decentralized nature of the system of graduate education, which constitutes a free market of intellectual labor," because

> The inequities of the system are now so great as to create the conditions for organization from below, by the victims of the system, organizations otherwise known as unions. Organization from below will

produce some of the same results as organization from above, but in the adversarial mode. It does not seem to me unthinkable that graduate schools should see it in their interests to invest existing or ad hoc agencies with overseeing functions, if only to mitigate the long-term effects of the unofficial system of graduate education.[37]

This statement is professional in the sense outlined by critics of professionalism as a mode of social power: if the free-market has made a mess of things, it is up to the enlightened elite to step in and "mitigate" the situation before the masses take their own (necessarily destructive) forms of action. Guillory's claims are especially striking given that most of the major positive changes made over the course of the last decade in his own professional organization, the Modern Language Association, have been spearheaded by graduate students and a few faculty allies like Cary Nelson. Here, as in "Preprofessionalism," Guillory's concern is with the backing up of political energies into the profession. "The System of Graduate Education" makes it clear, however, that the problem with this situation is not that it professionalizes (and thus invalidates) politics; rather, it's that it politicizes (and thus destabilizes) the profession.

Guillory's critique of professionalism as bad because it inhibits the individual practioner thus ends up enacting a form of professionalism that's bad because it concentrates institutional power in the hands of the very elites that seem to eschew it. As Fish suggests, the anti-professionalism common to professional identity in general achieves a "particularly pure" form in the literary professions, whose very professional object is putatively defined by its autonomy from such social determinations as the structure of professions.[38] And indeed, the anti-professional professionalism embodied in Guillory's call for something like academic company unions arises as the logical outcome of the fundamentally individualistic understanding of academic labor on display in "Preprofessionalism." In what is only a (usefully) extreme version of a more general professional logic, Guillory moves from upholding the purity of academic labor to implying that collegiality is something we must *prevent*, at least in those lower reaches of the profession where it might produce "adversarial" effects. We needn't be satisfied, however, with either the bad professionalism that Guillory critiques or the bad professionalism that he enacts. On the contrary, the very specter of graduate student organization behind Guillory's call for (hierarchical) professional organization might help us to rethink our pedagogical imperatives with an eye towards engendering a good version of professionalism. Such good professionalism would both reject the asocial understanding of academic labor and help head off the crisis of collegiality that this understanding engenders. Towards this end I will argue, in the remainder of this essay, for partially reorienting our understanding of professional training around the aspect of academic work that is the most socially and institutionally determined and hence, in Guillory's terms, the most suspect: administration or service.

Forty/Forty/Twenty

> One ground of my argument concerns an area of professional life for which virtually no faculty member is trained: collegiality.
> —Lauren Berlant, "Collegiality, Crisis, and Cultural Studies"

Paying graduate students for one semester of administrative work during the course of their training would have at least three pedagogical advantages. First, it would give students an introduction to an important element of their future work as academics: the traditional "20 percent" (with research and teaching each accounting for another 40) of my section title. Second, it would provide them with a sense of the institutional forces at work within colleges and universities, assuring that they arrive at their first job with the edge taken off of their institutional naiveté. Finally, and perhaps most importantly, it would provide some version of the training in collegiality that, as Berlant's epigraph to this section points out, currently doesn't exist. While the first of these pedagogical benefits would have the virtue of acquainting students with an already existing element of academic labor, the second and third would be aimed at ultimately changing the culture of the profession by breaking down academics' sense of administrative work as institutionally and socially constrained, and hence the opposite of what creative mental labor should be.

The most obvious objection to this plan is that it would load yet another requirement onto students' already full plate: in addition to showing that they've published and taught, job applicants would have to demonstrate that they've done interesting administrative tasks. This is why I insist that this work be paid, and balanced with a one-course teaching reduction. Of course we need to intervene in "the ruthless productivity speedup" that more and more characterizes graduate training.[39] In order to do so, however, we must discuss more concretely the sorts of professional training that will best suit our students both for the job market and for the work they will do once they obtain a job. Thus the teaching reduction, since most graduate students (certainly the ones at the sort of large state university where I work) already do far more teaching than they need to apply for jobs. (Indeed, the most insuperable objection to this plan is likely to come from university administrations who see graduate students as a labor force and wouldn't find it cost-effective to redirect their labor from teaching to the sorts of work that faculty already do.)

More to the point, many graduate students *already* perform administrative service, some of it paid (full or part-time, short- or long-term, inside or outside their home department) but much of it not. In the programs I'm familiar with (Chicago, where I got my PhD, and Missouri-Columbia, where I work), students serve on departmental graduate student committees and university-wide organizations of graduate laborers; they participate in searches for new faculty; they help edit journals (sometimes paid, sometimes not); they organize conferences and colloquia. Instituting a paid requirement would insure that *all* students participate in this unofficial economy at least once, while compensating those who already would have. Of course, the fact that such a volunteer system already exists itself raises some questions. First, why compensate students for something they already do for free? And second, would instituting payment for such work destroy the volunteer economy? Hopefully, these two questions answer each other. Students who already would take on administrative duties will continue to do so even when it's not paid for the same reasons—collegiality, a desire for organizational impact, scholarly interest—that they always did, while others will satisfy their service requirement and be done with it. The benefits to both kinds of students would thus be partial, but important: volunteers would get a course reduction that they otherwise wouldn't have, while non-volunteers would be drawn out at least once in their graduate career (and might even decide that they like it). In other words, graduate students would behave much like faculty members already do, all having in theory the same service obligation but some putting their shoulders to the wheel more assiduously than others. This points to a related question: why pay graduate students for something that faculty members do without compensation?[40] This objection is based on a spurious analogy, however. Compared to graduate students, faculty members *don't* perform uncompensated service work, but are compensated both directly (in merit raises) and indirectly (in the fact that we're paid a salary and benefits rather than on a per-course basis). If anything, then, a paid administrative requirement would in a small way help to offset the inequities engendered by universities' reliance on low-paid graduate labor.

Such questions aside, reorganizing the system of graduate student service work on a partially paid basis would involve some difficult practical questions. For instance, what would count as a semester's worth of service? Working for a journal for a semester obviously would, but how about organizing a conference (which arguably requires just as much effort, but on a more concentrated timetable)? How about administrative activities that come with their own calendar—activities such as academic hiring, which necessarily overlaps fall and spring semesters? How would departments allot administrative tasks when some, as would no doubt be the case, turn out to be more popular than others? While problematic, however, these problems don't seem intractable. Indeed, they seem to be mostly on the order of other decisions that departments already make: some students get to serve on hiring committees while others do not; some teaching duties are more popular than others, and have to be assigned on a competitive basis. And my conversations with students at the University of Missouri who already shoulder their share of administrative tasks lead me to believe that the headaches for departments and their Directors of Graduate Studies would be outweighed by the benefits to students and to the profession as a whole.

Chief among these benefits would be a sense that academic work can transcend the isolating, solitary regime sketched so convincingly by Damrosch. One student who's held various offices in Missouri's English Graduate Students Association (EGSA) points out that collegiality is sometimes in short supply among graduate students in English:

> One big thing that has struck me is that, in general, many English grad students are apathetic to the department's workings, beyond their own work. This probably applies to my fellow grad students more so than professors, mostly because I know the former more than the latter. But my sense is that your typical English graduate student, when faced with some sort of chore—whether it's carrying boxes of books for the EGSA book sale or teaching a service learning class—would rather come up with some cynical reason why, say, service learning is wrong or stupid and thus not worth his/her time, than actually participate in the activity. Certainly there are friendships among grad students, but there seem to be few students who will do the thankless work that can help the Department as a whole.

This student errs only in assuming that this "individualist mentality" is less common among faculty members: as Damrosch points out, graduate school both selects for and reinforces precisely this quality in future academics.[41] As another student suggests, the disjunction between "intellectual" and administrative activities is both greater in a discipline like English ("There seems to be a tacit understanding of [their] interconnectedness in other fields") and built into the educational process: "It has been a source of wonder to me that early experience of this fundamental part of our future professional lives is so little emphasized." This student offers a useful illustration of what she means about other fields:

> The following example typical to another field in academia might be fitting: when I was a theater student as an undergraduate, my degree required that all students be trained not just as actresses but as "techies"

(people trained in the technical aspects of stage work like sets, lights, and costumes), no matter which of the two fields we had chosen for a career. The philosophy behind this was that if you don't know what's going on behind you, backstage, with lighting, props, sets, music, and all other technical matters while you're acting onstage, you won't be able to act competently. Focused on their acting, many actresses did not keep up with their techie studies yet still managed to graduate. I don't know if the best techies made the best actresses, but of all my former theater colleagues, the women who kept up as techies are the most employed today and since.

What separates such a program from most graduate training in English is that its directors understand it as not only fostering individual creativity but also training people for the sorts of work necessary—literally—to set the stage on which creative activity occurs.

Granted, administrative work can often be a lesson in limitations. One student, for instance, describes how organizing a graduate student conference forced her to give up a topic she liked in favor of one that was more popular and, ultimately, better suited to the interests of the department as a whole. Another, active in committees at both the department and the university level, notes that she has seen "a lot of stagnation," with groups "accomplishing very little and twiddling away whatever power and influence they potentially have." Such experiences carry, of course, their own pedagogical charge. "In sacrificing intellectual ideals to political and economic realities," the conference organizer writes, she was "performing an exercise in the compromises that are so vital to the machine of academia—compromises that, from what I have witnessed, are guaranteed parts of a professor's career." Administrative experience teaches people, as another student noted, about "the shape their ideas take under constraints of institutional resources; policies; faculty, staff, departmental, and grad student support; politics; and monies." This is a valuable lesson, one academics too often learn, to their dismay, *after* starting a job. Beyond such lessons in realpolitik, however, it's also worth noting that compromise is an element of the collegiality currently in short supply in academia. If, as Berlant writes, it is "[s]ometimes . . . hard to find anyone who comes into a meeting not knowing how they're going to vote,"[42] this is because academics' proprietarily Roarkian relationship to their work trains them to think that they are bringing the truth out of the desert, rather than thinking together with other people.

Moreover, administration need not be solely an exercise in compromise and limitations; it can also foster intellectual growth. A graduate student conference, for instance, can provide—despite Guillory's jaundiced view[43]— a chance for students to see and enter the larger world of their discipline, to test and sharpen their ideas with people not constrained by their local assumptions. More importantly, it can provide an opportunity to do so not in the proto-professional role of somebody's student, but as a professional in one's own right, an academic hosting fellow academics. This can be a hugely empowering experience: the moment when one stops thinking of oneself locally and passively and begins to identify and contribute to scholarly conversations. Gerald Graff makes a similar point in his riposte to Guillory, "Two Cheers for Professionalizing Graduate Students." "I suspect I would have matured more quickly as a scholar and writer," Graff contends,

> if I had been encouraged to try to publish one or two of my course papers. Even at the graduate level, writing only for your teachers is infantilizing. There's nothing like a real audience (even if only of journal editors who send rejection notices) to force students to consider readers who don't share the pet assumptions of their teachers.[44]

Although Graff too worries about speedup, he doesn't share Guillory's limiting assumption that the professional machinery of English studies like conferences and publications necessarily distort scholarship. On the contrary, he stresses how such machinery can *improve* scholarship.[45]

University of Missouri graduate students who've worked on one of the journals published out of the department support this view. One reports, for instance, that working as an editor has enabled her to "recognize the difference between good and bad work." This recognition puts her way ahead of Howard Roark, who after telling his Dean that he has nothing to learn from the history of architecture delivers, with no irony, an impromptu lecture on what's wrong with the Parthenon.[46] What this student realizes, and Roark doesn't, is that learning how not to do something is still learning; that one's relationship to other work in one's field need not take the rigidly dichotomized form of either mindless subordination or (equally mindless) insubordination. In addition to providing an empowering lesson in what she calls "intellectual responsibility"—"What I say as an assistant editor is not simply something that comes out of my mouth, but has repercussions for the article, for the author, for the subject area, for the journal, for its sponsoring organization, and for the discipline"—this student's administrative work has also taught her lessons she can use in her own research. One might, of course, say that what she has learned are a set of conformist codes that will submerge her individual creativity. The student, however, demonstrates a more sophisticated view, arguing that her experience has actually helped her to distinguish her own judgements from those of others: "I can recognize," she goes on to say, "when my criteria for [differentiating between good and bad work] are my own, and when they are criteria that have been trained into me by my teachers and by the current mode of discourse in my discipline." Another student with editing experience attributes similar advantages to a position that requires her to "manage and even delegate work to my 'superiors'" in the profession:

> Although some situations still make me feel like I am assuming a role beyond my true qualifications, this experience has given me a professional confidence different from anything I could have gained in the classroom. As a result, I am more willing to send out my essays to journals and better prepared for the responses. I am also more confident when approaching other scholars at conferences.

This student adds that she thinks she "will be better prepared to interview for jobs because of [her] experience." We can go further than this, and speculate that she will be better prepared to take up a job when she gets one; that she will be of more use to her department, her colleagues, and herself due to her institutional experience; and that she'll experience a less vertiginous sense of disconnection between her scholarship and her other activities as an assistant professor.

Jeffrey Williams has recently taken issue with our reliance on the category "smart," arguing that it has overrun the academic imaginary and prevents us from articulating other measurements of academic merit.[47] Although we may never get rid of the category (and may not want to—after all, who doesn't want to work with smart colleagues?), we need to actively supplement it with other qualities. How are we to do this, however, if our machinery of professional formation is geared so single-mindedly towards scholarship? Indeed, part of the task that lies ahead is figuring out what categories besides smartness we want to encourage. What, for instance, does "collegiality" mean? What should it mean? In the preceding argument I have been as guilty as anyone of leaving it undefined, although I hope that I have at least suggested something like a respectful acknowledgement of those around us as co-workers, an acknowledgement that requires taking service work as more than a distraction.

Of course, we can go too far in extolling service work; much of it is a distraction, and sometimes it is even busy work. There are, however, aspects of service work that build spaces for intellectual activity, both by individuals and by groups. Such spaces too often don't get built because of the profession's ingrained prejudice against its own professional protocols. On a broader political level, this state of affairs has left us ill equipped to cope with the ongoing transformation of the university: we complain about administrators but don't want to do the work necessary to take back faculty governance; we feel that we are striking a blow against the corporatized university by writing witty essays exposing its deficiencies. If the graduate student union movement has taught us anything, it's that change only comes about through organizational labor. In this sense, the conjunction between professionalization and politicization in Guillory's recent discussions of the academic job crisis seems worth considering. It's unlikely that requiring administrative experience from our graduate students will radicalize the profession, but it's possible that it might help to channel the profession's political energies more effectively. Beyond this, it might help to improve the quality of our institutional life, and maybe even lay the groundwork for more collaborative forms of scholarship. My own experience has been that graduate students who go in for administrative or service work tend to be not the dullest but the savviest members of their cohorts; maybe it's time to make this process less self-selecting and more systematic.

Notes

1. I am tailoring my remarks towards PhD students who plan to become academics. Despite calls to rethink the logic behind this assumption, it remains for now a practical one where most of our students are concerned. Moreover, I believe my suggestions won't hurt—and may help—those who ultimately find jobs outside the academy. See also Jennifer Wicke, "I Profess: Another View of Professionalization," in *Profession* (2001): 52–57.
2. John Guillory, "Preprofessionalism: What Graduate Students Want," *Profession* (1996), 92.
3. Ayn Rand, *The Fountainhead* (New York: Signet, 1993[1943]), 21.
4. Rand, *The Fountainhead*, 22.
5. Rand, *The Fountainhead*, 679.
6. Rand, *The Fountainhead*, 679.
7. Rand, *The Fountainhead*, 76.
8. Rand, *The Fountainhead*, 61; *emphasis* added.
9. See Sharon Stockton, "Engineering Power: Hoover, Rand, Pound, and the Heroic Architect," *American Literature* 72.4 (2000): 813–41; and Michael Szalay, *New Deal Modernism: American Literature and the Invention of the Welfare State* (Durham, NC: Duke University Press, 2000), 75–119.
10. David Damrosch, *We Scholars: Changing the Culture of the University* (Cambridge: Harvard University Press, 1995), 7.
11. Damrosch, *We Scholars*, 12, 59.
12. Damrosch, *We Scholars*, 85.
13. Damrosch, *We Scholars*, 140–85.
14. Damrosch, *We Scholars*, 177–78.
15. See Robert Connors and Cheryl Glenn, *The St. Martin's Guide to Teaching Writing* (New York: St. Martin's, 1992).
16. See Wayne Booth, *The Vocation of a Teacher: Rhetorical Occasions, 1967–1988* (Chicago: University of Chicago Press, 1988); and Jane Tompkins, *A Life in School: What the Teacher Learned* (New York: Perseus, 1996).
17. *Workplace*, an on-line journal (http://www.louisville.edu/journal/workplace/index.html), provides a vivid exception to this dichotomizing tendency, largely because its focus on academic labor repositions the classroom at the center of institutional politics. Evan Watkin's *Work Time: English Departments and the Circulation of Cultural Value* (Palo Alto, CA: Stanford University Press, 1989) and Gerald Graff's *Beyond the Culture Wars: How Teaching Can Revitalize American Education* (New York: Norton, 1992) likewise represent (very different) attempts to think teaching and institutional critique together. For those interested in the current state of the conversation(s) on teaching English, I recommend recent issues of *workplace, College English*, and *Pedagogy*.
18. Damrosch, *We Scholars*, 76.
19. Lauren Berlant, "Collegiality, Crisis, and Cultural Studies," *Profession* (1998), 108.

20. The Preparing Future Faculty (PFF) program (sponsored by the Council of Graduate Schools and the Association of American Colleges and Universities), with its commitment to teaching and service as necessary elements of faculty training, stands out as an important exception to this rule. PFF's trans-institutional nature has numerous strengths, not least its stress on acquainting students from research universities with the institutional realities of different kinds of programs. To the extent that it remains limited to certain programs in certain fields, however, PFF provides a model but not a substitute for the kinds of things we can—and, I am arguing, should—be doing in our own departments. For information on PFF and related programs, see its web pages at http://www.preparing-faculty.org/

21. Guillory, "Preprofessionalism," 91.

22. Guillory, "Preprofessionalism," 98, 92.

23. Guillory, "Preprofessionalism," 97.

24. See Cary Nelson, ed., *Will Teach for Food: Academic Labor in Crisis* (Minneapolis: University of Minnesota Press, 1997).

25. Guillory, "Preprofessionalism," 92.

26. Guillory, "Preprofessionalism," 94, 92.

27. Guillory, "Preprofessionalism," 98, 98, 94.

28. Guillory, "Preprofessionalism," 97, 98, 98.

29. Rand, *The Fountainhead*, 579.

30. Guillory, "Preprofessionalism," 98.

31. Chris Newfield originally encouraged me to consider this point.

32. See Gregg Lambert, "What Do Graduate Students Want?: John Guillory and that Obscure Object of Desire," *Minnesota Review* 52–54 (2000): 249–62.

33. See John Guillory, "The System of Graduate Education," *PMLA* 115.5 (Oct. 2000): 1154–63.

34. Guillory, "The System of Graduate Education," 1159, 1162.

35. Guillory, "The System of Graduate Education," 1162.

36. Guillory, "The System of Graduate Education," 1160.

37. Guillory, "The System of Graduate Education," 1163.

38. Stanley Fish, "Anti-Professionalism," *New Literary History* 17.1 (Autumn 1985), 99. See also Bruce Robbins, *Secular Vocations: Intellectuals, Professionalism, Culture* (New York: Verso, 1993).

39. Gerald Graff, "Two Cheers for Professionalizing Graduate Students," *PMLA* 115.5 (Oct. 2000), 1192.

40. Someone posed this question to me when I proposed an earlier version of this essay's argument to the audience at the Open Hearing of the MLA Ad Hoc Committee on the Professionalization of PhDs held at the 2000 MLA Convention in Washington D.C.

41. See Damrosch, *We Scholars*.

42. Berlant, "Collegiality, Crisis, and Cultural Studies," 115.

43. Discussing graduate student conferences, Guillory avers that "I am not dismissing these new institutional forms or their contents"—a demurral that might carry more force if it were not issued in the process of describing these conferences as avatars of the "prematurely professional" and "reductively political" world of preprofessionalism. See Guillory, "Preprofessionalism," 94.

44. Graff, "Two Cheers for Professionalizing Graduate Students," 1192.

45. Linda Hutcheon likewise questions this aspect of Guillory's argument in a recent issue of the *MLA Newsletter*, writing that "[i]n my view it is a question not of publishing but of *how much* publishing is required. From my own early experience and from what students tell me, submitting one's research to peer review and having it pass successfully can provide an enormous psychological boost. Success as a scholar can lead to new confidence as well as ensure a necessary engagement in (and contribution to) the public debates of the field." See Linda Hutcheon, "Professionalization and Its Discontents," *MLA Newsletter* 32.4 (Winter 2000), 3.

46. Rand, *The Fountainhead*, 23-24.

47. See Jeffrey Williams, "Smart," Society for the Study of Narrative Literature Convention, Atlanta, GA (April 8, 2000).

CHAPTER 8

Class Work

*Site of Egalitarian Activism or
Site of Embourgeoisement?*

SHARON O'DAIR

Is the college composition classroom a site where professors offer not just a set of skills to be mastered but also "a form of cultural citizenship and politics," which aims to reconstruct "democratic public life" so that "subordinate groups . . . have the opportunity to govern and shape history rather than be consigned to its margins?"[1] For most of us, the answer to this question is obvious. Of course the college composition classroom is a site for such activism: our pedagogy should be counter-hegemonic, the literacy our students achieve should be critical, and all of us should seek positive change in our communities, indeed in the world. To be sure, some problems are "now commonly recognized" in putting such Freirean theory into practice among undergraduates in the United States, as Richard Miller points out;[2] it is difficult, for instance, for some of us to agree that "basic writers are very much like Freire's peasants."[3] But neither the problems nor the recognition of them has unsettled the power of critical literacy in the composition classroom. Today, compositionists "focus . . . almost exclusively on ideological matters," as "writing proficiency has dropped from view as a key purpose."[4] Undoubtedly, says Jeff Smith, the various strands of critical literacy are now the "Standard Model" of pedagogy, aimed at all students, whether or not they are prepared to engage it.[5]

Since the late 1980s, voices have protested the institutionalization of this "Standard Model"—I have cited several in the preceding paragraph—and they have done so principally, and in my view correctly, by inveighing against the bad faith of the middle-class professorate while, at the same time, pointing out how deeply critical literacy conflicts with the goals of students and of higher education itself. In this essay, I add my voice to theirs, not as a compositionist but as a literary critic interested in the theory and workings of social class, particularly education's role in maintaining and reproducing class distinction. I do so, too, because I am suspicious of standard models, and, like Kathryn Bond Stockton, I wonder why "academics, who trade in fresh views," are content to repeat "set claims" and therefore to establish their students as "the target of political zeal that works by way of mantra."[6] Like Stockton, I want to "restore surprise" to our deliberations by focusing on details, in this case, by addressing what seems to me a contradiction in many of the essays in *Teaching Working Class*, a fine collection recently edited by Sherry Lee Linkon.[7] In so doing, I will offer an understanding of "class activism" that focuses less on the putative emotional needs of working-class students, of whatever ethnicity or gender, and more on the ways hierarchy and distinction are reproduced *within* as well as outside of the various institutions of higher education. As a corollary, I would like to suggest that it is possible and even desirable for most people to lead culturally and intellectually satisfying lives without spending four, six, or eight years in post-secondary education.

The contradiction I find in many of the essays occurs in the contributors' responses, implied or explicit, to the question, "toward what end are we easing our students' transition to higher education by engaging in counter-hegemonic pedagogy?" Ann E. Green wonders, "Do we want our working-class students to become bourgeois? Do we want our 'bourgeois' students to drop out of school and experience a less privileged life?"[8] The formulation of these questions assumes that with "school" comes a more privileged, a better life, an assumption I will question at the end of this essay, but here I wish to point out that many of the contributors *do* and yet *do not* want their students to become bourgeois—they want to ease their transition and they want them to succeed in the middle-class institutions of higher education;[9] at the same time, they seem not to want them to accept certain norms of those institutions—standard English, taste, manners, and the like. The latter position is stated most strongly by Caroline Pari, who, in response to her own educationally driven assimilation, has set out "to develop a pedagogy that critically challenges assimilation" into the middle class.[10] Challenging the transition, however, cannot make the transition easier for students to make; but in any case, the contributors seem to understand that the transition "will never be seamless unless the research university becomes a working-class institution, responsive to (rather than merely sensitive to) racial and ethnic diversity."[11] Many of the contributors join Joseph Heathcott in proposing such a transformation of the academy,[12] but I do not know how many of them agree with him that it is unlikely to occur.

Of course, if one cannot transform the research university into a working-class institution, a proposition I will return to later in this essay, one can attempt to transform the bourgeoisie, what the university produces. It is possible, therefore, to argue that when the contributors say they want their students to become bourgeois without acceding to certain bourgeois norms, what they mean is that they want them to form a new kind of bourgeoisie, one that is culturally different from the WASP bourgeoisie of the United States, but a bourgeoisie nonetheless. Some evidence of this position emerges in the essays. In addressing working-class students, says Green, "my biggest challenge and responsibility in the classroom [is] to insist that 'wholeness is possible,' that it is possible for working-class students or African-American students or Latina students to maintain connections with their home cultures and languages while still learning the skills that will bring them success in the academic world."[13] In this, Green might be seen as promoting language instruction that, as one of the anonymous readers of this essay puts it, recognizes "the contextual legitimacy of [students'] home dialects" and teaches "them not to be ashamed of them." An important yet modest goal, the encouragement of such bidialectism should not be difficult to accomplish in the college classroom, since, as Miller suggests, undergraduates are already well aware of "these competing spheres" of linguistic competency and their differing valuations.[14] Many, like me, figured out the difference in elementary school, and, as I have explained elsewhere,[15] this awareness led me to the kind of agency promoted by Janet Zandy in *Liberating Memory*, in which upward mobility does not extract "as its cost familial and historic memory," in which the newly bourgeois can "trace the inscription of class on their lives and on their work."[16]

But this goal is not quite what Green has in mind; for Green herself, "wholeness" is a bigger project,

> a feminist pedagogy that critiques classism and racism and sexism and homophobia and accounts for class, race, gender, and sexual preference, without denying either me or the students subject positions, without reducing or losing anyone's multiple and varied subjectivities.[17]

What is not considered by Green, however, is the possibility that classism, racism, sexism, or homophobia may be promoted and valued in her students' "home cultures," and that in critiquing such biases, she may be encouraging the kind of alienation from family and culture she purports to abhor. It is well known, for example, that many Muslims and fundamentalist Christians are strongly sexist. Many fundamentalist Christians and African Americans are homophobic. "Homosexuality is the greatest sexual taboo within the African diaspora," writes Delroy Constantine-Simms, a taboo enforced institutionally by Afrocentrist and Christian teaching and expressed popularly in rap music and film.[18] The taboo has resulted in "deep" antigay feelings among African Americans, particularly among the religious, the less affluent, and the poorly educated,[19] but also among the intelligentsia, who tend to "excuse black homophobia" by relegating it "to the domain of hegemonic whites."[20] According to Black lesbians Cathy J. Cohen and Tamara Jones, "homophobia within the Black community" is a "problem" of sufficient magnitude that years will pass before "Black communities are transformed" and homophobia eradicated; "there remains much more work to be done."[21]

If sexism and homophobia characterize many "home cultures," so, too, does classism. Many working-class families are classist, and not just in the putatively normative sense of looking down on those below them on the socio-economic scale. As sociologist Michèle Lamont argues persuasively, workers "are very aware of the distinctive disadvantages of their position," but such awareness is not the only element of their class consciousness, which is formed as well by a morality that produces "workers' sense of worth" and allows for "a detailed critique of upper middle class people . . . their lack of personal integrity, lack of respect for others, and the poor quality of their interpersonal relationships."[22] Working-class families revel in such moral critique, as I can attest and as Laurel Johnson Black suggests: as a child, she devoured the stories her father told, in which "the 'stupid rich bastards' almost always 'got it' in the end, outwitted by the poor little guy."[23] My mother often expressed her dislike of the professional middle class—the physicians and educators who told her how to live and raise her children—even as she pushed me to join it, and her conflicted attitude, like Black's father's, is not uncommon among workers, whether Black or White, according to Lamont's research: "middle class people have a position that deserves to be emulated, but their values are not always to be respected."[24] These examples suggest, therefore, a possibility Green does not consider: that a respect for others' values or for "multiple and varied subjectivities" is part of bourgeois good taste, like Jazz at Lincoln Center, and therefore that the "wholeness" she seeks for her students is, in fact, to be achieved by persuading them to subscribe to a set of values identified in particular, though not exclusively, with the professional middle class.

If this unacknowledged possibility accurately describes reality—and recent scholarship concerning students' resistance to critical literacy, such as Miller's, Russel Durst's, or David Seitz's, suggests that it does[25]—then what the contributors seem to be talking about is not the construction of a culturally different bourgeoisie, such as that envisioned by Zandy, in which upward mobility does not require the loss of "familial and historic memory,"[26] but rather, in a move that must strike us as familiar, the moral transformation of aspirants to that status, an age-old function of the academy. For this reason, the professed desire of many of the contributors to transform the academy into a working-class institution strikes me as nonsense. For two other reasons, that desire frightens me. First, those who propose it do not describe the bases on which such a working-class university might operate or what such a working-class university might be. For example, the recommendation that the research university be "responsive to (rather than just sensitive to) racial and ethnic diversity"[27] offers no blueprint for change, but more fundamentally, its terms do not match any sociological definition of class that I know. Second, those who propose it do not describe what might be the costs of such a transformation. This seems an especially important question, as Stanley Fish points out with respect to the politicization of literary criticism:

> when you exchange one activity for another, you lose something, and although you might mask the loss by calling the new activity by the old name, the phenomena that came into view under the previous dispensation will have disappeared in your brave new world. Maybe they should disappear, maybe the pleasures particular to close literary analysis are too esoteric and over-refined in a time of great social urgency, but we should at least have a clear idea of what would be at stake were we to think of ourselves as politicians first, and literary critics second, if at all.[28]

In this time of great social urgency, perhaps literary critics and compositionists should not be concerned about standard English, the intricacies of logical argument, or even the writing process; perhaps they should think of themselves as politicians first, and literary critics or compositionists second, if at all. But like Fish, I think we should have a clear idea of what is at stake if that is what we do, if that is what we become. And what seems to be at stake here is not just literary criticism or a fine writing style but also the value of intellectual accomplishment and distinction. How far do we go in promoting egalitarianism in the academy? How many students who require remedial instruction in English and mathematics should we admit to undergraduate study—40 percent? 60 percent? More? Should we confer master's degrees in English on students who demonstrate an inability to punctuate or to construct subordination? In striving above all to give our students voice, should we change our job titles from "literary critics" to politicians, or, as Susan Peck MacDonald puts it, to "newspaper reporters, tabloid TV hosts, social workers, or psychological counselors?"[29] Should we concentrate our professional lives on what Stephen North calls "academic consciousness-raising?"[30]

I see myself as a literary critic and an intellectual, and the job description I read when I set out upon this career did not include teaching composition to first-year graduate students or leading a consciousness-raising group composed of first-year undergraduates. But before you dismiss me as an uncaring, neo-conservative elitist—or even as just a garden variety elitist produced by a literature program, described recently by Peter Elbow[31]—please consider how working-class students might judge our apparent desire to abandon our expertise and distinction in the name of egalitarianism or the attempt to create a vaguely defined working-class university? I suggest that they would judge us fools. As Durst, Miller, and Seitz make clear, and as many of the essays in *Teaching Working Class* make clear—indeed, as we all know—the vast majority of working-class students are in college because they want better occupational opportunities. They perceive higher education as a way to achieve such a goal, and that perception is rooted in their understanding that higher education will help them gain access to and perform better in the weird bourgeois or professional worlds they wish to enter. That perception may be somewhat hazy, and they may not grasp, for example, that a degree in and of itself is no guarantee of better occupational opportunities or that standard English is the lingua franca of bourgeois and professional life, but when they do grasp those facts, they will feel cheated when they recall that their composition instructor purposefully decided not to initiate them into academic discourse but instead to value the language and knowledge they already knew.[32]

I do not question the motives or good will of instructors like Caroline Pari; I do not, for example, wish to claim that such instructors fail to help their students master standard English because they want them to remain working-class. I think such instructors are caught between a rock and a hard place, between their commitments to egalitarianism and their commitments to intellectual discipline and achievement. Because they are given students who have not been taught that in this society, standard English is useful in gaining access to the professions or to business, as well as in communication generally, and because their commitments to egalitarianism trump their commitments to the intellectual norms of their discipline, such instructors opt for the delaying strategy evident in many of the essays in *Teaching Working Class*. Rather than provide crash courses in English grammar and usage, which many if not most of their students might fail, a situation that would not contribute to egalitarian outcomes, instructors reconceive their goals for the composition classroom, which becomes, ideally, a site to pursue personal and political transformation, "education as a form of activism,"[33] and in reality, a site to ease the transition of their working-class or minority students into the academic and middle-class worlds by trying to accomplish two or three tasks at once: therapy, activism, and language instruction.

What is not considered, however, is how long this process ought to continue—one semester? two? three? more?—or, more fundamentally, whether the continued delaying of the students' transition to the academic and middle-class worlds is not, in fact, irresponsible and antitithetical to their ambitions. Empirical evidence—what we have of it, since composition studies, driven by postmodern theory, has largely abandoned empirical research[34]—suggests that a student's writing "will get somewhat better whatever the teacher does"; a student, concludes J. Hillis Miller, "learns to write by writing."[35] Accordingly, argues Fish, in the composition classroom "practice has nothing to do with theory, at least in the sense of being enabled and justified by theory."[36] And therefore, if "practice makes perfect [and] you learn to write by writing," then a pedagogy justified by "normative notions of correctness"[37] is just as useful to the development of literacy—and even, perhaps, of critical literacy, for one can only be critical if one is literate—as is a pedagogy justified by activism, for example, one that "critiques classism and racism and sexism and homophobia"[38] or that offers "a form of cultural citizenship and politics."[39] To the extent that the former offers more time to read and write than the latter or more effectively than the latter acculturates working-class and minority students into academic discourse, the former is, arguably, better pedagogy than the latter.

Recently, Howard Tinberg concluded that "composition . . . does not know what to do with the working class."[40] Noting, as I do here, that compositionists are split "between a conviction that first-year composition remain a site for critical literacy and social action and the conviction that it be the place to acculturate students into the academy," Tinberg offers two solutions to this contradiction, only the latter of which, I believe, offers much promise to compositionists or their students:

> In arguing that such a split exists in composition . . . we forfeit the possibility of a third way: that critical literacy can serve both purposes. Cannot students serve both community and the academy? Is it not possible to be thoughtful citizens in both the classroom and the world beyond the classroom? Having said as much, we might also consider this possibility, although many of us will find it uncomfortable to acknowledge: four years or more of college may not be the best option for everyone—and a productive life awaits others who choose to bypass that experience. Is obtaining an undergraduate or graduate degree a prerequisite for a good and satisfying life?[41]

Tinberg's description of "a third way" is formulated to garner quick assent from his audience; the rhetorical questions do not admit of a negative answer. But it seems to me that critical literacy cannot serve both purposes, because, as Andrew Levison argues, a "vast cultural chasm" exists "between college-educated and blue-collar America," one that is "created not by differences in knowledge or intelligence but by the fact that the two groups live in fundamentally different worlds."[42] Like standard English, critical literacy is part of the cultural world of the college-educated, and mastering it requires of working-class students as much acculturation—or, we might say, submission to authority, our authority—as does mastering standard English. Indeed, writes John Michael in a recent critique of counter-hegemonic pedagogy, an instructor's "egalitarian principles are largely irrelevant in the classroom," a site where "differentials of knowledge, of authority, and of institutional power may be useful tools in persuading students and opponents to see the error and ignorance of their ways"[43]—the error and ignorance of, for example and as I noted above, the sexism of fundamentalist Christians, the homophobia of African Americans, or the classism of the working class. As Michael suggests, counter-hegemonic pedagogies like critical literacy are like any other pedagogy: "ineluctably violent (though the violence remains verbal) and intrinsically elitist."[44] Critical literacy is thus activist insofar as it actively promotes the judgments of the professorate and of the cultural world to which they belong, a cultural world that is recognized to be superior to the cultural world of the working class. And, as I have argued recently in *Class, Critics, and Shakespeare: Bottom Lines on the Culture Wars*, what principally constitutes the superior cultural world of the middle and upper classes are the legacies of higher education. Or, as I might amend Levison, what principally constitutes the superior cultural world of the college-educated is *college*.

For those of us interested in equity and justice, the question is how to ameliorate the invidious distinction between these two worlds. For the past forty years or so, the answer has been to increase access via formal education to the world judged superior. Higher education, which in 1945 offered a place to only one in five Americans aged eighteen to twenty-two, now can accommodate four out of five Americans in that age-group.[45] According to Claude S. Fischer and his associates, as well as to Michael Zweig, this expansion has reduced inequality among those who actually hold bachelor's degrees; for this group, "there is *no* connection between the occupational status of their parents and their own."[46] Unfortunately, fewer than 25 percent of Americans over age twenty-five actually hold bachelor's degrees, and college graduates are disproportionately drawn from middle- and upper-class families.[47] The latter is a trend that has *not* decreased as higher education has expanded, according to Todd Gitlin: in 1979, a student whose family's income fell in the top quarter was four times as likely to earn a bachelor's degree by age twenty-four as a student whose family's income fell in the bottom quarter. By 1994, such an affluent student was nineteen times as likely to do so.[48] As Zweig concludes, even today, after all of its expansion, higher education "mostly helps to stabilize classes and reproduce them across generations."[49]

Nevertheless, it is widely assumed that to succeed in the twenty-first century, it is imperative to hold a college degree; we live in the world Martin Trow predicted thirty years ago, in which "going to college" is deemed appropriate not just "for people of wealth or extraordinary talent or ambition" but also "for youngsters of quite ordinary talent and ambition, and increasingly for people with little of either."[50] Among the many reasons for this shift in expectations, including an increased emphasis on egalitarianism, equal opportunity, and racial and gender equity, perhaps the most important, as Fischer and his associates explain, is economic: "those who do not graduate from college—and even more so, those who have a high school education or less—face bleak prospects."[51] According to former President Bill Clinton, "every American needs more than a high-school education. . . . A college education is not a luxury."[52] Even students in high school recognize the existence of a "B.A. premium"; in 1992, according to the Office of Education Research and Improvement, fully 84 percent of all graduating high school seniors expected to obtain a bachelor's degree, and, according to the National Center for Educational Statistics, 59 percent expected to become professionals.[53]

Yet, according to Lawrence Mishel, Jared Bernstein, and John Schmitt, of the Economic Policy Institute, the explanation for the perceived financial benefits of the bachelor's degree may not be quite so simple as the oft-repeated suggestion that the new economy needs a better educated workforce and is willing to pay more for it. Mishel, Bernstein, and Schmitt report that while the average number of years of schooling among all workers increased from 12.0 in 1973 to 13.4 in 1994, there was "no growth in the hourly compensation paid per year of schooling" and, therefore, "all of the growth in average hourly compensation since 1973 can be attributed to more schooling."[54] For Mishel, Bernstein, and Schmitt, this situation is not rosy. It is

> analogous to earning a higher annual wage because one works more hours at the same hourly wage—working harder at the same pay. While it is certainly a good thing to be able to work more hours, it would be a far better situation if annual wages grew primarily because of higher hourly wages (and one might even voluntarily reduce hours). Similarly with education, it would be far more preferable if hourly compensation grew beyond the growth caused by more schooling, as was the case in the early postwar period.[55]

What "the B.A. premium" reflects, perhaps, is as much the result of credential inflation as of the actual skills certified by the degree in question. In any event, the sociologists and economists cited above make it clear that higher education offers upward mobility only to a small portion of the working class; the expansion of higher education in the postwar period benefited primarily the middle and upper classes.

Colleges and universities have been and continue to be part of middle-class culture. And even if former President Clinton, the high school seniors cited above, or the contributors to *Teaching Working Class* are correct in their assumptions that access to higher education will become universal, colleges and universities will continue to be part of middle-class culture. Or at least, the colleges and universities that produce the middle and upper classes will continue to be part of middle-class culture. If some colleges and universities produce degree holders destined for jobs as janitors, bartenders, and retail clerks, then perhaps we will be able to say we have achieved a "working-class university," one that is part of working-class culture and thus offers a seamless transition to working-class students. Such an achievement, however, may not be worth shouting about, although I am sure many will disagree. Many think a degreed janitor an excellent outcome; a person who has been trained in critical literacy will be a better and more responsible citizen. Yet, like Renny Christopher, also writing in *Teaching Working Class*, I am skeptical that such an outcome is likely.[56] Such an outcome cannot occur when high schools graduate 70 percent of their students without adequate academic preparation for college[57] and when universities such as California State University, Stanislaus, where Christopher taught for many years, do not do much better, graduating many of their working-class students "without giving them basic skills (particularly the ability to write standard English and to do mathematics beyond prealgebra)," much less the kinds of abstract, analytic skills that lead them to become "autonomous thinkers with a sense of their intellectual worth."[58] What we have in the degreed janitor is not a critically literate janitor, but a janitor whose skills approximate those his grandfather possessed after finishing high school. In this case, the degreed janitor will have as little use for composition, critical or otherwise, as Daniel Green's students at "Service U" have for "literature," works they find entirely uncompelling and, indeed, useless.[59]

What we also have in the degreed janitor, however, is evidence that in the twenty-first century, we cannot talk about class and higher education without talking about class *in* higher education. We can no longer ignore "what is a major class division in American higher education: the gap between first-tier, selective-admissions schools and second-tier, open registration, two- and four-year colleges . . . that represent the majority of institutions."[60] A discussion about class at Princeton University is different from a discussion about class at the University of Alabama, at Fort Hayes State University, or at Long Beach City College. And a discussion about class at Long Beach City College should not occur without implicating Princeton or the University of California in the construction of it. Once we do so, we will see that solutions to the problem such as that proposed by John Alberti—to ensure even broader access to higher education[61]—can only fail: universal access does not undermine but enhances the prestige, selectivity, and power of elite institutions.[62]

Instead, I think, it is time for society to rethink its attempt to ameliorate via ever-increasing amounts of education the invidious distinction between the working class and the middle and upper classes. This strategy fails all but a few, who are absorbed into the middle and upper classes, and it does not achieve its goal of ameliorating class difference, as our postwar history shows. In 1972, Christopher Jencks and his colleagues judged that "the egalitarian trend in education has not made the distribution of income or status appreciably more equal over the past 25 years."[63] By 1984, according to Magali Sarfatti Larson, the numbers revealed far worse: "the postwar tendency toward equalization of educational opportunities has been accompanied by *greater, not lesser* inequality of income distribution."[64] And the past two decades, to put it mildly, have only intensified that correlation, have only intensified both income inequality and the desire to attend college. Furthermore, the expansion of education and of higher education in particular arguably exacerbates class difference by consolidating the cultural world of the middle and upper classes, among which higher education is already effectively universal, and by reinscribing for the working class the superiority of middle- and upper-class culture. At the same time, and ironically, the expansion of higher education has deformed or diluted the intellectual mission of the university, and threatens to turn English professors into social workers or the functional equivalent of high school teachers. It is time, I think, for us to face the fact that college is not for everyone: the way to ameliorate the invidious distinction between the classes is not by offering a few more people access to the middle class but by accepting that middle-class culture is not superior to that of the working class.

Middle-class culture is individualistic, hierarchical, and consumerist. As I have argued elsewhere,[65] the educational system, and higher education in particular, preserves and reproduces that culture, including its consumerist proclivities: *American Demographics* reports that "education is a stronger predictor of shopping than income"[66] and Juliet B. Schor adds that "controlling for other factors . . . the more education a person has, *the less he or she saves.* Each additional level of education (going from a high school diploma to some college, for instance, or from a college degree to a postgraduate credential) reduces annual savings by $1,448."[67] Working-class culture, in contrast, places less emphasis on the individual and more on the group, whether clan or, as is the case today, the family, and is thus less competitive, hierarchical, and consumerist than middle-class culture. As Levison puts it in commenting on Lamont's work, which I have cited above, "the values that workers can accurately be said to share as a group"—for example, privileging family over work (which, significantly, is not a "career") and valuing strength of character more than material success—are "not only not objectionable but are, in fact, profoundly admirable."[68]

Such persons do not need a college degree to enable them to lead good and satisfying lives, but they do need to be valued by society. Seeing positive images in the media of people like themselves would be nice, but more importantly, they need to be offered excellent primary and secondary education, as well as excellent secondary and post-secondary vocational training. Indeed, they should be offered the opportunity, as Randall Collins argued in 1979, to be recruited into managerial and professional positions through performance on-the-job.[69] In addition, they need the opportunity to organize in unions, and they need to be given a share of power in political parties and in the polity generally, in which case they might show that, rather than an educational issue, "the distribution of income is a legitimate political issue," as Jencks and his colleagues pointed out thirty years ago,[70] and as the Great Depression and the New Deal made clear seventy years ago. For these reasons, I would like to propose that the college composition classroom become a site for "class activism" by promoting the value and worth of working-class people and working-class culture. If the college composition classroom is a "slim point of entry from one world into the next," as Tinberg thinks,[71] then that classroom ought to be a site where the differences between those worlds are clearly expressed, and expressed without privileging the middle-class world of the university. Such frank talk—as well as opportunities for political participation and viable alternatives for training and work, including efforts to decouple occupational opportunity and higher education—would enable working-class students to get out of the university classroom if they do not want to be there, if they are there only because there are no alternatives and because it seems they need a bachelor's degree in psychology to become a bartender. Such frank talk would enable those who do want to be there to accept our help in teaching them how to become middle class.

Notes

1. Henry Giroux, "Literacy and the Politics of Difference," in *Critical Literacy: Politics, Praxis, and the Postmodern*, ed. Colin Lankshear and Peter L. McLaren (Albany: SUNY Press, 1993), 367, 368, 367. See also James A. Berlin, *Rhetorics, Poetics, and Cultures: Refiguring College English Studies* (Urbana, IL: National Council of Teachers of English, 1996); Patricia Bizzell, *Academic Discourse and Critical Consciousness* (Pittsburgh: University of Pittsburgh Press, 1992); Paolo Freire, *Pedagogy of the Oppressed* (New York: Continuum, 1970); and Ira Shor, *Empowering Education: Critical Teaching for Social Change* (Chicago: University of Chicago Press, 1992).

2. Richard E. Miller, "The Arts of Complicity: Pragmatism and the Culture of Schooling," *College English* 61 (1998), 11.

3. Bizzell, *Academic Discourse and Critical Consciousness*, 133. See also Joe Marshall Hardin, *Opening Spaces: Critical Pedagogy and Resistance Theory in Composition* (Albany: SUNY Press, 2001), 103.

4. Russel K. Durst, *Collision Course: Conflict, Negotiation, and Learning in College Composition* (Urbana, IL: National Council of Teachers of English, 1999), 5; and Susan Peck MacDonald, "Voices of Research: Methodological Choices of a Disciplinary Community," in *Under Construction: Working at the Intersections of Composition Theory, Research, and Practice*, ed. Christine Farris and Chris M. Anson (Logan, UT: Utah State University Press, 1998), 117.
5. Jeff Smith, "Students' Goals, Gatekeeping, and Some Questions of Ethics," *College English* 59 (1997), 107.
6. Kathryn Bond Stockton, "Review: Reading Details, Teaching Politics: Political Mantras and the Politics of Luxury," *College English* 64 (2001), 110, 109.
7. Sherry Lee Linkon, ed., *Teaching Working Class* (Amherst: University of Massachusetts Press, 1999).
8. Ann E. Green, "Writing the Personal: Narrative, Social Class, and Feminist Pedagogy," in *Teaching Working Class*, ed. Linkon, 16.
9. Linda Adler-Kassner, "The Shape of the Form: Working-Class Students and the Academic Essay," in *Teaching Working Class*, ed. Linkon, 91–2; Green, "Writing the Personal," 16–7; Richard A. Greenwald and Elizabeth A. Grant, "Border Crossings: Working-Class Encounters in Higher Education," in *Teaching Working Class*, ed. Linkon, 29, 30, 35; Joseph Heathcott, "What Kinds of Tools? Teaching Critical Analysis and Writing to Working-Class Students," in *Teaching Working Class*, ed. Linkon, 114; and Sherry Lee Linkon, "Introduction: Teaching Working Class," in *Teaching Working Class*, ed. Linkon, 6.
10. Caroline Pari, "'Just American'? Reversing Ethnic and Class Assimilation in the Academy," in *Teaching Working Class*, ed. Linkon, 125.
11. Heathcott, "What Kinds of Tools?," 114.
12. Adler-Kassner, "The Shape of the Form," 100–5; Green, "Writing the Personal," 17; and Greenwald and Grant, "Border Crossings," 29, 30.
13. Green, "Writing the Personal," 16–7.
14. Miller, "The Arts of Complicity," 24.
15. Sharon O'Dair, "Class Matters: Symbolic Boundaries and Cultural Exclusion," in *This Fine Place So Far From Home*, ed. C. L. Barney Dews and Carolyn Leste Law (Philadelphia: Temple University Press, 1995), 203.
16. Janet Zandy, "Introduction," in *Liberating Memory*, ed. Janet Zandy (New Brunswick, NJ: Rutgers University Press, 1995), 1.
17. Green, "Writing the Personal," 17.
18. Delroy Constantine-Simms, "Is Homosexuality the Greatest Taboo?" in *The Greatest Taboo*, ed. Delroy Constantine-Simms (Los Angeles: Alyson Publications, 2001), 76.
19. Earl Ofari Hutchinson, "My Gay Problem, Your Black Problem," in *The Greatest Taboo: Homosexuality in Black Communities*, ed. Delroy Constantine-Simms (Los Angeles: Alyson Publications, 2001), 5.
20. Dwight A. McBride, "Can the Queen Speak? Racial Essentialism, Sexuality, and the Problem of Authority," *Callallo* 21 (1998), 367.
21. Cathy J. Cohen and Tamara Jones, "Fighting Homophobia versus Challenging Heterosexism: 'The Failure to Transform' Revisited," in *Dangerous Liaisons: Blacks, Gays, and the Struggle for Equality*, ed. Eric Brandt (New York: The New Press, 1999), 97, 100.
22. Michèle Lamont, *The Dignity of Working Men: Morality and the Boundaries of Race, Class, and Immigration* (New York: Russell Sage Foundation, 2000), 148, 245, 147.
23. Laurel Johnson Black, "Stupid Rich Bastards," in *This Fine Place So Far From Home*, ed. C.L. Barney Dews and Carolyn Leste Law (Philadelphia: Temple University Press, 1995), 15.
24. Lamont, *The Dignity of Working Men*, 129.
25. See Durst, *Collision Course*; Miller, "The Arts of Complicity"; and David Seitz, "Keeping Honest: Working-Class Students, Difference, and Rethinking the Critical Agenda in Composition," in *Under Construction:*, ed. Christine Farris and Chris M. Anson (Logan, UT: Utah State University Press, 1998).
26. Zandy, "Introduction," 1.
27. Heathcott, "What Kinds of Tools?" 114.
28. Stanley Fish, *Professional Correctness: Literary Studies and Social Change* (Oxford: Clarendon, 1995), 69–70.
29. MacDonald, "Voices of Research," 115.

30. Stephen North, "Rhetoric, Responsibility, and the 'Language of the Left,'" in *Composition and Resistance*, ed. C. Mark Hurlbert and Michael Blitz (Portsmouth, NH: Boynton/Cook, 1991), 132. See also Peter Elbow, *Embracing Contraries: Explorations in Learning and Teaching* (New York: Oxford University Press, 1986), 85–98.

31. Peter Elbow, "The Cultures of Literature and Composition: What Could Each Learn from the Other?," *College English* 64 (2002): 540–43.

32. Pari, "'Just American'?" 129.

33. Linkon, "Introduction," 9.

34. See MacDonald, "Voices of Research"; and Ray Wallace and Susan Lewis Wallace, "Readerless Writers: College Composition's Misreading and Misteaching of Entering Students," in *Reforming College Composition: Writing the Wrongs*, ed. Ray Wallace, et al. (Westport, CT: Greenwood Press, 2000).

35. J. Hillis Miller, "Composition and Decomposition: Deconstruction and the Teaching of Writing," in *Composition and Literature*, ed. W. B. Horner (Chicago: University of Chicago Press, 1983), 52.

36. Stanley Fish, *Doing What Comes Naturally: Change, Rhetoric, and the Practice of Theory in Literary and Legal Studies* (Durham: Duke University Press, 1989), 355.

37. Fish, *Doing What Comes Naturally*, 355, 353.

38. Green, "Writing the Personal," 17.

39. Giroux, "Literacy and the Politics of Difference," 367.

40. Howard Tinberg, "Review: Are We Good Enough? Critical Literacy and the Working Class," *College English* 63 (2001), 353.

41. Tinberg, "Review," 354.

42. Andrew Levison, "Who Lost the Working Class?" *The Nation* (May 14, 2001), 31, 32, 31.

43. John Michael, *Anxious Intellects: Academic Professionals, Public Intellectuals, and Enlightenment Values* (Durham, NC: Duke University Press, 2000), 53, 56.

44. Michael, *Anxious Intellects*, 56.

45. Claude S. Fischer, et al., *Inequality by Design: Cracking the Bell Curve Myth* (Princeton: Princeton University Press, 1996), 152.

46. Fischer, et al., *Inequality by Design*, 153; Michael Zweig, *The Working Class Majority: America's Best Kept Secret* (Ithaca, NY: ILR Press, 2000), 44.

47. Todd Gitlin, *The Twilight of Common Dreams: Why America Is Wracked by Culture Wars* (New York: Henry Holt, 1995), 225; Zweig, *The Working Class Majority*, 44–5.

48. Gitlin, *The Twilight of Common Dreams*, 225.

49. Zweig, *The Working Class Majority*, 45.

50. Martin Trow, "Reflections on the Transition from Mass to Universal Higher Education." *Daedalus* 99 (1970), 3.

51. Fischer, et al., *Inequality by Design*, 155.

52. Quoted in Erik Lords, "Clinton Uses a Commencement Address to Stress the Value of Attending College," in *The Chronicle of Higher Education* (June 23, 2000): A34.

53. Cited in Kenneth C. Gray and Edwin L. Herr, *Other Ways to Win: Creating Alternatives for High School Graduates* (Thousand Oaks, CA: Corwin Press, 1995), 5, 8-9.

54. Lawrence Mishel, et al., *The State of Working America* (Armonk: M. E. Sharpe, 1997), 25, 24.

55. Mishel, et al., *The State of Working America*, 26.

56. See Renny Christopher, "Teaching Working-Class Literature to Mixed Audiences," in *Teaching Working Class*, ed. Sherry Lee Linkon (Amherst: University of Massachusetts Press, 1999).

57. Gray and Herr, *Other Ways to Win*, 54–8.

58. Christopher, "Teaching Working-Class Literature to Mixed Audiences," 220, 219.

59. Daniel Green, "Opinion: Abandoning the Ruins," *College English* 63 (2001): 283–85.

60. John Alberti, "Returning to Class: Creating Opportunities for Multicultural Reform at Majority Second-Tier Schools," *College English* 63 (2001), 563.

61. Alberti, "Returning to Class," 581–82.

62. See John Guillory, "The System of Graduate Education," *PMLA* 115 (2000): 1154–63; and Sharon O'Dair, "Beyond Necessity: The Consumption of Class, the Production of Status, and the Persistence of Inequality" *NLH* 31 (2000): 337–54.

63. Christopher Jencks, et al., *Inequality: A Reassessment of the Effect of Family and Schooling in America* (New York: Basic Books, 1972), 261.

64. Magali Sarfatti Larson, "The Production of Expertise and the Constitution of Expert Power," in *The Authority of Experts: Studies in History and Theory*, ed. Thomas L. Haskell (Bloomington: Indiana University Press, 1984), 43.
65. See O'Dair, "Beyond Necessity"; and Sharon O'Dair, *Class, Critics, and Shakespeare: Bottom Lines on the Culture Wars* (Ann Arbor: University of Michigan Press, 2000).
66. John P. Robinson, "When the Going Gets Tough," *American Demographics* (February 1989), 50.
67. Juliet B. Schor, *The Overspent American: Upscaling, Downshifting, and the New Consumer* (New York: Basic Books, 1998), 76.
68. Levison, "Who Lost the Working Class?" 27.
69. See Randall Collins, *The Credential Society: An Historical Sociology of Education and Stratification* (New York: Academic Press, 1979).
70. Jencks, et al., *Inequality*, 264.
71. Tinberg, "Review," 360.

The Actualities
of Media Interventions

CHAPTER 9

Media, Activism, and the Classroom

Teaching Black Feminist Cultural Criticism

JACQUELINE BOBO

Theory is rendered tangible in Black women's cultural work. Praxis, often talked about but little understood, moves from abstract concept to palpable form, and slippery ideas such as consciousness, agency, self-determination, transformation (both individual and cultural), indeed, even the idealistic word "empowerment," become real and achievable. Vivid examples of these principles that are so necessary for social and political activism—the essence of Black feminism—are portrayed in three dynamic documentaries: *A Place of Rage* (1991), directed by Pratibha Parmar; *Fundi: The Story of Ella Baker* (1981), directed by Joanne Grant; and, *Gotta Make This Journey: Sweet Honey in the Rock* (1983), directed by Michelle Parkerson.[1]

Although the films focus on the lives of extraordinary women, the central issues they raise concern the political activities of influential Black women as they sparked catalytic events within historic moments. The women portrayed include poet and social critic June Jordan and professor and political activist Angela Davis in *A Place of Rage*, civil rights revolutionary Ella Baker in *Fundi: The Story of Ella Baker*, and *Gotta Make This Journey*, which features Bernice Johnson Reagon, cultural scholar and founder of the highly respected a cappella music group Sweet Honey in the Rock. Each film superbly achieves the desired effect of political films: they contain mutually reinforcing components of historical exegesis, inspiration, and a call to action.

The films are ideal for classroom use. The production aspects engage students in the subject matter and sustain their interest throughout the approximately hour-long showings. Together with supporting print material and analysis during lectures before and after the showings, these three films have proven extremely valuable to convey ideas, theories, concepts, and even histories, that are little known to the majority of dominant society. Even for students who have taken a number of Black Studies courses and who have studied in allied areas, the information contained in these films offers new material. Many times, after seeing these films, students are upset that they were not introduced to the material earlier in their academic studies. These documentaries ignite spirited discussions and stimulate students' interest in pursuing similar subjects.

I've used the films effectively in a variety of undergraduate teaching contexts: as part of a lower division entry-level course in the Women's Studies Program that satisfies general education requirements, and enrolls between 120 and 150 students; as part of an upper division course on Black women filmmakers, enrolling students from a range of disciplines, including Women's Studies, Black Studies, and Film Studies; and, *A Place of Rage* has proven especially useful for an upper division production-oriented course entitled "Representation and Activism," where students "make media."

The lower division entry-level course attracts students from across the campus for a variety of reasons ranging from the time the course is offered to the fact that the Women's Studies course will satisfy a particular general education requirement. Many students are not majors and are not predisposed to the objectives of the course, which is an introduction to Women's Studies, with an emphasis on grounding students in feminist theories. The upper division course, "Black Women Filmmakers," tends to draw students who have a desire for the specific information. After the first course meeting, invariably, word-of-mouth information attracts students wanting to add the course. Even though the course is not specifically geared toward Film Studies majors, being housed as it is in the Women's Studies Program and by necessity accommodating students with no prior background in film concepts, Film Studies majors are encouraged to take the course because the majority of the films are created by independent filmmakers. Consequently, much can be learned about the pragmatics of film conception and production without the distractions of high-gloss mega-million dollar construction, such as that seen in mainstream Hollywood productions.

The upper division production oriented course, "Representation and Activism," is one I designed to assist students understand the rudiments of representation. If students are shown the skeletons of image creation, and allowed to try their hands at media making in a safe environment, then they understand more fully that images don't just happen, that they are constructed, and are imbued with powerful meanings.

History, Politics, Representation

A Place of Rage is a 53-minute documentary that interconnects historical resistance movements with political, social, and cultural activism. The director, Pratibha Parmar, is a British resident of Indian heritage who was born in Nairobi, Kenya and is a founding member of Black Women Talk, one of the first Black women's publishing houses in Britain.[2] Parmar funded and distributed *A Place of Rage* through public television station Channel 4 in Great Britain. Her stated goal in the making of the documentary was to preserve the legacy of Black women's contributions in the far-reaching struggles and triumphs of civil rights movements: "It's about reclaiming Black women's role in the past. It also says there are lessons to be learned for today. First about the way women were treated in those movements and secondly, about the leadership role they continue to play today. Angela Davis' work in the Black women's health movement, or June Jordan's writing around international issues, including Palestine and the Gulf War, are two examples."[3]

The film features commentary from artists who lived through the events portrayed. Black feminist author Alice Walker stresses that Black women were essential to freedom struggles and "were the pillars of the Movement." Walker offers examples of women such as Septima Clark, who founded citizenship schools in the South so that Black people could learn to read and write, and in the process, overcome one of the institutionalized impediments to their right to vote.

Yet another artist tells of the inspiration she received from the works of June Jordan and the autobiography of Angela Davis. Filmmaker Trinh T. Minh-ha, director of the highly regarded films, *Reassemblage* (1982) and *Surname Viet, Given Name Nam* (1989), points to the formidable resistance these women faced in Movement activities, noting that the majority of the opposition to Black women came from "men who call themselves radicals. They seem to view the fight mainly in terms of competition." Trinh T. Minh-ha concludes that despite their significant contributions, "Black women are invisible in most accounts of the Movement."

The primary focus of *A Place of Rage* is the public personae and political/cultural histories of June Jordan (1936–2002) and Angela Davis. At the time of her death Jordan was Professor of African-American Studies at the University of California, Berkeley and the author/editor of twenty-eight books, essays, and novels for children. Jordan had also written the libretto for the

1995 opera *I Was Looking at the Ceiling and Then I Saw the Sky*. June Jordan was widely acclaimed for her cogent essays and speeches on behalf of poor people, the disenfranchised, those without a public voice, and as someone who could be counted on to fight against injustice wherever it might occur.

In the documentary Jordan speaks of the evolution of her profound understanding of the persistent malevolence so rampant in society. Jordan remembers that as a young child she learned how "one word could make a life or death difference." The example she gives is that of the word "Negro" in front of "neighborhood." Even though the police would not come to Negro neighborhoods when assistance was requested by the residents, states Jordan, the police entered Negro neighborhoods and homes whenever they wanted with unconditional license to use unnecessary force. Jordan's constant observance of this legally sanctioned brutality hardened her, she states, "into a permanent place of rage."

In 1969, as a young Black female teaching at a major research university, Angela Davis entered into the public consciousness. Davis was a faculty member in the Philosophy department at the University of California, Los Angeles. Davis was also completing her PhD at the University of California, San Diego, writing her dissertation under the direction of Marxist professor Herbert Marcuse. The Regents of the University of California—the governing body of the nine campus statewide system—voted to terminate Davis from her position, the stated reason given was Davis' membership in the Communist Party, U.S.A. Davis and her lawyers filed an injunction that prohibited the Regents from firing her for political reasons. However, despite the court injunction, the Regents later voted not to re-hire Davis for the coming year. All of these actions were played out in the national headlines.

Angela Davis is a lifelong political activist who had grown up in the segregated South in Birmingham, Alabama, studied at Brandeis University with Marcuse, traveled to Europe to study with the leading philosophers in Germany, including Theodor Adorno, and had returned to the United States to complete her PhD at University of California, San Diego. Davis had also worked with others to form the organization Lumumba-Zapata College at University of California, San Diego, named for the assassinated Congolese revolutionary leader Patrice Lumumba and the Mexican revolutionary Emiliano Zapata. Davis also became a member of the Che-Lumumba Club, the Black component, or "cell" of the Communist Party, U.S.A. Che Guevara was a hero of the Cuban Revolution. While a faculty member at UCLA, Davis was a founding member of the Soledad Brothers Defense Committee. The Soledad Brothers were three Black men—George Jackson, Fleeta Drumgo, and John Clutchette—who were active in fighting for prisoners' rights and had been accused of killing a guard at Soledad Prison, located in California, in January 1970.

On August 7, 1970, Jonathan Jackson, the 17-year-old brother of George Jackson, entered a Marin County, California courtroom, heavily armed with guns that were legally registered to Angela Davis, and took over the courtroom. Jonathan armed three Black men in the courtroom—James McClain, a prisoner accused of assaulting a prison guard; Ruchell Magee, who was imprisoned in San Quentin and in the courtroom testifying on behalf of McClain; and, William Christmas, also imprisoned at San Quentin and in the courtroom to testify in McClain's defense. The four Black men left the courtroom with five White hostages: the judge, the prosecutor, and three female jurors. San Quentin guards fired on the van containing the four Black men and the hostages, which was stopped at a roadblock. Killed in the gunfire from the San Quentin guards were Jonathan Jackson, James McClain, William Christmas, and judge Harold Haley. Several others were wounded.

Because some of the guns used by Jonathan Jackson were registered to Angela Davis, she was charged with murder, conspiracy, and kidnapping. When Davis learned of the shootout, fearing for her life, she fled the state and became the first female placed on the FBI Ten Most Wanted Fugitives List. Davis eluded capture for two months, subsequently spent a total of 16 months in prison, endured three months of a trial by jury, and on June 4, 1972 was acquitted of all charges. Currently, Angela Davis is Professor in the History of Consciousness Program at the University of California, Santa Cruz.[4]

Archival footage of the events that forever lodged Davis in political history serve effectively as *zeitgeist* in *A Place of Rage*, allowing viewers to see not simply a present-day historical figure, but the spirit of the times in which government actions against an individual such as Angela Davis and other political activists could occur. Communities and college campuses across the country were in a constant state of outrage over contested actions such as the country's involvement in the Vietnam war, the police killings of Black students at Jackson State University in Mississippi, and the deaths of the student protestors at Kent State in Ohio at the hands of the National Guard.

The formal construction of *A Place of Rage* sets it apart from traditional documentaries. Noticeably, voiceover narration is refreshingly absent. In a telling moment in the film, the transition from present-day Davis speaking about her imprisonment is juxtaposed with visuals of her in prison in the 1970s being interviewed behind a bulletproof glass for a British documentary. The voiceover narrator is a British male who relates in ominous tones the circumstances surrounding the interview with Angela Davis. The segment is a poignant insight into the thoughts and, in retrospect, the constancy of the young Angela Davis: "All the educational opportunities that I had did not negate the fact that I am a Black woman, and that, as a Black woman, I continued to experience the oppression of my people. And continued to feel the necessity to involve myself as intensely as possible in that struggle to overcome oppression."

While allowing viewers entry to such a frightful moment so emblematic of the times, the voice of the male British narrator is a vivid reminder of the omniscient "voice of God" trope so prevalent in mainstream documentaries. In this instance, for a film so focused on redressing the "structured absence" of Black women from historic resistance movements, the deliberate omission of the authoritative male voice as a structuring device elsewhere in A Place of Rage becomes all the more compelling.

Throughout A Place of Rage lively contemporary music layers added commentary on the subject of Black people's lived experiences. Prince's "Sign O' the Times" (1987) speaks to the devastation of drugs and hopelessness in Black communities; Janet Jackson's "Rhythm Nation" (1989) is a spirited paean to Black youth; the Neville Brothers "Sister Rosa" (1989) is heard as background to shots of a media installation of photos and personal items featuring Black women, and the words give thanks to Rosa Parks for her contributions to the freedom struggles of Black people; and, at the conclusion, the song by the Staple Singers, "If You're Ready, Come Go With Me" (1973), in the closing shots of present-day Angela Davis and June Jordan, is an invitation to activism.

Location shots of Jordan and Davis in their daily routines serve to humanize the women. These personal portraits are interspersed with shots of Davis and Jordan speaking about their histories and thoughts on contemporary issues such as the plague of drugs in Black communities, the military recruitment in Black and impoverished communities, institutional racism, specific infringements of Black men's rights and police brutality, solidarity between women of color, the need for greater attention to the rights of lesbian and gay people, and the evolution of their personal awareness of injustice and commitment to activist movements worldwide.

And, remarkably, the oratorical skills of June Jordan are brought to life in performance pieces that are intercut throughout the documentary. Taken from the published essays of Jordan, dramatic impact is conveyed through the personal magnetism of Jordan's spoken word delivery. The medium of spoken word is consciously politically grounded and combines the authority of language with the impact of performance. Crucially, the central element in spoken word is the text and its capacity to reconstitute pervasive images of particular social groups.[5] These performance interludes energize the documentary and are especially striking given the manner in which the director has "dressed the set," or mounted the performances. In a studio setting, poster-size photographs taken from Brian Lanker's *I Dream a World: Portraits of Black Women Who Changed America*,[6] are positioned in front of a stark sky blue backdrop, with Jordan speaking at a podium. A constantly moving camera traveling in an arc around Jordan captures both her and the women in the photographs, serving to present a collective voice of the women through the words of June Jordan.

A specific piece by Jordan that resonates well with students is her poem about individual rights, nations' sovereignty, rape, the sanctity of women's bodies, imperialist invasion of African countries, and peoples' willingness to fight back: ". . . in France they say if the guy penetrates/but does not ejaculate then he did not rape me/. . . which is exactly like South Africa penetrating into Namibia penetrating into/Angola and does that mean I mean how do you know if/Pretoria ejaculates what will the evidence look like/. . . and if/after Namibia and if after Angola and if after Zimbabwe/and if after all my kinsmen and women resist even to/self-immolation of the villages and if after that/we lose nevertheless what will the big boys say will they/claim my consent. . . . "[7]

At a later point in *A Place of Rage*, Jordan delivers another segment of the poem: Do You Follow Me:/We are the wrong people of/the wrong skin on the wrong continent and what/in the hell is everybody being reasonable about/. . . "*I am not wrong: Wrong is not my name*/My name is my own my own my own/and I can't tell you who the hell set things up like this/but I can tell you that from now on my resistance/my simple and daily and nightly self-determination/may very well cost you your life."[8]

At the beginning of *A Place of Rage*, Jordan speaks emphatically of the revolutionary changes brought about through Black people's freedom struggles: "Things have changed absolutely in my lifetime. And they changed because we made them change." Clear evidence of the force of group actions reverberates when Angela Davis recalls her imprisonment and the organized efforts of people on her behalf and against political repression: "As I look back on that era, the historical significance of my case was that people took the organizing seriously; got together, built committees all over the country, all over the world; sent letters and telegrams and petitions to presidents and governors and judges. In the final analysis, there was nothing the government could do to counter that force. And that is why I was set free."

The women presented in the three documentaries examined in this article are not victims. They are powerful, forceful people who worked with others to change history. Their life stories on film contradict the prevailing representations of Black women's lives. That the subjects of these documentaries are not presented as passive, hopeless, pawns of repressive social conditions is an important intervention, because the "victim motif" has been a staple of mainstream documentaries for decades.[9] Presenting members of previously underrepresented groups as victims also serves the interests of those in power because it perpetuates the myth that individuals do not have control over their lives and must wait for "saviors" in the form of those from the dominant culture.

Image creation and representation are not innocent processes and not without consequences. The way in which members of social groups are shown to the larger society can play a determining role in how these groups are treated socially, politically, economically, and institutionally. Important in this politics of representation is not only what is selected to be shown, but what has been withheld. For these reasons, it is critically important that particular social groups have a say in how the groups are represented. Putting in that which has been left out—*A Place of Rage, Fundi: The Story of Ella Baker, Gotta Make This Journey*—balances history and ensures that other perspectives are made public.

Agency, Activism, Empowerment

In the closing frames of *A Place of Rage*, June Jordan talks about the continuing necessity for activism: "Rage has lost its respectability since the 1960s. The thing that you had in the civil rights revolution was an absolute, upfront embrace of rage and a working with that. When you don't rage against the evils and the enemies against you, what you do is you turn in against yourself. And you begin to despair and give up and become suicidal. And that leads to this plague of drugs and drug abuse that you see taking our young people out in droves today."

Political and social activism can be effectively translated through cultural means. Angela Davis writes that cultural practices have a primary role in the socialization process. In her article, "Black Women and Music: A Historical Legacy of Struggle," Davis lays a foundation for the historical development of Black women's social consciousness. Davis confirms that music in Black life has both shaped and expressed a collective awareness of social and political conditions. During periods of intense movements for social change, Davis notes, music "has helped to shape the necessary political consciousness."[10]

The political force of Bernice Johnson Reagon and Sweet Honey in the Rock has given momentum and stability over several decades to numerous social movements, as exemplified so powerfully in *Fundi: The Story of Ella Baker* and *Gotta Make This Journey: Sweet Honey in the Rock*. In fact, the original song that Reagon composed for *Fundi*, "Ella's Song," accompanies other political documentaries, including *Yuri Kochiyama: Passion for Justice*

(1994), directed by Pat Saunders and Rea Tajiri; and, *Faith Even to the Fire* (1992), directed by Sylvia Morales and Jean Victor.[11]

The words for "Ella's Song" were inspired by the keynote address delivered by Ella Baker to the Mississippi Freedom Democratic Party delegation during their challenge to be seated at the 1964 Democratic National Convention held in Atlantic City, New Jersey. Throughout the summer of 1964, which came to be known as Mississippi Freedom Summer, activists from the organization Student Nonviolent Coordinating Committee (SNCC) had attempted to register Black voters in the traditional Democratic Party. Constantly blocked by White Southerners, the student voter registration volunteers created an alternate party, the Mississippi Freedom Democratic Party, registering 60,000 Black voters, and electing forty-four "freedom delegates" to the Democratic National Convention. Ella Baker was one of the lead organizers of the MFDP and its bid to be recognized as voting members of the convention.

During Baker's speech to the MFDP delegates, she referred to the sustained public outrage at the murders of three civil rights workers—Michael Schwerner, Andrew Goodman, and James Chaney—in Mississippi in the summer of 1964. When the bodies of the young students were located after a six weeks' search, the pathologist who autopsied the bodies said that Schwerner and Goodman, who were White, had been shot in the heart, and that Chaney "had been beaten to a pulp. . . . In my twenty-five years as a pathologist and medical examiner, I have never seen bones so severely shattered, except in tremendously high speed accidents or airplane crashes." Commenting on the deaths, Michael Schwerner's widow stated that the massive search for the students, which was only undertaken by the federal government after intense pressure from nationwide publicity, was because her husband and Andrew Goodman were White: "If only Chaney were involved, nothing would have been done."[12]

Many Black people were aware that as the federal authorities searched for the missing civil rights workers, they found bodies of murdered Black men in the rivers of Mississippi that no one had previously investigated because they had not been killed along with White men. Ella Baker was angry at the deaths of the young volunteers and particularly upset at the circumstances of young Chaney's death. Her sentiments were preserved in song and in the documentary *Fundi*. Baker resolved that: "Until the killing of Black men, Black mother's sons, becomes as important to the rest of the country as a white mother's son, we who believe in freedom will not rest until it comes."

Ella Baker (1903–1986) had a profound influence on several generations of social justice activists. In the 1940s, she was a field organizer for the National Association for the Advancement of Colored People, traveling throughout the South six months of the year organizing membership drives and working with communities to help them recognize their potential for collective action. Baker had an intimate knowledge of the South; she was born in Norfolk, Virginia and spent her formative years in rural North Carolina, graduating from Shaw University in Raleigh, North Carolina. Baker moved to New York right before the Depression and became involved in radical organizations there, notably, In Friendship, an organization she helped found, along with Bayard Rustin and Stanley Levison. In Friendship provided economic support to Black people in the South who faced financial hardships because of their political activism. Through working with Rustin and Levison and the organization In Friendship, Baker honed her progressive ideas about social change, refining the idea of group-centered leadership, that those involved in social movement organizations can be empowered to act on their own behalf if they participate in the decision making process.[13]

This political privileging of the "rank and file" members rather than the authoritarian head of an organization placed Baker in conflict with the directors of the NAACP and, later, the group for which she was the first organizer, the Southern Christian Leadership Conference. With admirable foresight, Ella Baker felt that the development of leadership capabilities within individuals would enhance their ability for long-term political action. Baker cautioned repeatedly against continual reliance on a "charismatic leader:"

> I have always felt it was a handicap for oppressed people to depend so largely on a leader, because unfortunately in our culture, the charismatic leader usually becomes a leader because he has found a spot in the public limelight. It usually means that the media made him, and the media may undo him. There is also the danger in our culture that, because a person is called upon to give public statements and is acclaimed by the establishment, such a person gets to the point of believing that he *is* the movement. Such people get so involved with playing the game of being important that they exhaust themselves and their time and they don't do the work of actually organizing people.[14]

These ideas were the principles behind the organization for which Ella Baker was the guiding force, the Student Nonviolent Coordinating Committee, the organization that became the inspiration for other activist groups in the 1960s, such as the Students for a Democratic Society. *Fundi: The Story of Ella Baker* skillfully blends archival footage of Baker's life promoting participatory democracy—group-centered leadership—and interactions with those who heeded her call for living and working in the communities where movement activities, such as voter registration drives, were taking place. One such person was Bob Moses,[15] who categorized Baker as the embodiment of "Fundi," a designation of honor originating from Swahili. The title refers to someone in a community who masters a craft, then passes on what they have learned by sharing it with others.

Bernice Johnson Reagon refers to Ella Baker as her "political mother" and uses her example of recognizing the potential for resistance to oppression in every individual. Reagon's goal, in the formation of Sweet Honey in the Rock, was to provide the inspiration that motivated people toward collective action for social change. It was her participation in the freedom movement, Reagon states in *Gotta Make This Journey*, that made her realize that songs can do more than make people feel good; they have the power to mobilize concentrated, large-scale opposition to varied manifestations of injustice.

Reagon emphasizes the tremendous courage of those who participated in the voter registration drives. The American public was aware of the large protest marches because these were the events attracting national media coverage, but the local campaigns for the right to vote cost many Black people, and others, their lives. As a consequence, Reagon's first singing group, the SNCC Freedom Singers, became a "singing newspaper," keeping people at the grassroots level informed of the activities in the small cities and towns where Black people were fighting for their constitutional rights.

Through these experiences, Reagon became a specialist in Black oral, performance, and protest traditions, earning a PhD in History from Howard University in Washington, D.C. In 1989, she was awarded a MacArthur "genius" Fellowship and is currently Distinguished Professor of History at American University and Curator Emeritus at the Smithsonian Institution, National Museum of American History. Reagon formed the a cappella singing group, Sweet Honey in the Rock, in 1973, taking its name from a parable in the Bible. According to the parable, there was a land that was so rich that when the rocks were cracked, honey would flow from them. Over the course of the group's thirty-year existence, over twenty women have at various times been members.

Gotta Make This Journey: Sweet Honey in the Rock, produced by Michelle Parkerson, is a broadcast videotape of Sweet Honey's ninth anniversary concert, held at Gallaudet College in Washington, D.C. It is a thoughtful documentary and much more than a typical concert tape. Compatibility is established between the programming of the concert and the structure of the videotape, so that the force of Sweet Honey builds throughout, not overwhelming the viewer. Careful attention is given to the rhythm and pacing of the video, matching the content of the songs with the narrative provided by the individual women as they are interviewed in the field segments of the documentary.

The six then-current members of Sweet Honey—Yasmeen Williams, Evelyn Harris, Aisha Kahlil, Ysaye Barnwell, Shirley Johnson (the sign language interpreter), and the group's founder and leader, Bernice Johnson Reagon—all express their commitment to Sweet Honey's political mission of creating awareness of specific human rights issues. Examples include the soundtrack provided by the group for *The Wilmington Ten—USA 10,000* (1978), directed by Haile Gerima. The song "You can break one human body, I see ten thousand Bikos,"[16] was composed by Reagon specifically for Gerima's documentary, and the song accompanies a series of photographs of anti-apartheid marches in South Africa. The comparison likens the repression in South Africa with the condition of those unjustly imprisoned in Wilmington, North Carolina, and, in turn, draws a parallel to acts of injustice throughout the world.

The three documentaries analyzed in this article offer textbook examples of the process of how representation becomes more than simply documentation. There is a specific emphasis on Black women as social agents actively committed to changing repressive conditions and working towards better lives. In the book *Women and the Politics of Empowerment,* editors Ann Bookman and Sandra Morgen offer a comprehensive assessment of the goals of empowerment:

> For the women whose lives form the subject of this book, empowerment is rarely experienced as upward mobility or personal advancement. . . . For these women, empowerment begins when they change their ideas about the causes of their powerlessness, when they recognize the systemic forces that oppress them, and when they act to change the conditions of their lives. . . . Fundamentally, then, empowerment is a *process* aimed at consolidating, maintaining, or changing the nature and distribution of power in a particular cultural context. This process is rarely a linear one. It takes twists and turns, includes both resistance and consent, and ebbs and flows as groups with different relations to the structures and sources of power come into conflict.[17]

In my work on Black female cultural producers, I have categorized them as comprising a cultural movement that is re-constituting the images of Black women in popular imagination and in the minds of Black women themselves.[18] Within this movement Black women have reclaimed a history that has been distorted or ignored; reconstructed and re-presented this history; documented the reconstruction by means of a cultural manifestation, whether in literature, film, television, dance, theatre, poetry, music, or some other form; and, shared the vision of this reconstruction through various methods of dissemination. The overarching goal is some form of social change or the re-configuration of the existing social order.

A Place of Rage, Fundi: The Story of Ella Baker, and *Gotta Make This Journey: Sweet Honey in the Rock* belong to a burgeoning tradition of films created by Black women that are instrumental in erasing destructive ideologies affecting Black women. The filmmakers are vital components of a configuration of activists that seeks to transform the status of Black women in popular imagination and in the minds of Black women themselves. Through meticulous concentration on Black women's history, faithfully representing their lives, Black women's films magnify female viewers' perception of their material circumstances, potentially motivating them toward activism, thereby strengthening their viability as a potent social force.

Notes

1. *A Place of Rage* and *Gotta Make This Journey: Sweet Honey in the Rock* are both available from the distributor Women Make Movies, http://www.wmm.com; *Fundi: The Story of Ella Baker* is available from First Run/Icarus Films, http://www.frif.com. Except where noted, all other referenced films are available from Women Make Movies.

2. Parmar's first film was an 11-minute video, *Sari Red*, about the killing of an Asian woman in Britain by White youth.

3. Melba Wilson, "All the Rage," *The Guardian* (October 3, 1991): 19. Parmar also directed *Khush*, about South Asian lesbians and gay men living in India and Great Britain; and, with the novelist Alice Walker, Parmar directed the film *Warrior Marks*, about female circumcision.

4. Valuable background information can be found in the following works: Bettina Aptheker, *The Morning Breaks: The Trial of Angela Davis* (New York: International Publishers, 1975); Angela Davis, et al., eds., *If They Come in the Morning: Voices of Resistance* (New York: New American Library, 1971); Angela Davis, *Angela Davis: An Autobiography* (New York: Random House, 1974).

5. For a cogent explication of spoken word and its unique distinction from performance poetry, see Evelyn McDonnell, "Divas Declare a Spoken Word Revolution," *Ms.* (January–February1996): 74–79.

6. See Brian Lanker, *I Dream a World: Portraits of Black Women Who Changed America* (New York: Stewart, Tabori and Chang, 1989). *I Dream a World* is also a traveling exhibition in various galleries throughout the United States.

7. June Jordan, "Poem About My Rights," in *Passion: New Poems, 1977–1980* (Boston: Beacon Press, 1980), 86.

8. Jordan, "Poem About My Rights," 87.

9. Mike Wayne, *Theorizing Video Practice* (London: Lawrence and Wishart, 1997), 211.

10. Angela Davis, "Black Women and Music," in *Wild Women in the Whirlwind: Afra-American Culture and the Contemporary Literary Renaissance*, ed. Joanne M. Braxton and Andree Nicola McLaughlin (New Brunswick, NJ: Rutgers University Press, 1990), 3.

11. *Faith Even to the Fire* is available from The Filmakers Library, http://www.filmmakers.com, *Yuri Kochiyama: Passion of Justice* is available from Women Make Movies, http://www.wmm.com.html.

12. Reported in Terry M. Anderson, *The Movement and the Sixties: Protest in America From Greensboro to Wounded Knee* (New York: Oxford University Press, 1995), 78.

13. See Charles Payne, "Ella Baker and Models of Social Change," *Signs: Journal of Women in Culture and Society* 14 (1989): 885–899; and Carol Mueller, "Ella Baker and the Origins of 'Participatory Democracy,'" in *Women in the Civil Rights Movement: Trailblazers and Torchbearers, 1941–1965*, ed. Vicki L. Crawford, et al. (Bloomington: Indiana University Press, 1993).

14. Ella Baker, "Developing Community Leadership," in *Black Women in White America*, ed. Gerda Lerner (New York: Vintage, 1973), 351.

15. Bob Moses remains motivated by the tenets and spirit of Ella Baker and has remained a movement activist. Moses initiated the "Algebra Project," begun in 1981, to give poor and educationally disenfranchised Black youth access to math and science literacy. For his constancy as a movement activist and innovator, Bob Moses was awarded a MacArthur "genius" grant in 1982. A PhD in Philosophy of Mathematics from Harvard University, Bob Moses shares his experiences in his memoir, *Radical Equations: Civil Rights from Mississippi to the Algebra Project* (Boston: Beacon Press, 2001), written with fellow activist and journalist Charles E. Cobb.

16. Steven Biko was a South African anti-apartheid activist who was murdered by White police officers. Biko's life is fictionalized in director Richard Attenborough's widely available film *Cry Freedom* (1987), starring Denzel Washington as Biko.

17. Ann Bookman and Sandra Morgen (eds.), *Women and the Politics of Empowerment* (Philadelphia: Temple University Press, 1988), 4.

18. For information about the films, distributors, and how to incorporate the films into various classes, see my books *Black Women as Cultural Readers* (New York: Columbia University Press, 1995), *Black Women Film and Video Artists* (New York: Routledge, 1998), and *Black Feminist Cultural Criticism* (Malden, MA: Blackwell, 2001).

CHAPTER **10**

Back to Cyberschool
Some of the Learning, None of the Fun

DAVID TREND

Tremendous changes have been taking place in education during the past decade—changes that have laid the groundwork for a radical technological transformation of schools in the coming years. As the "tidal wave" of baby boomers' children continues to move from elementary school to college levels, the digital mechanization of teaching is moving at a quick pace. But the introduction of technology into the nation's schools and universities could never have been imagined unless a fundamental transformation had occurred in the way education was organized, managed, and funded. It took the introduction of corporations into education to get the job done.

A confluence of several cultural, political, and economic factors made this transformation of education possible. The back-to-basics reform movements of the 1980s, rooted as they were in the liberal/conservative culture wars, concerned themselves largely with the content of education: the books, courses, teaching methods, school regulations, and values that made up the educational experience. With the ascendancy of Bill Clinton to the White House, the culture wars continued to be fought over issues ranging from the arts and entertainment to the personal behavior of public figures. But in education they went underground, leaving behind a residue of public discontent and suspicion that enabled structural changes in schools at local, state, and federal levels. Meanwhile, a college degree changed from an option to a career necessity for entrance into the middle class, and pressure grew to control skyrocketing tuition, even as new demands were placed on colleges to broaden the kind of education they delivered. As a result, institutions of higher learning began to change how they operated, often at the expense of their more traditional functions.

The economic context for these changes is significant—especially as budgets have taken such a nasty turn from 2000 to 2004. It began in the 1990s, when the number and magnitude of corporate mergers reached unprecedented levels. By the end of the decade, yearly mergers had topped $1-trillion—or more than 200 percent their 1996 level.[1] America OnLine merged with Time-Warner, MCI bought Sprint, Daimler-Benz purchased Chrysler, Westinghouse acquired CBS, and CBS merged with Viacom. With the so-called "triumph" of capitalism across the globe and the relaxation of international trade barriers, multinational corporations grew and prospered as never before. Meanwhile within the U.S. government, budget surpluses and the meteoric rise of the stock market fueled a media-driven belief that the booming economy could never go bust. On many levels, it seemed that the enlightened corporation was the engine of utopia. And given the centrality of "dot.com" in this transformation, technology was widely touted as the fuel for the utopian dynamo.

It should come as no surprise that as computer technology and Internet stocks captured the nation's imagination at the end of the 1990s, these values would be mapped onto education. But unlike past technological revolutions, the digital age was driven by the very institution that high-speed communication had helped to bring into existence: the multinational corporation. The result was the transformation of education to an unprecedented, yet largely under-acknowledged, extent. While the public had been wearied by a repeated cycle of emotional school-related debates over vouchers, school uniforms, and prayers at football games, the unquestioned value of technology in education offered a magical release, opening the door to a myriad of commercial enterprises, their methods of operation, and the underlying ideologies that motivate them.

The most dramatic factor driving the rush to technology in education was the anticipated growth of the student population. The so-called "echo boom" of offspring from the post World War II baby boomers hit the secondary school level in the late 1990s. The effect in California alone resulted in a need for 260,000 new K–12 teachers in the subsequent decade. During this period the number of college-age young people is expected to grow by 20 percent and the overall enrollments are projected to expand by 40 percent. This profound growth in the student population has occurred at a time when the original cohort of post-war college professors—hired to meet the demands of the original baby boom generation—has contracted through retirement. Finally, this decline in the established post-secondary workforce began taking place just as the facilities—the classrooms, laboratories, and campus infrastructure—of many colleges and universities built or expanded in the 1960s and 1970s required repair or replacement. In some areas, this has even necessitated the construction of new schools.

In the face of this apparent demand for professors and buildings, one might imagine that educational administrators would be planning new hiring initiatives and capital campaigns. Not so. Regrettably the residue of the "back to basics" reform movements of the 1980s, as well as negative public opinion generated by conservatives toward university based affirmative action, multiculturalism, "political correctness," and "tenured radicalism" created an atmosphere in which increases in educational funding became all but politically unthinkable, except for kindergarten and elementary school children. Coupled with the corporatization of education, the escalating state and federal fiscal crises of the 2000s have resulted in calls for greater efficiency in education rather than more school spending.

Rather than replacing retiring tenured professors, the number of temporary, part-time instructors has continued to grow, as increasing responsibilities have been heaped on graduate teaching assistants. Rather than constructing new classrooms, plans were developed to expand the usage of existing facilities. The most extreme consequences of this occurred at the community college level, where in some districts classes began to be offered twenty-four hours per day, every day of the year. Labor issues aside, this has created a highly compromised environment for teaching and learning— but one that is clearly more cost efficient than earlier models. Propelling this move to efficiency is a new breed of academic administrators, entering the university from the business sector or rising within the university due to their business expertise. As a result, those in decision-making positions within higher education are increasingly sympathetic to critiques of the university as fiscally bloated and unresponsive to "customer" demand. At the center of this corporatist reform resides the mechanization of instruction. New forms of distance learning, teleconferencing, computer-mediated instruction, Web and CD-ROM based curricula are being implemented to increase teacher productivity by enabling the instruction of larger groups of students and eliminating the need for duplicate presentations. Now these uses are being extended throughout the campus to enable web-based course registration, library use, syllabi postings, and exam schedules.

The Past is Prologue

Of course, the idea of mechanized instruction isn't new. In the 1920s and 1930s such "audiovisual" materials as sound recordings, slides, and films were widely used in K–12 schooling with the support of the Division of Visual Instruction of the National Educational Association. The newly emerging field of educational psychology supported these new media in the belief they improved students' experience of school and enhanced their ability to memorize concepts.[2] In the 1920s, the Division of Visual Instruction actively lobbied equipment manufacturers and film production companies to enter the educational market. It also worked to convince the military of the importance of audiovisual media, both as a means of training troops and also as a propaganda tool. Missing in these early formulations was any consideration of problematic ways that filmic media teach in one-directional, non-dialogical, transmission—especially when people were unaccustomed to engaging media critically. By 1945, the federal government had entered the picture, allocating support for audiovisual education in public schools through the Vocational Education Act. This merger of mind and machine was touted as an emblem of U.S. industrial, military, and intellectual might.

Like today, corporations drove the mechanization of education in vocational terms—as students were constructed as objects to be serviced, consumers to be won, and workers to be trained. As the first wave of the baby boom hit the classroom in the 1960s, video became recognized as a means of increasing teacher productivity. By simply eliminating the need for duplicate presentations, video could reduce teaching labor by up to 70 percent.[3] This idealistic vision of new "audio/visual" technology fit perfectly into 1960s educational reformism, while also complimenting U.S. cultural policy. In a domestic atmosphere of desegregation, urban renewal, and other liberal initiatives, efforts were made to eliminate the biases inherent in standard teaching methods. To de-emphasize differences of race, gender, and class, practices that stressed the structure of learning over culturally specific content were introduced into many schools. Educators uncritically seized upon media as tools for directly engaging student experience. They developed concepts of "visual literacy" to compete with what some viewed as oppressive print-oriented paradigms.[4] As one educational textbook of the era explained, many students "lack a proficiency and lack an interest in reading and writing. Can we really expect proficiency when interest is absent?"[5] Consequently, many teachers adopted photography and video equipment to teach subjects ranging from social studies to English composition.

With the economic downturns of the 1980s and the ascendancy of the Reagan/Bush government came sweeping indictments of liberal programs. Supply-side analysts blamed schools for the nation's inability to compete in world markets, while ironically arguing for reductions in federal education and cultural budgets. Because they often required expensive equipment, media programs were terminated in the name of cost reduction, as renewed emphasis was placed on a "back to basics" curriculum. This did not mean that television disappeared from the classroom, only that its more complicated, hands-on, applications were replaced by simple viewing.

The type of media that survived the early 1980s differed greatly from its utopian predecessors. Stripped of any remnants of formalist ideology, video again was reduced to its utilitarian function as a labor-saving device. This redefinition of "television as teacher" paralleled distinct shifts in production and distribution. These were outgrowths of large-scale changes in the film and television industry brought about by the emergence of affordable consumer videocassette equipment. For the viewer, home recording and tape rental allowed hitherto unknown control over what was watched. The same was true in the classroom. For the instructional media industry, the previously costly process of copying 16mm films was quickly supplanted by inexpensive high-speed video duplication. The entire concept of educational media products began to change, as films could be mass-produced on a national scale (in effect "published") like books. Market expansion in this type of video was exponential. So profound was the technological change that 16mm film processing labs from coast to coast went out of business overnight. The shape of education was changed forever.

Computers didn't become a serious part of K–12 schooling until the 1990s, with the broad-based distribution of personal computers in the home, the development of network technology, and the popular advocacy of computers in education by such public figures as Al Gore and Bill Gates. Like cable television, the Internet was touted as a means of bringing the outside world into the classroom, while connecting students to resources previously unimagined. In its early stages of implementation, school computerization was also regarded as a means of leveling the cultural differences among students—much as "visual literacy" had been promoted. These attitudes fit well within the progressive belief that digital media could deliver a world of great equity and freedom.

Cyberschool

Is the current craze for computers in the classroom simply an extension of this historical faith in educational mechanization, or it something more? The business interests that have the most to gain in this matter assert that fundamental structural changes and paradigm shifts are occurring that necessitate new technological approaches to schooling. This could be dismissed as simple self-interestedness were it not for the great influence of high tech corporations in educational policy discussions leading up to the dot.com crash. Meanwhile, parents exposed to an endless barrage of effusive media reports and advertising about the "information society" and the need for "digital literacy" were petrified (and remain so) at the idea of their kids missing out. So it's a double whammy. As parents pressured schools to adopt

technology, schools became institutional customers for educational products and venues for promotions targeted at students. It was like an entrepreneurial dream come true. But there have always been limits to the ways
that K–12 schools can change. Given their role as day-care for underage
youth, the fundamental structure of schools and the school day will not
change significantly. Since elementary and secondary schools are also primarily regarded as a site for general academic or vocational education, the
fundamental balance in curriculum among humanities, science, and math
offerings will similarly resist significant change. At the same time expensive
computer technologies and maintenance have created tough educational
funding choices for the forty-seven states currently in fiscal deficit.

This raises the issue of what is being taught with computers. Although in
growing numbers of K–12 schools computers are used to augment instruction of traditional subjects, just as often "computer literacy" is taught as an
end in itself. Not everyone is happy about these electronic literacy programs,
especially in an age in which school budgets are falling and the late 1990s
craze of digital utopianism is in a similar decline. As the practice of teaching students how to read and critique the medium has grown and been
promoted, many educators believe that its methods are shallow and that it
diverts resources from much needed basics. While such arguments originally were heard from conservative reformers two decades ago, now they
come from progressive educators as well. Jonathan Sterne states that "the
very idea of computer literacy is conflicted at its core: while educators clearly
intended computer literacy as the ability to control machines, the language
of literacy can easily degenerate into the project of creating consumer populations for communications technologies."[6] While traditional literacy programs are premised on the ability to both read and write, digital literacy
tends to focus only on using or viewing software programs, websites, and
CD-ROMs. The key notion of writing or producing exists only as an intellectual response, rendering digital literacy programs lessons in consumption.
As David Bolt and Ray Crawford write, "When you put computer literacy
before literacy, the only thing you are doing is turning out people who do
not have a complete facility with either. The computer, for all of its audio
and graphic qualities, is still primarily a written medium."[7] Finally, school
economists assert that digital literacy programs are especially damaging for
disadvantaged schools, which feel pressured to add computer-oriented
courses at the expense of other offerings.

Cyberschool Divided

Within the United States serious technological inequalities persist in the
nation's schools. To some extent these inequalities parallel larger disparities

in school funding. Yet there are other independent causes relating to differences among schools in support for technology upkeep, cultural attitudes toward technology, and actual (as opposed to assumed) local needs for the technology. It is also worth noting that the digital divide is not a binary construction, but a complex continuum with much variation.[8] Technological differences among schools are far more significant than those among adult individual users, considering the importance of schooling in determining life-long patterns of learning and behavior.

In his farewell address to the 2000 Democratic National Convention, Bill Clinton proudly stated that 95 percent of the nation's public schools had been connected to the Internet. Clinton failed to mention how many schools had *only an Internet connection*—and little else in terms of network or computer capacity. The reality is that the majority of the nation's schools do not have directly allocated funds for telecommunication, nor do they possess the infrastructure to support the computers they might receive from industry or government. Getting connected is important, but so is having an internal network and workstations, which regularly need service and replacement. Donations or equipment grants of computers can be wonderful for schools—until the need is recognized for ongoing technology budgets and technical support personnel. Most schools still lack this broader compliment of resources. Of those that do, many have faculty that are unprepared to utilize computers in the classroom. By 2003, claims of school internet connection by the U.S. Department of Education had reached 99 percent, although a gap of 36 percent existed between primarily White schools and African-African/Latino schools.[9] Overall, more than 60 percent of all schools lacked a full time technician to maintain their technology.

Owing to the interest in the digital divide from the federal government and private groups like the Benton and Markle Foundations, significant public attention was focused in 2000 on the issue of wiring and equipping the nation's schools. Then, the biggest danger was that wiring the schools might become in the public mind a substitute for actual school financing reform.

Unfortunately as federal and state budgets dwindled in the years that followed and foundation stock portfolios fell to pennies on the dollar, the great promise of equipping and wiring all schools was never fulfilled. In 2002, the Bush administration announced that it would begin to dismantle its digital divide programs, eliminating both the "Technology Opportunity Program" and "Community Technology Initiative." Hence, after several years of progress, by most accounts the digital divide is again beginning to worsen.

Ironically perhaps, there is one aspect area of the new digital age that turns the digital divide on its head. While students in wealthy or predominantly White or Asian-American schools far exceed others in use of new computer applications that promote higher order thinking, those same students are the lowest users of remedial drill-and-practice software. These so-called "drill and kill" programs are used 50 percent more by the poor, 30 percent more in Latino schools, 300 percent more by African Americans, and 300 percent *less* in private schools.[10] Paradoxically, the students using the remedial software end up spending more time at school using computers than the non-remedial users.

The Wired University

College is its own story altogether—one in which mechanization and corporate influences are transforming institutional organization, governance, curriculum, and research in profound ways. In a report entitled "The Virtual University," great changes during the current decade were predicted by senior administrators and business people from a diverse range of institutions that included, among others, IBM, Lotus, Educom, the National Science Foundation, Pew Charitable Trusts, Sloan Foundation, and the American Federation of Teachers, as well the universities of California, Hawaii, Illinois, Michigan, Minnesota, and Virginia.[11] The document anticipates a restructuring of post-secondary education in the first decade of the twenty-first century, as conventional residential four-year colleges and universities change or go out of business. These will be replaced by "a global electronic campus, which students enter via a computer and thereby telecommute from home, a dormitory room, the workplace, or a community center," and "the continuing education and training provided by employers and community organizations."[12]

Echoing many of the familiar refrains about a rapidly changing technological work world, the report projected the need for employees to retrain for "six to seven different careers in the course of a life time" and that within five years 75 percent of all workers will need retraining. Computer skills, currently used by 65 percent of workers, would be used by 95 percent of employees in the first years of the new millennium. These changes in the world of business, work, and information will generate new demands from students. As Twigg and Oblinger put it, "Students expect to participate in a learning environment that fosters measurable improvement in their skill development, not just during college, but also throughout their careers. Students are increasingly selecting curricula that enhance their chances of both initial and sustained employment."[13] This pressure will force traditional colleges and universities to change their offerings and modes of curricular delivery as they seek "a competitive edge in a student based—or consumer driven—market."[14] Finally, since it will be difficult for bureaucracy-laden universities to change quickly, much of this new education will be delivered by private enterprises like ITT Technical, Heald Institute, and the University of Phoenix. As the lumbering bureaucracies of public colleges and universities have scrambled in recent years to accommodate these changes, more nimble private for-profit versions of the virtual university are popping up everywhere, the most ubiquitous of which is the University of Phoenix. With 50,000 students, it is already the largest private university in the country. However, it has not accomplished this success by establishing anything resembling a campus. Many University of Phoenix students take their courses on-line or at drop-in locations at any of its ninety satellite locations, mostly located in rented office space. Catering to the growing adult population of people (euphemistically termed "life-long learners") anxious about their job skills, the University of Phoenix has no tenured faculty.[15]

Although in 2000 it looked as though all of this might come true—and "brick" universities would be replaced by "click" universities—the scenario has lost some of its steam. While the decline of the dot.com phenomenon popped the utopian bubble that drove much of the digital hysteria and hype, the more longstanding growth of the information economy has continued. As a consequence, many colleges and universities shelved plans for huge technology purchases and distance learning investments. But just as many continued, albeit at a more sober pace. Matthew Serbin Pittinsky asserts four fundamental reasons for the sustained interest in digital media:

1. a growing interest in the individual learner and the ability of on-line programs to serve individual needs;
2. the move of technology from the classroom to the front office to help schools with such things as Web-based advertising, access, registration, grade posting, payroll, etc.;
3. the desire to reach new markets and revenues through extension programs and other online offerings; and
4. the responsibility to serve new constituents, special populations, and individual/groups wanting long-term updating of course knowledge.[16]

But these are only the most obvious examples of a much broader phenomenon taking place inside almost all colleges and universities, as campus after campus begins to slowly expand vocational/technical curricula and reduce academic/humanistic offerings. This reapportioning of instructional content is accompanied by incentives to technologize teaching, or in some cases requirements to do so. In the most benign instances, this might mean simply posting a syllabus on the Internet or being available to students via e-mail. Elsewhere, faculty are encouraged to translate course materials into video formats or software programs that can be accessed on demand or from remote locations.

These practices present potential problems in the way they fragment or extend academic labor, remove instructors from the pedagogical process, and permit growing levels of administrative monitoring, control, and intervention in the way education takes place. In a widely reproduced essay "Digital Diploma Mills," David Noble discussed the worrisome implications of the new virtual university. He writes,

> What is driving this headlong rush to implement new technology with so little regard for the pedagogical and economic costs, and at the risk of student and faculty alienation? A short answer might be the fear of getting left behind, the incessant pressures of "progress." But there is more to it. For universities are not simply undergoing technological transformation. Beneath that change, and camouflaged by it, lies another: The commercialization of higher education. For here as elsewhere technology is but a vehicle and a disarming disguise.[17]

According to Noble, universities are undergoing a change that has been occurring for the last two decades, as the university is transformed from a relatively autonomous non-profit educational provider into a significant site of corporately regulated capital accumulation. In a two-stage process that began with the commodification of research, the university has become increasingly reliant upon and influenced by the mandates of commercial product development. This began in the wake of the 1970s oil crisis and the concomitant decline in heavy industry, as business and political leaders began to recognize the potential in value-added goods, service industries, and "knowledge-based" products. The latter recognition of "intellectual capital" as a potentially lucrative form of currency both enabled and benefited from the information technology boom of the last decade. What's new in more recent years is the second stage of this transformation, in which the educational function of the university is similarly co-opted and commodified, both in the way curricula are organized and delivered, as well as in the development and sale of copyrighted videos, courseware, CD-ROMs, and Web services. The final piece has been the near complete technologization of campus administration.

Ultimately, the digitization of higher education represents much more than a labor issue. More than one commentator has suggested, following *The Virtual University* reasoning, that computer networks will eliminate the need for costly campuses, troublesome faculty, and the numerous other inconveniences that define college. David Cohen writes that "this technology would eliminate the need for universities to provide daycare for superannuated adolescents: The costly and burdensome administration of dormitories, health services, counseling, and related services could be reduced or eliminated."[18]

These many changes within higher education are producing a highly charged and polarized discourse. Technology will not enter all colleges in the same way or for the same purposes. As in the K–12 arena, the most advanced kinds of computer "courseware" are currently developed and used for basic or remedial instruction, especially in language skills. Such materials are used most in community colleges, which operate with the mission of imparting basic skills to large numbers of students. Less dependent on students seeking complete four-year degrees, community colleges also generate the majority of "distance" learning offerings.

University extension programs are the second largest users of computer-based instruction, with research universities and liberal arts colleges entering the computerized instruction game last. Here the university administration plays an important role, not only in encouraging mechanization to take place, but in providing the infrastructure and support personnel to facilitate the process. Finally, claiming an interest in serving the "individual" student, many instructional packages now have the ability to monitor when and how students use them. This allows administrators and corporations to employ "data mining" on large cohorts of students to analyze product use patterns—presumably in the interest of improving the software. It also allows faculty to see how much time students are spending studying and doing on-line homework, generally with no notice to the student that such information is being collected. To the developers of Prometheus Software, this allows "instructors to assess the depth of student interaction to a course."[19] This is poor pedagogy, superficial analysis, and an invasion of privacy—and the practice is quickly increasing.

The Road Ahead

Faculty and students who find themselves in a changing technological environment face the choice of engaging or resisting that change. The discourse of technology is fond of predicting the future with an air of certainty, suggesting that no alternative paths are possible. Yet the history of anti-trust suits brought against the radio and telephone industries, the community-based campaigns that have imposed regulations on the cable companies, and more recent efforts for democratic internet policy have shown that the business world's version of technological utopia is not always the one that prevails. As Michel Foucault has written, power is hardly an absolute force that flows uniformly in one direction.[20] Instead it is a malleable substance with many currents and with an eternal possibility of reversal for change. Just as new relationships with entities outside the university constitute cause for worry and concern, they also can be seen as opportunities for positive growth and innovation. The challenge is to engage the possibilities that these new technologies offer, while being cautious of how they may silently undermine the institution.

The most obvious changes enabled by information technology within universities are structural, with many institutions adapting buildings to new purposes, equipping new labs, identifying new degrees or curricular emphases—to facilitate computer-oriented instruction and research. The use of computer databases and multimedia instruction is transforming the design of libraries and classrooms. Regardless of one's feelings about the Internet, networked communication is altering the way students and faculty study, teach, research, and socialize inside and outside the university. The net is also enabling scholarship that once took place in the isolation of discrete campuses to become networked into an integrated matrix of knowledge.

This has obvious implications for instruction. To begin with, interdisciplinarity, which for decades was resisted by traditional scholars with interests in preserving protected domains of knowledge and the intellectual hierarchies they held in place, is now so integral to the digital experience that it seems natural. From hyperlinked texts that enable the immediate referencing of ideas throughout the library to Web pages that combine information in written, pictorial, and aural form—notions of linguistic singularity or objective decontextualization seem increasingly remote. At the same time, it is important to note that the curricular interdisciplinarity evoked by digital media also is increasingly celebrated by cost-cutting administrators as a means of reducing instructional labor by compression. Now language programs are compressed into schools of "communication" as multiple art and design specializations are merged into "digital imaging" programs. Hence with each new interdisciplinary program or major that is developed, a countervailing concern needs to be raised for what may be lost in a zero-sum game.

The digitization of instruction offers important opportunities to bring new volumes of material to students and to connect learning in multimedia dimensionality to worlds outside the classroom. Networked bulletin boards, chat rooms, and Web-based virtual spaces offer the ability to bring students together to exchange ideas and collaborate in ways that only the most skilled teacher might engineer in a physical classroom. At the same time, instruction mediated by a computer can also engender distraction, laziness, and alienation if students become disengaged in a multimedia classroom or if they lose motivation in the solitary confines of a remote home computer. Indeed, one of the little publicized actualities of the much-touted revolution in distance learning is the majority of students who begin such courses never finish them. Hardly the future of instruction for all students, professionals who conduct distance learning courses report that such formats work primarily for students with a supervening reason to use the network, such as physically handicapped students, residents of rural communities, or homebound child care providers. The good news is that similar insights have seeped into other parts of the university as well. Consequently the mania to replace "brick" with "click" instruction has modulated considerably in the last three years, with most professors and administrators recognizing the value of the computer and Internet to enhance rather than transform their practice. Today digital media are often found as supports to traditional classroom instruction, offering online syllabi, homework options, course-related chat bulletin boards, or opportunities to discuss issues with the instructor.

The Knowledge Factory

Increasingly higher education is regarded as the prime site of knowledge production in the information economy, as corporations build partnerships and licensing agreements with colleges and universities around the world. Partly a function of the university's growing willingness to conduct paid commercial research, these relationships also are driven by the changing character of commodities themselves. In a world in which images and concepts are assuming more economic significance than conventional goods and services, centers of idea production become centers of income production. Jeremy Rifkin states that "tangible property is becoming increasingly marginal to the exercise of economic power, and intangible property is fast becoming the defining force in an access-based era, "and "ideas in the form of patents, copyrights, trademarks, trade secrets, and relationships—are being used to forge a new kind of economic power composed of mega suppliers in control of expanded networks of users."[21]

On one level this produces numerous new funding opportunities for research efforts in the form of grants, capital contributions, endowed professorships, building campaigns, and even the development of new schools and colleges. Unfortunately this is hardly an equitable form of development, as science and engineering programs, and other computer related disciplines, enjoy the lion's share of these benefits.

Even more significantly, disciplines in the arts, humanities, and social sciences fall victim to an incremental decline, as new, more lucrative, research opportunities pass them by in favor of more directly profitable areas. Some of this has begun to change very recently. In 2003, the venerable National Research Council (NRC) issued a 250-page report announcing the emergence of a powerful interdisciplinary alliance between researchers in information technology and the creative arts.[22] Asserting that similar alliances had produced inventions like photography, film, new forms of architecture, product design, computer animation, digital music, electronic games, and interactive communication, the NRC, with uncharacteristic fervor, argued for the speedy development of such partnerships as those existing at MIT, Carnegie Mellon, University of Califonia, Irvine, and University of Califonia, San Diego. The NRC document represents the first major intellectual endorsement of such partnerships.[23] In fundamental terms, the NRC is using its reputation to encourage interdisciplinary collaborations—practices that are often discouraged or distrusted at many research centers for their "impractibility."

The point is that information technology is transforming educational institutions at all levels, and that these changes are not autonomous transformations. Information technology is no longer merely an enabler for deeper social technologies. Much of this essay has dealt with the way digital media are facilitating the growing privatization of the university and its transformation into an educational marketplace. Schools become sites for commerce, students turn into commodities, and research shifts to product development. Yet at the same time, great potentials exist in the way information technology is causing schools and universities to scrutinize themselves and become more focused on such issues as the relationship between teaching and research. Ultimately, technology can serve as an important catalyst for the reconceptualization of educational institutions, if it can be seen in such a way.

Notes

1. Russell Mokhiber and Robert Weissman, "Focus on the Corporation," *Multinational Monitor* (Nov. 6, 1998), 2.
2. See Anne De Vaney, "Can and Need Educational Technology Become a Postmodern Enterprise?" *Theory and Practice* 37 (Winter 1998): 72–80.
3. Robert M. Diamond, "Single Room Television," in *A Guide to Instructional Media*, ed. Robert M. Diamond (New York: McGraw-Hill, 1964), 3.
4. The terms "visual literacy" and "media literacy" have been employed in a variety of differing contexts during the past two decades. The formalist media literacy of the 1970s should not be confused with the critical media literacy movement of the 1980s and 1990s.
5. Linda R. Burnett and Frederick Goldman, *Need Johnny Read? Practical Methods to Enrich Humanities Courses Using Films and Film Studies* (Dayton: Pflaum, 1971), xv.
6. Jonathan Sterne, "The Computer Race Goes to School," in *Race in Cyberspace*, ed. Beth Kolko, et al. (New York: Routledge, 2000), 192.
7. David Bolt and Ray Crawford, *The Digital Divide: Computers and our Children's Future* (New York: TV Books, 2000), 114.
8. See Mark Warschauer, *Technology and Social Inclusion: Rethinking the Digital Divide* (Cambridge: MIT Press, 2003).
9. Roy Mark, "School Web Access Soars, Digital Divide Still Remains," (Oct 19, 2003) http://earthwebnews.com
10. Warschauer, *Technology and Social Inclusion*, 131.
11. Carol Twigg and Diana Oblinger, *The Virtual University* (Report from a Joint Educom/IBM Roundtable, Washington, D.C., Nov. 5–6, 1996). Available online: http://www.educause.edu/ir/library/html/nli0003.html
12. Twigg and Oblinger, *The Virtual University*, 1.

13. Twigg and Oblinger, *The Virtual University*, 5.
14. Twigg and Oblinger, *The Virtual University*, 6.
15. Michael Margolis, "Brave New Universities," *First Monday* 3 (May 1998). Available on-line: http://www.firstmonday.dk/issues/issue3_5/margolis/index.html
16. Matthew Serbin Pittinsky, *The Wired Tower: Perspectives on the Impact of the Internet of Higher Education* (New York: Prentice Hall, 2003), 6.
17. David F. Noble, "Digital Diploma Mills," *First Monday* 3 (January 1998). Available on-line: http://www.firstmonday.dk/issues/issue3_1/noble/index.html. Not all of Noble's work has been well received; see "Online," *Chronicle of Higher Education* L (Oct. 3, 2003), A28.
18. David Cohen, "Educational Technology and School Organization," in *Technology in Education: Looking Forward Toward 2020*, ed. Raymond S. Nickerson and Philip P. Zodhiates (Hillsdale, NJ: Earlbaum, 1988), 238–39.
19. Mark Mullen, "Web-Based Courseware and the Pedagogy of Suspicion," *Radical Teacher* 63 (2002), 16.
20. Michel Foucault, *Discipline and Punish: The Birth of the Prison* (New York: Vintage, 1975), 225.
21. Jeremy Rifkin, *The Age of Access: The New Culture of Hypercapitalism, Where All of Life is a Paid-For Experience* (New York: Putnam, 2000), 57.
22. National Research Council, *Beyond Productivity: Information Technology, Innovation, and Creativity* (Washington, D.C: National Academies Press, 2003).
23. National Research Council, *Beyond Productivity*, 5.

CHAPTER 11

Where in the World is the Global Classroom Project?

TyANNA K. HERRINGTON

Introduction

Of the utopic promises of the Internet, the declaration that space and time would become less restrictive is one of the most intriguing. It seems logically acceptable that the Internet would eliminate the confines of physical space, allowing boundless exploration of cyberworlds and unlimited room for thought, learning, communication, and interaction. As a site of pedagogy, the Internet does deliver on some of this promise to undermine the limits of space and time. In fact, the whole precept that used to drive education, that students would meet their instructors in physical spaces within the confines of a specific time and within the physical proximity of their class-mates, is certainly fractured from our current expectation of the "classroom" experience. Teaching on the Internet has become commonly acceptable and expectable.

Yet to transverse physical boundaries of actual space for teaching classes creates as many challenges as it alleviates. My collaborative partner, Yuri Tretyakov (European University at St. Petersburg and Russian Academy of Sciences) and I (Georgia Institute of Technology), with the support of our institutions, developed and effected the Global Classroom Project, our at-tempt to take advantage of a virtual site of pedagogy to bring together students from St. Petersburg, Russia and Atlanta, Georgia, USA to work collaboratively to examine issues in cross-cultural, digital communication in an experiential learning environment. The project has continued to develop each semester since its debut in spring 2000 and recently we have been joined by collaborative partners from the Blekinge Institute of Technology in Karlskrona, Sweden: Jane Mattison, Shiela Feldmanis, and Gösta Viberg, whose students have become part of the project since 2002. Teaching an online class across cultures and national borders in a cybersite of pedagogy, despite the theoretical utopic premises of the Internet, actually implies multiple sites, which in turn create differences in administrative, educational, and cultural influences on course content and the processes of communicative interaction. Our experiences have shown us that those who use cyberspace as a site of pedagogy must nevertheless be tied to the limitations imposed by the grounded reality of their home bases, thus they should carefully consider both the physical impact of place as well as the theoretical.

Where online spaces allow a different kind of interaction than has ever been possible in a traditional classroom, they also can highlight more prominently the problems that cannot be alleviated easily or efficiently in the absence of face-to-face interaction. Online teaching forces us to find new ways to cope with the absence of elements of the traditional classroom: face-to-face interaction, greater focus of student attention on informational content, and control over time and space for interaction. Despite the difficulties, cyberspace as a site of pedagogy allows us to bring together students who otherwise would never have opportunities to work with each other across digital, cultural, and global boundaries.

In this essay, I describe issues regarding the interactions between online teaching and the spaces in which it occurs, in this case in an international arena. Although the following text focuses on a cross-global project, many of the conditions we encounter are either similar to those of others who teach in online sites within national, state, or institutional boundaries, or highlight common issues of concern for those who eventually will teach in web-based international or multi-disciplinary forums. I hope that readers will find it applicable to their own needs or interests.

Global Classroom Project Description: The Site of Pedagogy

The Global Classroom Project is an ongoing enterprise that provides a forum for experiential learning for students in diverse areas of the world. Students examine issues in cross-cultural, digital communication while experiencing aspects of the content they simultaneously examine. Participants are both undergraduate and graduate students whose disciplinary interests include humanities studies, technical communication, information design and technology, human computer interaction, and technical engineering fields.

The class site is embodied in WebBoard Web-based communication software that allows separate visual spaces for class assignments, class discussions, student small group collaboration, and linguistic questions and discussion. Students work together to analyze issues in communication and produce analytical reports in hard copy and digital form, preceded by supportive documents such as proposals, article analyses and discussion, and annotated bibliographies. Student collaborative groups are made up of students of diverse nationalities, requiring that they work together to overcome communication difficulties in order to produce end-products that reflect their shared analyses. The Global Classroom Project tests questions related to itself, its site of pedagogy, cultural spaces that influence the communication that occurs and the effects of the digital form on cross-cultural communication and classroom interaction. Its site of pedagogy, disembodied in the physical sense, becomes embodied within the communication process of its participants.[1]

Site, Place, and Cultural Space

The Internet provides a mechanism to teach in ways that were not possible before, but it also generates a means for encountering new difficulties. Using the Internet allows us to teach classes across cultural and national boundaries, a new opportunity. But with this opportunity come the difficulties inherent in teaching culturally and nationally diverse classes of students, not unlike the complexities encountered in land-based classes that cater to multi-national student groups.[2] Because the connection point of an international class, by its nature, cannot exist in a physical space, its site is embodied in the connections between and among course participants; this "sitelessness," in theory, provides freedom from the cultural constraints of any one locale. But in truth, students', instructors', administrators', and countries' cultural influences continue to act on the formative spaces from which participants interact. Therefore, where technology makes possible an international site of pedagogy in cyberspace, it also infuses complexity and accompanying difficulty. Particpants' differing cultural traits, communication and learning styles, administrative structures, technological capabilities and accessibility, and skills in communicative interaction do not evaporate in an ephemeral technologically-induced place, but the impact of these differences is often amplified when participants are brought together. And even though participants make their connections in the ether, they remain physically, culturally, and most often, ideologically and psychologically in their own cultural venues. Ironically, the achievement of connection that technology makes possible brings with it the difficulties that result from that possibility.

In addition, using the Internet can emphasize the variances among the broadly differing sites from which students and instructors generate class participation and that in itself adds difficulty. The point of this piece is to illustrate why teaching in an Internet-based "site of pedagogy" not only does not eliminate the cultural differences by creating a meeting place without physical "sitedness," but instead emphasizes the importance of the physical sites from which participants generate their communication. In doing so, I also hope to illustrate the importance that the pedagogy that forms the basis of the Global Classroom Project was developed jointly through instructors' collaborative negotiations to adapt and readapt to the demands of a learning forum for cross-cultural, digital communication, keeping both the ephemeral and land-based sites in mind.

The Experiential Site of Pedagogy

Much has been written about how students can benefit from learning through experience, from John Dewey's early support of "learning by doing," to Ettienne Wenger's work on learning communities, among others.[3] Experiential pedagogy can be well served by using a virtual site that allows students to experience cross-cultural, web-based communication while learning about it. In assessing the effect of site when developing online pedagogy it is important to understand that virtual space is only one of the many sites in which students will learn.

Examining an experiential learning site's effect on both the pedagogy itself and the students' responses to it can help provide a means for categorizing the elements of that experience that are helpful, difficult to cope with, and frustrating, but it is the essence of the experience that provides a means for student learning. Wenger notes that "A history of joint enterprise is an ideal context for . . . leading-edge learning, which requires a strong bond of communal competence along with a deep respect for the particularity of experience."[4] Locating the tangible experience within the realm of abstract aspects of communication can sometimes provide tools to respond to students' practical concerns in order to give footholds for progressing forward with the more abstract difficulties of online experiential learning. With that in mind, I first delineate some of the difficulties in fusing landscape with cyberspace, then I treat separate categories concerning complexities in working with issues regarding time, language, and the broad category of culture, focusing more specifically on technology access, experience with power, and cultural and seasonal influences such as weather, differing semester schedules, and breaks. Although the categories are divided to aid analysis, their influences are never cleanly separated from one another and in actual experience, create quite an impact as they intermingle.

The Fusion of Landspace and Cyberspace

Teaching in cyberspace can heighten the effect of cultural difference because students who participate in classes from their home countries face no demand to adapt to another society as they would if they were physically located in a different nation's dominant culture. Students and instructors can maintain independent cultural ties to their own nations while simultaneously working online in a space that brings each of these societies together. The continuing challenge is to find ways to bring each of our three cultural processes together online in a way that allows for communicative expression reflecting the cultural demands of each of the participating cultures. Courses must be developed with truly collaborative and equal input from each of the participating professors, representing the needs of their students, administrations, and cultures. The process of developing shared courses is often time-consuming and requires extensive discussion and negotiation, but is essential for successful course structuring.

Effect of Landsite

A teaching site's physical space can create a sense of comfort or discomfort that affects the nature of the course taught in it, which is so for online classes as well, even though the site of pedagogy exists in cyberspace. Research noting the effect of computer placement in relation to the instructor and on student-to-student interaction indicates that online interaction can be strongly affected by the physical elements of computer classrooms in which students work.[5] For those of our students whose online interaction is exclusive to computer classrooms or lab sites on campuses, we must consider the differing effects of their land-based physical spaces in which they work. Moreover, with an online course that moves across international boundaries, we deal with both the impact of physical place and culture as well as that of cyberspace; universities that provide students with comfortable, effective working spaces and the supplies and equipment to function well in online classes also provide them with an advantage. The relative advantages and disadvantages resulting from cultural difference that either supports or hinders student participation in computer-based classrooms must be taken into consideration when planning courses for students who work from unequally equipped or unequally supported landsites.

Differing Administrative Treatments of "Site"

Another aspect of complexity that arises when moving from a land-based course to a site in cyberspace is administrative treatment of the new form of course. Some institutions maintain administrative limitations on what kind of course credit can be given for cyberclasses. And the experiential nature of Internet courses such as ours is very difficult for students whose concern over grades is high throughout the semester. Often, even when they understand and appreciate the benefits of a non-traditional teaching and learning style, standard course evaluations do not often allow for reflection of the different nature of an online course and may resonate negatively, even where students may not intend a negative result. This may, in turn, generate an unsupportive administrative response to the course. Where teaching a land-sited course is a relatively secure prospect for both students and instructors, a course sited in cyberspace carries some level of risk. Participants undertaking online course development should consider this issue as they plan their course structure.

Despite the need to consider the consequences of participating in an online course, there are administrative benefits as well. The Internet provides a site of pedagogy that overcomes some of the administrative limitations that each group would likely experience in its home institution. Where each separate national group can be catalogued under a specific administrative course notation and credit hour requirement that allows it to maintain its own format that meets its institution's administrative demands, it can simultaneously engage with another national group meeting a different set of administrative demands. Not only does teaching online allow us to join students from three countries and three diverse cultures, it also is a means to join students with varying disciplinary interests because we do not rely on physical presence in a dominant school system or cultural setting. In addition, providing courses online makes it possible to support cross-disciplinary training, even within the same institution, without affecting the student enrollment numbers or curricular requirements from each school or department.

The material that follows illustrates the interdependent nature of actual place and the virtual site of course experience, focusing particularly on how time, language, and culture, arising from the locus of the society from which students and instructors connect, can both cause complications and simultaneously be complicated by online interaction.

Effects of Time in Site Relationship

Theoretically, the Internet makes time irrelevant since it provides information and space for communicative interaction that is accessible at any time of day or night from any place in the world. A lack of dependence on temporal sameness for teaching makes it possible to provide classes for students from three countries who live in three different time zones; there is an eight hour time difference between St. Petersburg and Atlanta, a two-hour difference between St. Petersburg and Karlskrona, and a six-hour time difference between Karlskrona and Atlanta. Temporal boundaries exist regardless of the ability to connect students across time and the space, given the overwhelming influence of "place." In many ways, the Global Classroom Project participants' association with time is influenced by the trappings of the places in which they physically interact in the class.

Variously, administratively, seasonally, and culturally, the concept of time is created by "place," a very important element in constituting a site of pedagogy. Adaptation to administrative restrictions, in fact, has made it presently unworkable to arrange synchronous interaction for classes. Each university has its sets of limitations on class and room scheduling, especially when it comes to arranging time for whole class use of computer classrooms and labs. These administrative restrictions are directly related to "place" in the sense that each country's educational structures create demands on its institution and each institution's demands vary from the others. In addition, the time schedules for university courses differ radically from country to country. Effectuating an online course in collaboration with participants in various locales requires adaptation to the administrative needs of each of the participating countries and is part of the challenge of dealing with the realities of the site of pedagogy that goes beyond our virtual site in cyberspace. In this instance, the result is that our sense of time stays relative to place in a very real way and each group of students participate in the class processes within their own distinct experiences of "real-time."

Each group of students is also sited, in actuality rather than virtually, within a seasonal structure that affects they way they interact in class and with each other. Meeting in a virtual site cannot overcome the effects of weather on class participation, even in the form of virtual attendance. Russia and Sweden are well known for their cold winters that can make it difficult for students to come to class at certain times of year. Even Atlanta can experience bad weather days that increase traffic accidents and hamper traffic flow into the city, which can keep students away from computer classrooms. Students who depend on technology access within class walls are greatly affected by these conditions. Few students in St. Petersburg have access to their own computers and instead depend on computer labs at the university for joining class. And though more students in Karlskrona have online access away from the university setting, immediate computer use is still not as prevalent as it is in Atlanta; neither students at the Blekinge Institute or the European University are required to buy computers for schoolwork as they are at Georgia Tech. Students' time away from classes and the computers during differing holiday break times complicates participation even more. Even in a virtual setting, access to computers can make the physical site of pedagogy as important as the virtual site.

"Real-Time" Dominance

All of the effects of administrative, seasonal, and cultural difference on construction of time have less significance, however, than the ongoing struggle to replace an actual sense of time with that of a virtual nature. In fact, students find that actual time is so dominant that their greatest difficulty in the course is to develop the ability to keep track of a virtual schedule for class collaboration, necessary for communicating to group partners whose days begin and end in differences of up to eight hours. Students must adjust to timelines for corresponding with each other, which have little to do with their real-time class experiences. Students who post at inopportune times can become frustrated by working without the immediacy of online correspondence. Their actual sense of time can be so powerful that it overcomes their ability to shift to a virtual sense of time through intellectual willpower. Students whose task is to break through the difficulties of cross-cultural communication find that their frustration with the asynchronous nature of cross-global online communication severely impairs their ability to communicate and collaborate effectively and efficiently in virtual settings.

The very nature of the struggle for communicative interaction, though, is at the basis and purpose of the Global Classroom Project. The opportunity to use a virtual site of pedagogy for bringing together students of disparate cultures to work collaboratively implies introducing pedagogical experiences that students have not yet encountered. And the difficulty that they confront is a part of that experience. Using technology to bolster active learning is well supported, and using virtual space as a site of pedagogy does, of course, provide opportunity.[6] It is through virtual connection that students can begin to learn how to overcome those very difficulties to communicate across cultural, temporal, and digital boundaries.

Linguistic and Technology Issues in a Place of Cultural Interaction

As illustrated above, a virtual site for interaction does not alleviate communicative difficulties. It can also accentuate the effect of linguistic problems. In fact, linguistic barriers once again relate to actual, culturally influenced space since students' thoughts and communicative abilities develop within the countries in which their first language is dominant. At present, classes in the Global Classroom Project are taught in English. Russian students take their course in the project primarily as English language classes, where Swedish students take the course for technical communication, writing, and English language. American students enroll in technical communication. English language dominance is not necessarily our preference for the course, and we would like to develop another iteration in which students could participate in communication that shares each other's languages. At present, American and Swedish students who enroll in the course know little if any Russian, and Russian and American students know little Swedish.

An additional barrier exists with computers that are not configured to recognize Cyrillic characters that are used in Russian, and even Unicode, claimed to be a means for universal character recognition, has failed to make Russian language characters recognizable by all computers. As a result, we continue to teach the course in English, while instructors in Russia and Sweden work directly with students to aid them in English language development.

Both the Russian and Swedish students are well skilled in English language and communicate successfully with each other and the Americans, but they certainly bear a greater burden of translating and interpreting American English in addition to working with course content. The linguistic challenges of the course surface in several forms. Communication is much more time consuming for Russian and Swedish students, so their work load is doubly difficult when they have responsibilities to participate in class article discussion and collaborative project content development. To help balance the workload, American students are required to do the overall editing work for collaborative projects; we ask them to post in non-colloquial language, and to limit the length of posts in order not to over-burden other students. In addition, we maintain a section on the communication site for linguistic questions and answers. Although these measures help to provide balance, they do not solve a greater problem with linguistic dominance.

Similarly, American and Swedish students have greater access to technology. Where Swedish and American students can access computers in their universities or at home at any time, Russian students usually have access only during class time. Both Swedish and American students have a high level of comfort with computer technology, most having used it throughout their grade school and high school years before ever entering university systems. Many Russians, however, receive their first computer training when they enter the university.

Power Distributions in Cybersited International Settings

A virtual environment may actually bring out cultural difference, and sometimes cultural conflict, particularly when addressing issues of access and power. Despite claims that "hegemony provided by geography has disappeared" with the use of online distance teaching,[7] inequalities still exist. The dominance of English certainly gives American students greater power than their Swedish and Russian counterparts have. And, as previously noted, both the Swedes and Americans have greater access to the technology that drives the class.[8] These benefits provide some students with a relatively high level of power to control class activities. At times Americans' ready access to linguistic and digital communication can lead them to be impatient with students who take more time to read and respond to collaborative interaction, which can lead to attempts to overpower their collaborative group members and control project work. There are also times when Russian participants, graduate students with serious course goals, become impatient with their American or Swedish colleagues when courses consist of undergraduate participants. At times it is the Russian or Swedish students whose work ethic pushes them to take charge of group work. Ours is a constant struggle to relay to all students their responsibility to request and support participation from all collaborative partners and this is a large part of the challenge for teaching the course.

Ironically, where the participants' physical sites have a broad effect on online class interaction, the sometime lack of actual place can also take a toll. The following observations note how the absence of the structure that is otherwise inherent in traditional land-based courses can negatively affect course provided in the virtual realm.

Cultural Structures and Sites of Pedagogy

The boundaries of time and space in a traditional classroom provide structure that is not inherent in online classes. Sometimes these boundaries contain students in a way so that they can work together more efficiently simply because they physically share a common place and time. Instances where they also share a common nationality, or more precisely, acceptance of the structure of the dominant nationality with which a place is associated, can lead to a relatively efficient basis for group collaboration. When we teach in cyberspace, in an attempt to truly share the space and eliminate dominance of one culture or one culture's structural boundaries, we have to deal with the chaos that results from students' attempts to follow the rules of their own cultures as they work in collaboration with others who are doing the same with theirs. Students learn to understand differences in cultural communication styles and to respond more effectively as they progress through the course, but the process of developing understanding can be slow and difficult. For example, Russian students can sometimes use very direct language structures, which American students may characterize as abrupt and off-putting, while the American style of softening negative response can be misleading. More specifically, Russian students use and expect a direct response regarding negotiated plans for project development. When an unacceptable idea is put forth a Russian student might respond by writing, "I don't like this idea," or "This is not a good idea." An American student who wants to express the same negative reaction, might instead write, "Yeah, this is a good idea, but we might consider another instead," misleading the Russian counterparts to believe that the idea is accepted rather than rejected. A cyberspace site of pedagogy forces a more direct focus on these kind of cultural communication style differences because it absences the behavioral and facial expressions that would otherwise accompany speech and could soften the impact of textual communications alone.

National Experience in Actual Sites of Pedagogy

There are other instances where the shared site of pedagogy, although strictly speaking, located in cyberspace, is more importantly physically connected to the national spaces that students inhabit. During the fall semester in 2001, students had just begun collaborative work together when, in the midst of a synchronous online class, the September 11 terrorist attack occurred in New York. Not only did the class discussion for that day turn to what was being revealed on television, but the rest of the work of the semester was affected by the students' response to the attack. Russian students were overwhelmingly sympathetic and supportive, but American students seemed to find it difficult to participate in any kind of class, whether on or offline, and virtually absented themselves from collaborative work for most of the semester.

In the midst of the fall 2002 semester, we experienced similar effects on class interaction when Chechen terrorists held hostages in the Moscow theater, essentially holding the country hostage as a whole. Later, when the Swedish students joined in their first interactions in class discussion, America had become internationally unpopular for the Bush administration's attack on Iraq. National location again was an important element in students' attempt to understand and characterize each other as collaborative partners, and the Swedish students, coming from a less directly involved player in international affairs concerning Iraq, seemed to become catalysts for class discussions that began to open up talk about national characterization and how it might affect the way we work together online.

Sighting the Ideal

Despite the difficulties of teaching across cultural boundaries in an online classroom, we believe that the struggle is worth the extra effort it takes. Our experiences with the Global Classroom Project have led us to hypothesize about elements that would provide optimal, cross-cultural communication in a digital site of pedagogy: equality in power and access, both linguistically and technologically; synchronous communication; stable, fast connections; robust visual and audible information for interaction; equal access to information; additional actual international exchange. Ideal circumstances are always that—merely an ideal—but we consider these areas a baseline from which to approximate beneficial qualities as much as possible.

Ideally, our site of pedagogy would include students who have a working knowledge of the language bases of all the participating nationalities. In our current circumstances, students would know or be learning Swedish, Russian, and English. The class would contain articles and other content material in all three languages, and students would create their class products in all languages as well. Students would alternate the language of content discussion and group collaboration in equal periods of time, giving no one group of students linguistic dominance over another. In addition, all students would have equal access to technology; each would have a home computer with 24-hour access to the Internet and equivalent training in technology use. Connections would be fast and stable, efficient and effective for all students. In this way, as with linguistic issues, no one group of students would have technological dominance over another and all students could participate in the online site of pedagogy with ease and efficiency.

More importantly, in our ideal site of pedagogy, students would share robust visual and audible forms of information. They would be able to port movies and music to each other, explaining what these forms of communication mean to their national cultural constituency. They would be able to represent themselves and their national sites with as much specificity as possible so that students would experience each others' cultures to the extent that is possible through online connections.

In a course at its best, students would have equal access to information that would allow them to participate fully in classes. At present, Russian students can be limited in their access to Western textbooks and articles, which can be expensive to import across international borders. As American intellectual property law becomes more restrictive on fair use of information, even for educational purposes, our ability to copy and distribute common works for shared student use is hindered dramatically. Ideally, all students would have equal access to the research and course materials that help them understand issues in the study of cross-cultural communication.

Of course, in the optimal situation, students would also be able to physically travel to each national site and experience the different cultures and institutional structures first-hand. But even then, communicative ability would only be aided by students' experience of each others' national sites, rather than created by their experiences in them because it is culture rather than place, whether online or off, that allows or inhibits communication and exists regardless of the siting of pedagogy.

Conclusion: Cultural Effects on Sites of Communication

Communication issues are tied to culture and culture is tied to the spaces we can never leave behind. Our language and expression come from place, which both embodies and is embodied by its culture. Our limitations and abilities come from our cultural training and backgrounds. We relate to the world around us based on our cultural expectations. Our ability to communicate and understand what is communicated to us is determined by our cultural expectations. A site of pedagogy is really nothing more than a site of communication supported by means to create commonality for understanding the course content that is being communicated. In other words, communication requires a commonality of sign and symbol to the extent that the communicants have the same subject in mind when sending and receiving messages. In a course that focuses on cross-cultural, international communication, commonality of understanding that forms communication is much less related to "sitedness," whether on or offline, than it is to mutual experience and attempts to find common expressions to relate communicative content as closely to a shared concept as possible. Learning how to make commonly understood communication possible is less a pedagogical task of transferring information than it is of providing a means and method for joint communication experience. Thus, the Global Classroom Project focuses less on a site of pedagogy as a point in cyberspace than it does on the intangible place for shared communicative experience among students. In order for students to understand each other and work together collaboratively, they have to find a common ground of communication and experience upon which to build their analytical work, they have to develop at least a minimum of cross-cultural understanding. When theory is reified in acts of creative production, students have no choice but to develop some form of functional means for mutual understanding, as difficult as it may be under the circumstances of the course. Therefore, our cybersite of pedagogy forces us to adapt and thrive because to communicate, we have no other choice.

Notes

1. For in-depth descriptive detail on the Global Classroom Project, see TyAnna Herrington and Yuri P. Tretyakov, "The Global Classroom Project: Trouble-Making and Trouble-Shooting," in *Online Education: Global Questions, Local Answers*, ed. Kelli Cargille-Cook and Keith Grant-Davie (Amityville, NY: Baywood Publishers, 2004).
2. See Kirk Amant, "Integrating Intercultural Online Learning Experiences in the Computer Classroom," *TCQ* 11 (summer 2002): 289–315; Emily A. Thrush, "Bridging the Gaps: Technical Communication in an International and Multicultural Society," *TCQ* 2 (summer 1993):

271–83; and Elaine E. Whitacker and Elaine N. Hill, "Virtual Voices in 'Letters Across Cultures': Listening for Race, Class, and Gender," *Computers and Composition* 15 (1988): 331–46.

3. See David H. Lempert, *Escape from the Ivory Tower: Student Adventures in Democratic Experiential Education* (San Francisco: Jossey-Bass, 1995); Ettienne Wenger, *Communities of Practice: Learning, Meaning, and Identity* (New York: Cambridge University Press, 1998); and David Wolsk, "Experiential Knowledge," *New Directions for Teaching and Learning* 94 (summer 2003): 89–95.

4. Wenger, *Communities of Practice*, 214.

5. See Thomas Barker and Fred Kemp, "Network Theory: A Postmodern Pedagogy for the Writing Classroom," in *Computers and Community: Teaching Composition in the Twenty-First Century*, ed. Carolyn Handa (Portsmouth, NH: Boynton-Cook, 1990); Carolyn Boiarsky, "Computers in the Classroom: The Instruction, the Mess, the Noise, the Writing," in *Computers and Community*, ed. Carolyn Handa (Portsmouth, NH: Boynton-Cook, 1990); and Roxanne Kent-Drury, "Finding a Place to Stand: Negotiating the Spatial Configuration of the Networked Computer Classroom," *Computers and Composition* 15 (1998): 387–407.

6. Ann Hill Duin and Ray Archee, "Distance Learning via the World Wide Web: Information, Engagement, and Community," in *Computers and Technical Communication*, ed. Stuart A. Selber (Greenwich, CT: Ablex, 1997), 156–62; and Katrina A. Meyer, *Quality in Distance Education: Focus on Online Learning* (San Francisco: Wiley, 2002), 24–6.

7. James Cornford and Neil Pollock, *Information Technology and Organizational Change* (Philadelphia: The Society for Research into Higher Education and Open University Press, 2003), 2.

8. For a discussion of how the technology itself can burden users in subtle political ways, see Johndan Johnson-Eilola, "Wild Technologies: Computer Use and Social Possibility," in *Computers and Technical Communication*, ed. Stuart A. Selber (Greenwich, CT: Ablex, 1997), 101–8.

CHAPTER 12

History in the Digital Domain

MARK POSTER

Digital Disciplines

What is at stake in the alteration of the material structure of cultural objects from the paper forms of manuscript and print to the digital form of computer files? In particular, how is the change affecting academic disciplines which rely upon stable forms of symbolic records? More specifically still, how is the discipline of History affected by the digitization of writing? Is digitization simply a more efficient means of reproduction, storage and transmission of documents, whose availability in space and time is enhanced for the application by historians of research techniques and methods? Or does digitization cause an alteration for historians in the constitution of truth?

N. Katherine Hayles suggests that digital culture introduces into the epistemological procedures of the Humanities and Social Sciences a logic of pattern and noise, one that contrasts with an older logic of presence and absence.[1] In the digital domain of zeros and ones, everything is in principle immediately present and at the same time always distant, mediated by information machines.[2] Digital information is on the server, in cyberspace, on the hard disk, in RAM, never palpable to beings ensconced in a Newtonian universe. By contrast, in the world of atoms, an epistemology of presence and absence prevailed at least since Plato introduced a hierarchy in which voice receives privilege over writing. In the domain of atoms—let us call it for convenience, the analogue world—truth consists in a certain relation to presence, either presence in the consciousness of an embodied speaker, or in the representation of that consciousness in voice, or, finally, in the representation of that voice in a printed or handwritten text. The epistemology

211

of the analogue, or its ideology if you prefer, is that of an original that is defined as subsisting in consciousness: truth exists in consciousness in the first instance. Voice, handwriting and print sustain that epistemology through the supplement of representation. Derrida's critique of this epistemology inserts deferrals in time and space within the ideology of presence, revealing its repressed underside as the position of absence. Deconstruction remains within the epistemology of presence/absence, complicating its intentions, reversing its priorities, unsettling its metaphysic of the origin, without, however, discarding its terms.

If digital culture constitutes an epistemology of randomness/pattern, it inserts a new logic of truth within a cultural world caught up in an older binary of presence/absence. One might say that now, in the era of information machines, in an age when cultural objects reside within such machines, the strategy of interpretation shifts to the question of the pattern within the noise. Truth cannot find its origin in consciousness but in the interpretive process that sifts patterns from a background of noise. One might then also go along with Neal Stephenson in *Cryptonomicon* and give priority in the question of truth to the decoding of messages, to the extraction of patterns from the devised noise of encrypted signs.[3] In this case, one knows that a pattern exists, but the agent that formed the pattern is so removed from the presence of the signs—through the machinic mediation, through the encoding process, etc.—that decoding must look to the pure text, to the array of signs and apply methods like statistics and other algorithms that do not suppose an originating consciousness but only a pattern related to a language. Encrypted messages constitute a heaven of structuralist linguistics, one where meaning pertains solely to the string of symbols.

Epistemology is then complicated first by the deconstructive move to reverse the binary of presence/absence, then by the addition of the binary pattern/randomness. At issue is not the displacement of analogue truth systems by digital truth systems but the establishment of a field where both are at play, independently and in mixed forms. We have then a very messy situation confronting us.

Disciplining the Discipline

In this messy situation, with so much in the Humanities appearing up for grabs, uncertain and in turmoil, the ability of the discipline of History to respond to the challenge and opportunities of new media depend in part on how tightly the boundaries of the discipline are guarded, or how open historians are to new developments affecting their methods and assumptions. From the 1970s to the 1990s, the discipline of History shifted interest toward the social and the everyday, away from grand politics and intellectual history. Although many of these younger historians were Marxist in orientation, the empiricist epistemology that characterized political history changed very little in the shift to social history. Social historians, like their forebears, searched the record for conscious acts of agents.[4] Despite the shift of field to the social, historians, clinging to established methodologies, defensively rejected the theoretical innovations that coursed through the disciplines of the Humanities in the last third of the century. Borders of the discipline were closed to any hint of "fiction," of questioning the objectivity of the past, of introducing critically-oriented theories, and self-reflection on assumptions. Those who insisted upon doing so, like Hayden White, generally found themselves shunned or marginalized. Remarkably the same conclusion may be drawn concerning another shift of emphasis in the discipline: the turn in the 1990s to cultural history and global history. Although the field of inquiry is now radically different from what it was in the 1950s and 1960s, the epistemological rules remain the same.

A question that follows from this summary of the state of the discipline is who qualifies as a bona fide historian? As new media challenge many of the habits of the discipline, it is urgent to inquire about the readiness of the discipline to face what might be perceived as strange new procedures of inquiry. In this vein, most often academics in History Departments will respond to the question of membership in the guild, "Only those who have a PhD from a History Department." But at least in three quite prominent recent cases, Edward P. Thompson in British social history, Arthur M. Schlesinger in the political history of the United States, and Philippe Ariès in the cultural history of France, that criterion would not suffice: none earned a PhD in History.[5] In another criterion of qualification, many scholars from disciplines other than History write books which are taught in history courses at universities. These important exceptions to conventional judgment—and there are many more examples like them such as Herodotus and Thucydides—encourage us not to slough off the question with statistical probabilities but to open it to fresh inquiry.

If it is not possible to guarantee with certainty the historian's identity, perhaps an easier question might be, what qualifies as a work of history, as historical knowledge or truth? A simple answer might be those works which are accepted as such by historians. But then we are in an awkward logical circle, as the reader/listener might have noticed. In my experience, faculty in History Departments that offer PhDs in History, often utter, in relation to papers by students and even published works, the phrase "that is not history." This comment pertains not to the question of the coherence of the students' texts or the quality of their research effort but rather to the theoretical aspect of their work. Historians habitually draw a boundary around their discipline, excluding from it scholarly works which at least on the surface are historical in the simple-minded sense that they are about the past. In fact one might, with Foucault, designate the phrase "that is not History" as a discursive "rule of formation" of the discipline.[6] For example, students are often told in no uncertain terms that their work is "not history" when they deploy in their texts theories from poststructuralists.

Here are some instances of the problem from my own experience. In a job talk at my university a young historian presented a paper on the historical conditions of Lacanian psychoanalysis in the 1920s, the relation of the emergence of French psychoanalysis with legal institutions. Distinguished members of the department voted against hiring her using the argument that Lacan "is not history." In another instance, a graduate student at the University of Toronto told me that her adviser urged her not to include Foucault's name in her dissertation, not even in a footnote, because "that is not History." Or again, some years ago I presented to my department the proposal of a distinguished colleague from the French Literature Department at my campus who wanted to give a course in the History Department on the relation of History to Literature in the eighteenth century, an age when the demarcations between the two discourses was murky at best. This was an easy one: many colleagues demurred with the phrase "this is not History." And one more example: while attempting to qualify with enough undergraduate credits for entry into a graduate program in History, I took a course in 1963 on European history at St. Johns University in Queens, New York from an instructor who was also a priest in the Catholic Church. He announced to the class, much to my naive surprise, that prominent historians of the day, (he mentioned the most distinguished American historian of France of the day, R. R. Palmer of Princeton University), regarded two categories of scholars as automatically "not historians": Communists and Catholics. Although such judgments are not often aired in official journals and at panels of the convention of the American Historical Association, they are commonplace in the practice and decisions, in the institutional activity, of History Departments. Keeping the boundary of history defended against fiction, theory, non-Protestants, non-liberals is the difficult work of the gatekeeper. These personal examples illustrate, I hope, not that gate-keeping ought to be abolished but that historians have an overly narrow sense of what may be included within their safe boundary. So today, when digital culture introduces its new conditions of truth, the discipline of History may need to rethink the location of its Maginot Line. It may behoove historians to redefine who and what are included in their club.

Historical Data

The digitization of texts, images and sounds presents several levels of problems for defining the nature of historical truth. The first concern in the minds of most historians is the fate of data that originally existed in print or manuscript forms. That data may now be located in digital files on the Internet. Roy Rosenzweig has shown how quickly historians have converted documents into digital files and posted them on the Internet.[7] One major archive, "American Memory," the online resource of the Library of Congress's National Digital Library Program (NDLP), contains over five million records. Full text digital versions of countless academic journals are available online for historians, especially from JSTOR (Journal Storage) and Project Muse.[8] Thousands of sites have been constructed on the Web by teachers of history and history enthusiasts, and by Civil War re-enactors, family genealogists, and other groups. These sites are constructed by a combination of professional historians and amateurs, raising the question of verifiability of documents to a new level of urgency. It is often not clear if documents on the Web have been put there by those holding PhDs in History. The pedigree of Web sites is notoriously uncertain. Nonetheless these sites, which are sometimes very popular, contain a rich trove of text, images and sounds.

In addition to worries about authenticity, another troubling aspect of history-on-the-Web is the increasing privatization of document collections and, even worse, the increasing concentration of media companies owning these databases. In a sense, access to historical documents has always presented difficulties for the scholar. Collections are often controlled by governments, corporations, and private individuals who may be reluctant for various reasons to open them to researchers. One skill not taught in graduate school but that remains essential for historians are strategies of overcoming obstacles to such collections. Legal hurdles are often most burdensome: copyright law, in one stroke, prevents access to vast classes of documents. Yet digitization changes the nature and extent of the difficulties. Since it renders distribution and copying cost free, the Internet lightens the burden of many research chores. One can access countless documents and locate information with great ease from home. Yet the great advantages of digital culture put in question many of the established systems of control. In response, the music and film industries lobbied hard to undermine the best features of the Internet with the passage in 1998 of the Digital Millennium Copyright law which significantly expanded corporate control of culture and, for historians, reduced access to data collections.[9] Digital culture thus opens a new political dimension to access, one that seriously affects historians, although I am not aware of any response to the DMC by the American Historical Association. In the first instance, then, digitization changes the nature of historical documents by rendering them easily available, introducing new questions of certification, and opening the issue of access to direct and controversial political questions.

A second aspect of the digitization of data is that it renders all documents potentially fluid, changeable at the whim of the reader/viewer/listener. At present many digital document formats are closed. Certain hypertext novels, for example, can be read and the reader can add "links" but the nodes of the story cannot be changed. Also, Adobe's pdf format forbids alteration of the document and additionally prevents cutting and pasting of passages. Many of the books and articles that have been digitized and are available online come to the reader in pdf format. JSTOR articles and Netlibrary books are in pdf. Using such closed formats perhaps promotes the widespread distribution of documents but preserves their original forms, some would say, their integrity. Inured to print media and paper formats, modern culture has for centuries abided closed formats. But digital culture lends itself more readily than print and broadcast media to open cultural objects, to the simultaneous reading and rewriting of texts, to viewing and reimaging of pictures, and to listening and transforming of auditory items. Word processing, image viewing and audio programs all allow and encourage the position of audience to become, at the same time, the position of author, artist and composer. Furthermore, the network of digital objects encourages these figures to become distributors. Functions that were separate in the print and broadcast ages of media, now are merged or at least have their boundaries blurred. Digital culture introduces principles of reception that echo the era before mechanical reproduction: the traditions of oral storytelling and folk music in which each reception was also a transformation. In the digital mode, these practices, once limited to the proximity of voice, now may disseminate globally. As a result, historical documents face a danger of losing their "integrity" and becoming open to continual transformation, surely a nightmare for historians.

Digital Archives

The archive has been central to the epistemology of History from its inception. For historians, travel to archives in the nineteenth century was analogous to field work for anthropologists, a sine qua non of professionalization. Archives gained new importance beginning in the 1970s with the trend toward social history. If nineteenth century historians, given the salience of the history of the nation state, consulted the collections of governments, late twentieth century historians, more concerned with previously ignored groups (the working class, women) and institutions (the family, the labor union) investigated legal documents, church registries, land-holding records.

Both political and social historians regarded the visit to the archive as a prerequisite of scholarship, investing in it great emotional energy.

In a pioneering study of the gendered nature of historical practices, Bonnie Smith demonstrates the emotional fascination of historians for archival work. She distinguishes the graduate seminar, characterized by a mood of civic rationality, from the journey to the archive where historians found "love, melodrama, and even obsession."[10] The trip to the archive was most arduous, especially in the nineteenth-century. Historians viewed themselves in heroic terms, overcoming dangers, costs and inconveniences to access ill-sorted records and the authentic traces of the past. In this context, emotions were easily incited. Even the legendary founder of modern history, Leopold von Ranke, was affected. He described his experience in the archive thusly: "Yesterday I had a sweet, magnificent fling with the object of my love, a beautiful Italian, and I hope that we produce a beautiful Roman-German prodigy. I rose at noon, completely exhausted."[11] The archive was the occasion for a most masculine flurry of emotion. Smith concludes her analysis by indicating the imbrication of archives with truth and feeling: ". . . archives became the richly imagined repositories of knowledge and the guarantors of truth. . . ."[12] One can also conclude that social historians from the 1970s onward, including many women, continue to associate truth with feeling, albeit in a more complex mixture of gendered experience.

The physical form of documents as print and manuscript papers conditions the architecture of the archive. Papers require an enclosure safe from the elements of nature and papers that are rarely consulted, such as those in archives, likely will be housed in an obscure location and given little attention in their arrangement. By their nature archives of paper are off-putting, remote, inaccessible and poorly organized. Digital archives, by contrast, require no journey at all, only "surfing" with "Navigator" or "Explorer," metaphors that conceal the absence of travel in space. Such repositories may be "searched" with the ease of database algorithms, with a tap on the keyboard or a movement of a mouse. Information can be extracted from them with simple cut and paste operations of the word processor, not the arduous copying by hand or even machine. The new archive far less likely elicits feelings of heroic conquest in men or analogous emotions in women. Perhaps the digital context will reduce the intensity historians invest in the archive and perhaps they will less likely fall under the illusion, characteristic of earlier generations, that archives contain the truth of the past, that the reassembly of their documents constitutes by itself, to quote Ranke, "the past as it actually was."[13] Perhaps digital archives will lessen the false objectivism of historians and afford a turn to a more self-reflective and constructivist understanding of the historical text.

In other disciplines, such as anthropology, literary criticism and art history, scholars have begun to investigate the media that contain cultural objects. Museums have attracted much attention in these fields as important constituents of the epistemological practice of the discipline. The way cultural objects are stored and are available for reception thus is understood to influence the kind of knowledge produced about them. Jacques Derrida muses about the influence of an e-mail archive on the early psychoanalytic association.[14] His use of the term "archive" is more general or metaphorical than the historians', including in the category any stored collection of information. In this sense, museums and public libraries would also qualify as archives. Using Derrida's definition, an archive denotes a material collection of data and is distinguished from memory, although the brain is certainly a material being and memory changes its chemistry however minutely. If other disciplines than history have been most interested in the functioning of the archive, historians have focused attention on memory. In recent years, they have explored oral history and testimony as a continuation of the trend toward social history but also in new directions such as the question of historical trauma.[15] While historians have wrestled with questions of the epistemology of memory, and addressed the comparison of written/print records with oral evidence, they have paid much less attention to the archive and its potential transformation into digital forms.

Curious about the recognition by historians of the importance of the archive to their disciplinary truth, I did some searches of online journals, using the latest technology of the California Digital Library. I searched for the word "archive" in the texts and titles of articles in some of the leading journals of the field: The *American Historical Review, History and Theory,* the *Journal of Modern History, French Historical Studies,* and the *Journal of Interdisciplinary History.* In the *AHR* going back to the 1960s, there were 119 instances of the word "archive"; in *History and Theory* (which went back only to 1998) and the *Journal of Modern History* combined there were 120. A search of the other two journals yielded not one result. Of the 239 mentions, only one raised questions about the archive in general in relation to historical truth. One may conclude that, compared to the great interest of historians in the question of memory and its relation to more permanent traces in paper, the media change of the archive has not aroused much concern.

But an older technology yielded slightly better results: an e-mail to a friend asking about the question of digitization of archives resulted in a reference that proved suggestive.[16] A German scholar, Wolfgang Ernst, compares digital archives with historical narratives in relation to archaeological evidence. He argues that inscriptions on stones from Roman antiquity confront the historian with bits of data, forming a kind of archive, which can only be absorbed in historical narratives by seriously violating the limits of the evidence at hand. He contrasts the mute, modular, partial, highly ambiguous shards of script that constitute a good deal of the "archive" of ancient history, with the pleasingly unified fullness of meaning in historical narratives, underlining "the dissonance between analytical archaeology and synthetical history. . . ."[17] Ernst speculates on a new history that would take its point of departure from hyper-text databases where modules of documents reside in heterogeneous juxtaposition. "Maybe the computer has the better memory of the past," he snidely suggests.[18] His polemic against narrative history however rejoins the profession's objectivist leanings. A synthetic model of archaeology and digital archives, in his mind, is closer to some form of facticity than the elaborated stories of conventional historiography. Digital archives for him returns history to a grounded methodology of fidelity to the documents, the old empiricist saw.

Ernst remains within the binary history/fiction. Perhaps digitization permits a move outside this opposition. Computerized databases suggest the inseparability of the discursive need for narrativizing (introducing "fiction") and the insistence to heed the material form of the information. Digital documents, for instance, require aesthetic choices about the display of the data, even in the matter of keyword indexing that greatly affects access to information. At the same time, digital documents remind the researcher of their inauthenticity, that they are not relics from the past but transcodings of a recent vintage.[19] In these ways, digital archives obey epistemological canons that depart from the familiar rules of usage associated with more conventional sources.

Historians Online

In addition to the digitization of historical documents, writings by historians are also migrating to computer formats and appearing online. Historians are publishing their work in online journals, print journals are available online, and even monographs and other larger works are being posted to Web sites. There are also a number of centers for historical research that treat directly the question of the new media, such as the Center for History and New Media at George Mason University. In all of these ways the writing of historians is increasingly present on the global computer network. One question persists from our earlier discussion of digital data: how does the user authenticate Web sites that contain historical writing? It is easy enough for someone to copy a piece from my Web site and place it on their own, under their own name, perhaps with alterations of their design. Such acts that were called plagiarism in the age of print (and which instructors are quite familiar with) will likely increase with digitization and the new principle of the variable cultural object.

Digital culture also facilitates new kinds of texts by historians, texts that combine audio and visual components.[20] Multimedia documents are as easy to create as linguistic texts. Ted Nelson's vision of "Xanadu," a global, hypertext library, put forth in the mid-1960s anticipated what has become the reality of the World Wide Web.[21] Some scholars in the William Blake Archive[22] put online the poetry of William Blake whose printed texts included drawings that were integral to the reading. They have utilized the Web to transfer, as faithfully as possible to the original print versions, work that appeared first in rudimentary multimedia forms. This form of transcoding, however, ignores the difference between print and digital media, taking advantage only of the propinquity of the Web as a means of dissemination. Gregory Crane's Perseus Digital Library,[23] covering ancient Greek and Latin writing, and others like George Landow (whose databases concern the work of Charles Dickens) deploy greater features of digital culture. Landow built multimedia databases including literary works, historical works that relate to the same period, and images from the period.[24] As many have argued, the transfer of texts to the Web, even limited to the juxtaposition of multiple media and cultural objects in a single database, introduces an associational logic of Web space that runs counter to the more linear logic of print. Hypertext promotes jumping from one site to another, with no hierarchical, tree-like structures, such as numbered pages or library catalogue files to control the narrative of discovery or research. It remains unclear how these features of digital culture—hypermedia and associational links—will affect the construction of historical narratives.

If the material form of the Web presents a challenge to the bookish discipline of history, it also poses a threat to the institutional procedures of certification. Anyone, even an undergraduate History major, can publish their work on a Web site for all to see. In one respect, Carl Becker's phrase becomes a literal reality: "everyman his own historian."[25] No obstacle stands in the way of publicly displaying historical scholarship. The practice of expert readers and referees in publishing houses and journals is bypassed by digital culture. Ease of publication poses an enormous problem for all the disciplines, including of course History. For the student or layperson, the Web offers exciting possibilities for distributing historical scholarship; for those in the discipline, the issue is more complex. To what extent will departments and campus review committees accept publication online for credit toward promotions and tenure? As economies of publishing discourage the printing of narrow monographs and revised dissertations, presses are beginning to issue "books" exclusively in digital formats. Will these publications earn the status of paper books? And as print journals are appearing in digital form, the lines are blurring between paper and online distribution. Again digital culture destabilizes established traditions of scholarly evaluation and review.

Life Online

Digital culture presents further difficulties for historians: not only are archives online and historical writings online but social life itself in part occurs on the Web and the Internet more broadly. Historical experience itself is in part digital. Personal letters take the form of e-mail. A great variety of chat rooms, bulletin boards, electronic cafes and public meeting rooms proliferate on the Internet. Guest workers in foreign lands and diasporic peoples in general utilize the Internet to maintain daily contact with family and friends back home. Young people expand their social contacts through instant messaging. Online games are a major activity for countless thousands. Wireless telephony is becoming digital. In some places, bandwidth is great enough to afford video conferencing. Millions exchange music files in digital form on the Internet. In fact, digital culture is designed for and characterized by remote intimacy, communication mediated by machines, in short, by virtual reality. Interlaced with RL (real life), VR (virtual reality) obeys rules that are significantly different from familiar forms of society. Most saliently, the historian's assumption about individual and group agency is sharply challenged by social encounters heavily mediated by networked computing, by information machines. The interface of the Net, where no one ever knows for sure who you are, presents an enormous problem of theory and methodology. How will historians write the history of life on the screen when it is uncertain who is acting and to what extent the actor is a human being, a machine, or some combination of the two?

An Example from Ethnography

One of the richest and most nuanced studies of social experience on the Internet is Don Slater and Daniel Miller's ethnography of Internet use in Trinidad, *The Internet: An Anthropological Approach*. Based on interviews with Trinis (as Trinidadians prefer to be called) in the late 1990s, the book contains numerous surprises: In Trinidad, the Internet is not understood as an extension of American imperialism, but as a facility completely adaptable to local conditions. Trinidad, as a third world nation, nonetheless has very high Internet usage. The only social category left out of Internet culture is the older population, a demographic trait that cuts across all nations. Trinis do not see the Internet as an intimidating, arcane technology but as easily assimilable to their existing cultural patterns. At the time of the study fully one-third of Trinis had Internet access at home and Internet cafes were ubiquitous in the urban landscape.

Miller and Slater provide a comprehensive overview of Internet use in Trinidad: which groups use it and how, which aspects of the Internet are most heavily used, how the political economy of Trinidad relates to the Internet, and, above all, how the history and culture of Trinidad link up with Internet use. They argue that the long history of Trini diaspora creates conditions ripe for Internet use: since Trinis are unusually dispersed around the globe they have a need for a cheap means of communication such as the Internet. The Internet enables, they claim, a solidification of the ethnicity of Trinidad. Further they show how Trinis represent themselves to the world by Web pages and other features of the Internet, another way that the Internet strengthens local identity. Finally they content that Trinis received the Internet as matching and enhancing local cultural practices. They practice "liming": "filling one's time with skilled banter, dancing and drifting on-wards to other places (a street corner, a club, someone's house, another island). . . . [It] was regularly cited as the Trini pleasure they most wanted to recover on or through the Internet."[26] And they did so in e-mailing and in chat rooms. The Internet for Trinis was not a strange technology that was learned with difficulty and seen as altering their behavior. Use of the Internet flowed directly from pre-existing cultural habits.

This very sketchy outline of Miller and Slater's surprising findings indicates the importance of empirical studies of Internet use. Their results contradict most assumptions about new media. However their work points to a problem with such inquiry: they proceeded from the assumption "that we need to treat Internet media as continuous with and embedded in other social spaces. . . ."[27] In other words, they assume that the distinction between the virtual and the real presents no epistemological hurdle to their investigation. Continuing from there, they simply interviewed Trinis about their use of the Internet. They inserted into their study the figure of the rational agent, one who deploys technologies, engages in practices, expresses cultural forms, and has full self-understanding of those experiences. Historians will find this agent convincing since it is the chief narrative conceit of historical writing. Yet it begs the very question that needs to be asked when humans engage with information machines and digital culture, to whit, what are the alterations in the cultural construction of the subject under such conditions? This question might not be answerable by historical agents who appear to have every motive to disavow it. If cultural practices generally tend to work at the unconscious level, then profound changes in cultural modes are even more likely to go deliberately unrecognized, if I can use that oxymoronic phrase. In the present case, Trinis know that they are Trinis but as *agents* cannot recognize that they became that way and are sustained in that identity through discursive practices embedded in fields consisting of relations of force. How likely would it be, then, for Trinis, or any other group, to ask, how, when I am chatting on the Net, do I know that my conversant is a Trini, and how, under those conditions, can I represent my true Trininess?

The historical and social science study of the media often concentrates on "effects," such as, does a TV show which depicts violence lead to violent acts by viewers? Or even, does the reporting in the media of actual violence in society, increase its incidence, as in copycat violence? These studies contain a dubious epistemological assumption of a sensationalist theory of action—sense data from outside is internalized by the subject, leading in some cases, to its reproduction. This epistemological principle becomes even more questionable, I contend, in relation to the Internet. Sensationalist theories of truth presuppose a pre-media agent who is affected by information as an external force. Cultural and social practices are far more complex than that. In any case the image of the subject presumed by such research is contravened by the multiple marriages of human and machine in digital cultures. We need instead to study the links and assemblages of humans with various media. Our categories are profoundly humanist and need to be modified to account for such mediated social experience.

Finally, there is a still more difficult question: digital culture mixes into other media cultures and to face-to-face relations, situations where humans are proximate and deploy primarily language as a medium. Humans are now going in and out of various different configurations of media situations. Questions then arise about how these transitions are managed and how each medium experience affects the others. One study that approaches this multi-media condition is Nancy Baym's work on soap operas.[28] Her text is noteworthy especially for its comparison of television viewing with Usenet participation, a broadcast and a digital medium, along with telephone conversation and proximate, voice dialogue. The book provides a model of how to approach the dense mediascape of the current conjuncture.

One last issue that I would like to call to the attention of historians and social scientists is the following: when you study the archive of a chat room in the effort to comprehend life online, all you have is the digital script, a script that does not represent a social act, but rather *is* that social act. True enough, reading a chat room archive misses the flow of text on the screen, which often combines several conversations in fast moving and intertwined complexity. But in any case such a text is quite different from say a transcript of a courtroom trial. The latter is a record of spoken dialogue by co-present agents concerning prior actions. The former—the chat room or archive—has no external referent: the archive is the entirety of the encounter or exchange. The agents in the chat room exist, while they are there, solely by their textual interventions. Language in the chat room, mediated by networked computers and software programs, constitutes the agent in the act of enunciation and only thereby. What analytic categories, one might ask, are required to render intelligible such a human/machine interface? What ontology of subject and object are capable of rendering coherent these bizarre, monstrous engagements?

Teaching History with Digital Technology

Digital culture upsets standards of the teaching of history in every way imaginable. Steeply rising anxiety over Web plagiarism, the intrusive e-mailing of questions to professors, posting of student work on Web pages, online evaluation and testing of students, online research and submission of work in the form of new media, distance learning—in these and many other ways, digital culture offers innovations in higher education at every level. Some of these innovations are relatively innocuous, like downloading online research or the use of e-mail or listservs to facilitate the administration of the class. Other changes, on the contrary, promise to transform basic aspects of the disciplines. The ease of students' exchanging and posting their own work introduces potentially fundamental alterations of educational experience. More cogently still, research on the Web introduces a logic of association, a horizontal epistemology of a "flat" discursive regime in which every site is equal, depending on the protocols of the search engine rather than on intrinsic quality or financial support. This replaces the hierarchical or vertical search logic of the card catalogue, the layout of the library, the linear material organization of the book, or the judgment of the professoriate and the discipline. In addition to the leveling effect of Web architecture, digital culture promotes an epistemology of the link and module. What becomes interesting in digital text is not so much the string of symbols but the connections made most often between pre-existing cultural objects, be they text, sound or image. In the analogue world, higher education promoted truth regimes of argument, rhetoric, comprehensiveness of research and the like. How will teachers inured to these epistemological habits evaluate a link between a picture and a module of text taken from some document? Will such a link even be considered an accomplishment of learning?

Historians are probably no better or worse than faculty in other disciplines in adapting to the classroom of the digital age. One aspect of the new circumstances that has achieved some attention is the creation of online learning tools. There are many examples of highly successful Web pages designed by faculty and graduate students to promote historical education. One thinks immediately of the University of Virginia Center for Digital History, with its projects on "the Valley of the Shadow" (concerning the

Civil War), "Virtual Jamestown" (an online tour of the colonial city), various digital databases such as "Virginia Runaways Project" (on escaped slaves), and "The Dolley Madison project" (a multi-media database about the President's wife). Countless historians have produced excellent teaching tools that, generally speaking, are open to all teachers in the field. One can only applaud these experiments in digital historical culture.

But other aspects of the application of digital culture to higher education may be less worthy of praise. In the field of distance learning there are also many important experiments. But here there are also serious dangers. Pecuniary impulses, so unconstrained in American culture, combine with digital technology to produce software packages for distance learning that undermine the basic principles of education: critical inquiry and academic freedom. The advent of digital culture has encouraged some entrepreneurial types to view higher education as little more than a potential market. Heedless of educational culture, these companies imagine they can improve on the efficiency with which information is transmitted from the mind of the teacher to the mind of the student. They need only capture the mind of the teacher in a digital recording system and transfer it to a software system by which it can be commodified and sold. This perversion of education is facilitated by digital culture and must be resisted by faculty in all disciplines.

History as Media History

The drastic novelties of digital culture suggest, at the very least, that the history of the media must become a major topic for historians. This apparently harmless innovation in the epistemological repertoire of the discipline ought to incite far less resistance than some of the other suggestions offered in this paper. Students of media from other disciplines would benefit greatly from comparative historical work. Too many studies of the Internet, for example, are flawed by a lack of perspective on the topic, becoming lost in the dazzling novelty of the new technology. Some important work has already been done on topics such as print (Adrian John's *The Nature of the Book: Print and Knowledge in the Making*); the telegraph (James Carey's *Communication as Culture: Essays on Media and Society*); photography, panoramas, and other visual technologies of the nineteenth century (Jonathan Crary's *Techniques of the Observer: On Vision and Modernity in the Nineteenth Century*); the telephone (Claude Fischer's *America Calling: A Social History of the Telephone to 1940*); film (*Cinema and the Invention of Modern Life*, edited by Leo Charney and Vanessa Schwartz); radio (Susan Douglas' *Inventing American Broadcasting: 1912–1922*); television (Lynn Spigel's *Make Room for TV: Television and the Family Ideal in*

Postwar America); and others too numerous to mention. Not all of these histories, it might be noted, are by historians.

Despite the appearance of many noteworthy studies in media history, the constitution of the field of the history of the media will be no easy task. One issue concerns the relation of media to one another and the relation of new media to old media. Bolter and Grusin have put forth an interesting hypothesis they call "remediation," the complex way new media attempt to disavow their novelty and assert it at the same time.[29] More than this, the question of the history of information machines, culminating so far in digital media, concerns issues of the materiality of the media, the relation of media to agents, the interface or subjects to objects, the question of humans to machines, the alteration of space/time configurations, the issue of artificial life and the changing boundary between life and non-life, and a plethora of other problems that fundamentally reconfigure the objects of historical analysis, the figure of the historian as subject of history, and the status of history as a truth regime. Media history raises no less a question than the history of the human and the non-human.[30] Digital culture, after all, imposes the question of information machines as agents, placing agency itself in question, a hard nut for historians to crack. Finally, the rapid pace of the introduction of digital culture suggests another kind of problem, one that I do not believe historians until now have dealt with: rapid change of media implies a rapid change of analytic categories, leading to the recognition of the tentative nature of all such epistemological tools. We are thus well outside the binary certainty/relativism, and in a new age of conditional truth regimes, a far cry from history "as it actually was."

Notes

1. See N. Katherine Hayles, "Virtual Bodies and Flickering Signifiers," *October* 66 (fall 1993): 69–91.
2. See Sadie Plant, *Zeroes + Ones: Digital Women + the New Technoculture* (New York: Doubleday, 1997).
3. See Neal Stephenson, *Cryptonomicon* (New York: Harper Collins, 1999).
4. See Mark Poster, *Cultural History and Postmodernity: Disciplinary Readings and Challenges* (New York: Columbia University Press, 1997).
5. Of the three, only Schlesinger held a post in a History Department.
6. See Michel Foucault, *The Archaeology of Knowledge* (New York: Pantheon, 1972).
7. See Roy Rosenzweig, "The Road to Xanadu: Public and Private Pathways on the History Web," *Journal of American History* 88 (2001): 548–79.
8. Project Muse puts complete text journals online. It was initiated by Johns Hopkins University Press and is available to students and scholars whose university libraries subscribe.
9. Michael L. Benedict discusses these issues regarding the revision of the Copyright Law of 1976 in "Historians and the Continuing Controversy over Fair Use of Unpublished Manuscript Materials," *American Historical Review* 91(1986): 859–81.
10. Bonnie Smith, *The Gender of History: Men, Women, and Historical Practice* (Cambridge: Harvard University Press, 1998), 116.
11. Smith, *The Gender of History*, 119.

12. Smith, *The Gender of History*, 128.

13. See Peter Novick, *That Noble Dream: The "Objectivity Question" and the American Historical Profession* (New York: Cambridge University Press, 1988).

14. See Jacques Derrida, "Archive Fever: A Freudian Impression," *diacritics* 25 (1995): 9–63.

15. See Dominick LaCapra, *History and Memory After Auschwitz* (Ithaca, NY: Cornell University Press, 1998); and Dominick LaCapra, *Writing History, Writing Trauma* (Baltimore: Johns Hopkins University Press, 2001).

16. The person in question is Dominick LaCapra who I thank for the reference.

17. Wolfgang Ernst, "Modular Readings (Writing the Monument): The case of *Lapis Satricanus*," *Rethinking History* 3 (1999): 53–73, 61.

18. Ernst, "Modular Readings," 62.

19. See Lev Manovich, *The Language of New Media* (Cambridge: MIT Press, 2001).

20. For an interesting discussion of the impact of digital culture on historians, see Vanessa Schwartz, "Walter Benjamin for Historians," *American Historical Review* 106 (2001): 1721–43. Schwartz argues that digital culture presents in a new way visual material in relation to textual material. She takes Benjamin's notion of the image as "flash" as an important reconceptualization of history.

21. See Theodor Nelson, "A File Structure for the Complex, the Changing, and the Indeterminate," in *Proceedings of the ACM National Conference* (New York: Association for Computing Machinery, 1965).

22. Http://www.blakearchive.org/

23. Http://perseus.mpiwg-berlin.mpg.de/

24. See George P. Landow, *Hypertext 2.0* (Baltimore: Johns Hopkins University Press, 1997).

25. See Carol Becker, *Everyman His Own Historian* (New York: Crofts, 1935).

26. Daniel Miller and Don Slater, *The Internet: An Ethnographic Approach* (New York: Berg, 2000), 89.

27. Miller and Slater, *The Internet*, 5.

28. See Nancy K. Baym, *Tune In, Log On: Soaps, Fandom, and Online Community* (Thousand Oaks, CA: Sage, 2000).

29. See Jay B. Bolter and Richard Grusin, "Remediation," *Configurations* 4 (1996): 311–58.

30. See Felix Guattari, "Machinic Heterogenesis," in *Rethinking Technologies*, ed. V. Conley (Minneapolis: University of Minnesota Press, 1993).

Contributors

Michael W. Apple is the John Bascom Professor of Curriculum and Instruction and Educational Policy at the University of Wisconsin, Madison. Among his most recent books are *Official Knowledge* (2000), *Educating the "Right" Way* (2001), and *The State and the Politics of Knowledge* (2003).

Stanley Aronowitz is a Distinguished Professor of sociology at the City University of New York and a passionate champion of organized labor. He has written fifteen books in all. The most recent are *The Last Good Job in America* (2001), *The Knowledge Factory* (2001), and *How Class Works* (2003).

Carol Becker is the Dean of Faculty and Senior Executive Vice President for Academic Affairs at the School of the Art Institute of Chicago. She is the author of numerous articles and several books, including: *The Invisible Drama: Women and The Anxiety of Change* (1990); *The Subversive Imagination: Artists, Society, and Social Responsibility* (1994); *Zones of Contention: Essays on Art, Institutions, Gender, and Anxiety* (1996); and, most recently, *Surpassing the Spectacle: Global Transformations and the Changing Politics of Art* (2002).

Jacqueline Bobo is a Professor in the Women's Studies Program and the Department of Black Studies at the University of California, Santa Barbara. Her publications include *Black Women as Cultural Readers* (1995), *Black Women Film and Video Artists* (1998), *Black Feminist Cultural Criticism* (2001), and *The Black Studies Reader* (2004).

229

Jeffrey R. Di Leo is Assistant Professor of English and Philosophy at the University of Houston-Victoria. He is editor and founder of the journal *symplokē*, and editor of a new book series published by the University of Nebraska Press entitled *Class in America*. His recent publications include *Morality Matters: Race, Class, and Gender in Applied Ethics* (2002), *Affiliations: Identity in Academic Culture* (2003), and *On Anthologies: Politics and Pedagogy* (2004).

Elizabeth Ellsworth teaches media theory, documentary, and media and social change in the Media Studies Program, New School University, New York City. As the 2002–2003 Julius and Rosa Sachs Distinguished Lecturer at Teachers College, Columbia University, she presented public lectures now incorporated into her forthcoming book: *Places of Learning: Media, Architecture, and Pedagogy*.

Henry A. Giroux holds the Global Television Network Chair in Communications at McMaster University in Canada. His most recent books include *Breaking Into the Movies: Film and the Culture of Politics* (2002), *Public Spaces/Private Lives: Democracy Beyond 9/11* (2002), *The Abandoned Generation: Democracy Beyond the Culture of Fear* (2003), and, co-authored with Susan Searls Giroux, *Take Back Higher Education: Race, Youth, and the Crisis of Democracy in the Post Civil Rights Era* (2004). His forthcoming book is *The Terror of Neoliberalism*.

TyAnna K. Herrington is an Associate Professor at the Georgia Institute of Technology. Although her books—*Controlling Voices: Intellectual Property, Humanistic Studies, and the Internet* (2001) and *A Legal Primer for the Digital Age* (2003)—treat legal issues, her Fulbright grant to Russia allowed development of the Global Classroom Project that electronically links students and faculty in Russia, Sweden, and America.

Andrew Hoberek teaches twentieth-century American literature and culture at the University of Missouri-Columbia. During his last two years in graduate school at the University of Chicago he worked as a full-time administrator in the university's Master of Arts Program in the Humanities.

Walter R. Jacobs is an Assistant Professor of Social Sciences in the University of Minnesota's General College. He has written numerous essays on race, media, and pedagogy. His book *Speaking the Lower Frequencies: Students and Media Literacy* is forthcoming from SUNY Press.

Nathalia E. Jaramillo is a doctoral candidate in the Graduate School of Education at the University of California, Los Angeles. Her research interests primarily center on the governing rule of capital to understand policy shifts in education and how critical pedagogy can be used to envision a world outside the precincts of capital.

Peter McLaren is a Professor of Education at the Graduate School of Education and Information Studies, University of California, Los Angeles. His many books include *Schooling as a Ritual Performance* (1999), *Che Guevara, Paulo Freire, and the Pedagogy of Revolution* (2000), and *Life in Schools: An Introduction to Critical Pedagogy in the Foundations of Education* (4th ed., 2002).

Sharon O'Dair is Professor of English at the University of Alabama. Author of *Class, Critics, and Shakespeare: Bottom Lines on the Culture Wars* (2000) and co-editor of *The Production of English Renaissance Culture* (1994), she is writing a manuscript entitled *Broken English: Egalitarian Dreams and Professional Realities*.

Mark Poster is Chair of the Department of Film and Media Studies at the University of California, Irvine, and a member of the History Department. His recent books are *The Second Media Age* (1995), *Cultural History and Postmodernity* (1997), *What's the Matter with the Internet?* (2001), and *The Information Subject* (2001).

David Trend is Director of the University of California's Institute for Research in the Arts and Professor of Studio Art at the University of California, Irvine. The former editor of the journals *Afterimage* and *Socialist Review*, Trend's books include *Cultural Democracy* (1997) and *Reading Digital Culture* (2001).

Index